御河

The Emperor's River

TRAVELS TO THE HEART OF A
RESURGENT CHINA

Liam D'Arcy-Brown

eye books

Challenging the way we see things

First published in Great Britain in 2010
by Eye Books Ltd
7 Peacock Yard
Iliffe Street
London
SE17 3LH
www.eye-books.com

Map by Lee-wan Jon
Cover design by Emily Atkins
Text layout by Helen Steer

British Library Cataloguing in Publication Data
A catalogue record for this book is available from the British Library

ISBN: 978-1-903070-70-3

Printed and bound by J F Print Ltd., Sparkford, Somerset.

Contents

5   Prologue

9   The Grandest of Canals

33   A Culture to be Proud of

63   Graffiti

119   Life's Bitterness

161   Predictions of Change

211   Water, but no Boats

249   A Canal Reborn

280   Appendix & Author's Note

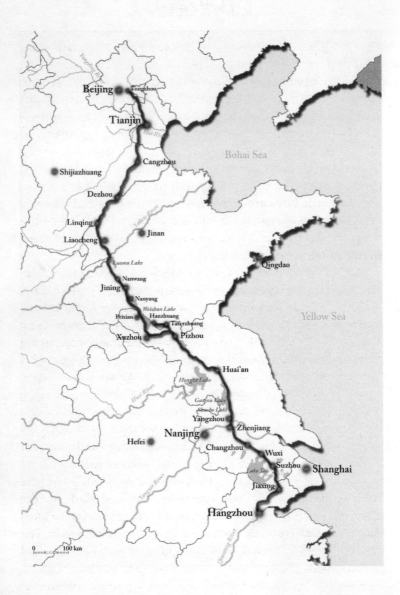

Prologue

When they were small our distant grandparents were terrified by tales of a skeletal French emperor called Boney, while across the Channel in France *le Croque-mitaine* skulked under the bed, ready to gobble up any child who misbehaved. The bogeyman still haunts children's imaginations. But if ever there was a figure calculated to strike fear into young hearts it was Ma the Barbarous, a cruel mandarin of seventh-century China who was said to eat the flesh of infants. It's rumoured that in parts of China to this day bad little boys are reminded of Ma's taste for children, a craving so voracious that families with young sons once built boxes of wood bound with iron and each night locked them inside to keep them from his clutches.

But Ma the Barbarous was not just a mythical ogre. In real life Ma Shumou had been a civil servant under Emperor Yang – ruler of what proved to be the cruel and short-lived Sui dynasty – tasked with the job of digging a great canal from the Yellow River to the southern city of Hangzhou. Such a responsibility was not to be taken lightly: already the emperor had commanded that any mandarin who opposed the project was to be beheaded. A levy was made of all men aged fifteen to fifty, and any who went into hiding were executed along with their entire family to the third generation. By such gentle means of persuasion, 3,600,000 labourers were swiftly raised.

Excavating a canal across the marshlands of eastern China proved an onerous job, and the greater part of Ma's workers were to die before it was complete. Exposed daily to the elements, even Ma himself became ill. His physician made a diagnosis: damp air had become trapped beneath his skin. The remedy, lamb fat mixed with almonds and herbs and cooked in the animal's breast cavity, turned out to be so efficacious, so delicious, that what had begun as a cure became a preference.

5

Those who wished to influence Ma had the dish prepared and offered up to him. Had matters ended there, Ma might have been remembered as a gourmand rather than a monster.

It was at this point that two wicked brothers, hearing that Ma's canal was set to destroy their family tombs, murdered a young boy and cooked his dismembered torso in place of a lamb. The dish was even more delicious than before! As rumours circulated of Ma's taste for child flesh, others who hoped to spare their own tombs began to kidnap boys for him to eat. Unfortunately, the effect of avoiding so many burial grounds was a canal with many unnavigable twists and turns, as Emperor Yang soon discovered when his magnificent dragon boats became grounded upon a shoal. Ma Shumou had made him look a fool, and for this most unforgivable of crimes he was chopped in two at the waist on the bank of the canal he had dug.

How far Ma deserves his gruesome reputation we cannot know, but what we are left with for certain is his legacy. His canal still exists, though its course was realigned long ago to serve Beijing, the capital city of the People's Republic. Known as the Grand Canal of China, it stretches farther than the distance from London to Tunis or from New York to Miami. It is mankind's oldest working canal: when Ma's labourers started work at the dawn of the seventh century they often found themselves redigging even earlier channels cut with Iron-Age tools while Confucius himself was alive. Its very existence has shifted the centre of gravity of a whole nation. It has determined China's history, its cargoes guaranteeing the power of the imperial elite. It has decided the fate of dynasties, and has dictated the site of the Chinese capital for much of the last millennium.

Today the Grand Canal means business. Two hundred and sixty million tons of freight pass along it each year, two-thirds the volume of the USA's entire waterborne freight and three times more than Britain's railway network carries. One hundred thousand vessels ply their trades upon it, and more than 100 million souls pass their lives along its banks. Since the start of Deng Xiaoping's reforms in the late 1970s, the Grand Canal has been fuelling China's economy. And if the Communist Party has its way, it might soon be the saviour of a country slowly dying of thirst as the earth's climate changes.

Just as parents have always told their children stories, so too have nations. The stories of how we came to be who we are give us a comforting sense of identity. In recent years the Chinese have begun to tell themselves a story about their Grand Canal, a story that merges a rediscovered pride in their heritage with a boisterous – and often worrying – nationalism. The course that China chooses to navigate will go a long way to defining all our futures. We should listen to this new story that China is telling itself, and try to understand why.

The Grandest of Canals

杭州　　　　　　　　　　　　　　　　北京

from Hangzhou to the town of Tangqi

Cradling the city of Hangzhou in one of her broad sweeps, the Qiantang River breathes serenely in and out. Already that morning she had inhaled a huge sigh of water, the world's largest tidal bore, deep into her lungs, and now a high tide lapped against her river walls. On her northern shore a mouth opened into that dangerous tideway. Willows shaded a pathway damp with brackish spray. There a scarlet pavilion, its roof like the capital "A" on a thousand-mile manuscript, marked the start of the Grand Canal of China. The confluence of these two waterways was more peaceful than I had imagined it would be, for the Qiantang was wide and the sound of her shipping simply dispersed into the vastness of the heavens. The buildings on the far bank shimmered through a mile of haze. A lone barge waited as the lockgates opened. It was a giant, its length hard to judge. One hundred and forty, one hundred and fifty feet long? The monstrous shiplock swallowed it whole with a silent gulp.

I took out a pen and made a rough calculation on the back of one hand. Beijing lay 1,115 miles away, and the canal here at its mouth was easily 50 yards across. Even assuming a minimal depth of twelve feet to float such great barges, 294 million cubic yards of spoil must have been excavated. But I had seen photographs of the canal further inland, where it could not have been less than three times as wide, and in places it was said to be eight yards deep. Those larger dimensions came to

9

a staggering 2.4 billion cubic yards in total and left the back of my hand more ink than flesh. The two figures averaged out at 1.3 billion cubic yards. Scholars of the Great Wall had estimated that it had taken 236 million cubic yards of rammed earth to build. Even at a conservative estimate, the Grand Canal was far and away the greater achievement. It was only the conspicuous proof of the labour that had gone into the Great Wall, redoubled by its photogenic beauty and the wildness of its terrain, that had made it the more popular of those two siblings, the extrovert *yang* to the canal's introverted *yin*.

For the moment, there in Sanbao Village, the Grand Canal of China was just a meek expanse of water. A string of coal barges was hitched like spent horses to the walls beyond the lock. There was chatter and laughter in their wheelhouses. The canal around them was motionless, ink-black with the run-off from a coal wharf. It skulked low that day as if condensed to liquid carbon by the heat of late spring. Then the ribbon of water turned west with the towpath, and factory walls became columns of pretty willows. I began to see other people out walking, watched cars slide along wide avenues, heard the babble of tourists aboard the shiny, new water buses. Hangzhou had become a modern city in the fifteen years since my last visit, a perky informality of apartment blocks. In the centre of town the temperature dropped so suddenly that passers-by looked up to the heavens as one and shivered. The sky, pregnant and lowering, began to spit. I hailed a taxi: a short drive away, a traditional waterside neighbourhood was rumoured to have survived the frenzy of reconstruction.

By the time our car reached Lishui Road the rain had strengthened. The driver turned his meter off while we waited for the worst to pass, more interested in spending the time in conversation than in charging the extra fare he was entitled to. He pointed to his licence, glued to the dashboard.

"My name's Cong Bian. Are you married?" I told him I had married just a week earlier. "I congratulate you! I'm married too, with a daughter, ten years old. She's living in Harbin while my wife and I are here working." So he wasn't from these parts? He waved his palm stiffly. "I'm from Heilongjiang. Can't you hear?" He spoke, now I paid attention, the crisply correct Mandarin of a Manchurian.

"So you don't understand the locals?"

"They speak Wu dialect. I can understand a little, after two years here, if they speak slowly." I too found the speech of eastern China incomprehensible, I admitted: the disparate tongues that go under the name of Wu dialect are unintelligible to Mandarin speakers just as Spanish is to an Italian or a Frenchman.

"We're both in the same boat in that regard", he mused. "In China we might say we are *tong shi tianya lunluo ren* – two vagrants thrown together under the same corner of the sky.

"We moved down here to the coast after I lost my job," he explained. "I'd worked in a factory, but the economic conditions in the northeast are poor. We've entrusted our daughter to her grandparents. This is the only way to earn money to put her through school, to save for our parents' old age, for our own retirement." But he did not want to talk about his old life in Manchuria, as though it pained him to be separated from his flesh and blood. The rain was easing off. Wiping away the condensation from a window he looked intently at our surroundings and changed the subject.

"This is Grand Canal Cultural Square, where the authorities have built the Grand Canal Museum. It's cost the city more than 100 million *renminbi*. Over there is Bowing to the Emperor Bridge. Very beautiful." Where were the old warehouses, the inns, the wharves and landing stages that had once stood where now there was an open plaza? "*Chuichule*," Cong Bian shrugged. "Demolished." He read my look of disappointment, and quickly added in consolation: "But Bowing to the Emperor Bridge is very old, the oldest structure in Hangzhou. Ming dynasty."

In his former life he had been an unskilled worker, and in his industrial hometown there was nothing so old, he said, or so enchanting. The bridge's triple arches soared, its steep granite steps reaching fully 50 feet in height before starting their descent to the far shore a hundred yards away. It was undeniably beautiful, even in rain that fell like water spilling from a calabash ladle (as the Chinese phrase has it), the last echo of the dozens which had once spanned the city's waterways. We both stared in appreciative silence at this reminder of how lovely China could be. On the misted windscreen Cong Bian drew two thoughtful strokes with a forefinger, the second running off at a broad angle from the first. They formed the character *ren*: human.

"I remember how in the 1980s, just as we were beginning to rediscover our history after the Cultural Revolution, state television broadcast a long series of programmes on the canal. The first was called *Two Strokes of the Writing Brush*. I still remember sitting as a child in front of a TV in my parents' work unit – they worked in a chassis factory – watching a man in a suit with a great map of China on the wall behind him. 'This first stroke, here,' he said, 'is the Great Wall. And this one is the Grand Canal. Here, where the two lines join, is Beijing, our capital.' The very character for 'human', you know, reminds us of what the Great Wall and the Grand Canal look like on a map of the People's Republic. You understand, we Chinese built that wall, dug this canal, brought human civilization to this land with our bare hands."

The rain eased, and soon we had said goodbye. The museum proved to be closed that day. Standing alone upon the bridge's crown, the water far below was still, betraying its slow drift only by the chemical which bled scarlet-red from a drain. Then, as that stain merged into the ripples, the blunt nose of a barge appeared beneath my feet. Her hold followed, sliding gracefully upstream with a cargo of gravel, and presently there came her wheelhouse. Behind her the dull dishwater became a wake of white foam. As the barge's bulk raised a bow wave from the meagre depths, the canal sucked at its own shallows to bring clouds of mud billowing to the surface like liquid smoke.

御河

So old are China's canals that their origins fade into fables. The oldest is the legend of the folk hero Yu the Great, who calmed the flood that once inundated the world. Yu dug and dredged for thirteen years, channelling the water out to sea and refusing to return home to rest despite the birth of his son and heir. That legend is known to all Chinese, for Yu's mass mobilization of Bronze-Age farmers can be seen as the true starting point of Chinese civilization. It is a civilization built upon a profound understanding of water and how to control it, as an unforgiving environment forced ingenuity upon the earliest ancestors.

For the pattern of rainfall in northern China was always intensely seasonal, with summer monsoons that filled watercourses to bursting and dry winters that tested the skills of reservoir builders. "Picks and shovels are as good as clouds, and opening a channel is as good as rain", goes one age-old saying. Running through the birthplace of Chinese civilization, the Yellow River was ever a capricious creature, her water bearing a staggering load of silt which raised her bed and choked her path, causing devastating floods. Even in the wetter Yangtze valley, where later generations would learn to cultivate paddy, water had to be stored and released through laboriously maintained works to ensure that rice seedlings had all the moisture they demanded at just the right points in their life cycle.

The Chinese proved more than capable of controlling that challenging environment, and with good husbandry the plains of the Yellow and the Yangtze became amongst the most densely populated places on earth. Kings and emperors mobilized millions to share in the work of flood prevention; ditches were dug to draw water into the fields, deeper channels cut to connect these to the great rivers. Long, long before China was ever a unified nation, junks were sailing out across those lands upon a labyrinth of man-made waterways.

The Grand Canal became the greatest of them all, and Hangzhou at its southern terminus one of the richest cities not just in China but on earth, its populace so large, so wealthy, that their gowns struck visitors as a solid screen of silk. Its markets were said to be piled high with gold and silver, the masts in its harbour as thick as the teeth of a comb. Flowers that never faded gave the city an air of everlasting spring. Today the West Lake that lies at its heart is one of the most beautiful sights in all China. Pleasure boats glide out from the wharves, and at dusk the locals promenade, or sit in silent embraces. Lined with weeping willows, hemmed in by hills speckled with temples, they have good reason to call it the finest lake in the world. On that first day of my journey I found a bench by the lakeshore and sat deep in thought. I recognized this place from my childhood, as though I had been predestined somehow to be there.

Not long into secondary school, you see, I had read ahead in my French grammar, beyond the present tense and into the past and the pluperfect, so that when my classmates were introduced to *avoir* and *être* verbs I was instead dispatched to a store cupboard to translate French pop songs. But my mind wandered from the lyrics of *Tous les Garçons et les Filles* and I began to potter around shelves piled high with old textbooks. One, *Beginning Chinese*, was a university primer, half in Romanized script and half in Chinese characters. Upon its cover was a sketch of a lake.

I spent hours poring over that book, copying its characters inexpertly onto the bare walls of a new home, staring into its pen-and-ink illustrations as though awaiting some revelation.

In Lesson One a besuited Mr Bai met a friend. Their meeting place overlooked a lake where people took tea on boats, and where a breeze ruffled the willows. A temple nestled in a fold of the hills, and a pagoda stretched up to heaven. *Beginning Chinese* became my subconscious template for China, a childhood ideal that did passable service for an entire country. It was just eight years later that I visited the People's Republic for the first time, by then a second-year student of Mandarin, and the image of the lake shrank to become just one element in a growing collage. I returned time and again to visit new parts, studying in Shanghai just as that dazzling city was finding its feet after the torpor of Mao's command economy. All the sights I saw, all the sounds and all the smells, became a sensual soundtrack to my life. But of all the memories, it was to the cover of *Beginning Chinese* that my thoughts turned as I sat on that bench in Hangzhou. The illustration had come to life, correct to the last detail as if it had been the artist's very pattern. I slid into a jetlagged half-sleep. A young man sat down beside me.

"Mr Bai?" I asked dreamily. No, he answered, his surname was not Bai; had I mistaken him for somebody? Yes, I said, I had once come across a Mr Bai in a book, who wore a suit just like his. We talked about my reason for being in China.

"*Weishenme?*" he asked. "Why? Why this big Grand Canal journey? And why now, at such an important time?"

Yes, it was an important time. only five days earlier I had taken my wedding vows in a church in the English shires. Rebecca and I had been together for ten years, and it had felt right to marry before being parted for several months. A fair-weather traveller raised in temperate York, I wanted to set out after the worst of the spring rains had passed and reach Beijing before August's heat. Our wedding day turned out to be a beautiful late-April afternoon, but we had spent only four days together before driving to Heathrow. Then Rebecca had had a nosebleed and spotted my shirt with blood, and our goodbyes had been of tender bewilderment.

"Why the Grand Canal?" I repeated distractedly. "Perhaps it would have been better if...." Uncertain, my voice trailed off. Glimpsed from the air the canal region had been a daunting tangle of threads teased out over the plains, each as fragile as a rivulet of rain upon a dirty window. I had taken in its sheer scale and wondered whether I had made the right decision. So why *was* I here?

It was apparent that the Chinese were increasingly focusing attention on their Grand Canal. With each new website and museum, with the completion of every canal-widening scheme and the founding of preservation societies up and down its length, China was beginning to look at the canal with fresh eyes. The sudden interest hinted at deeper currents, and I wanted to discover what these might be. Besides, just as in Chinese medicine the pulse is the most valuable diagnostic tool so there could hardly be a better place to gauge the state of the nation than upon this artery linking its economic heart to its seat of government.

Hearing of my plans to follow the Grand Canal, friends and relatives had joked and told me how much I would love Venice. Yes, and there were other grand canals – one more in Alsace, yet another in Ireland – but China's was the very grandest. Why nobody had thought to follow it from source to terminus left me lost for an explanation. Since a gap had first opened in the bamboo curtain, writers had crossed China by train, sailed the Yangtze, bisected the country by road, walked the Great Wall. Only the Grand Canal, inconspicuous behind a workaday façade, remained a missing piece of the Chinese jigsaw. I suspected too that the journey would be a personal challenge, a test of that idealized China I still carried from the cover of *Beginning Chinese*.

In preparation I had read everything I could find on the canal, a scant library amounting to a few volumes in Mandarin and even less in English. I had pored over atlases, scoured libraries for the faded wayposts of earlier travellers, had memorized a list of nautical terms, but there my knowledge ended. And so, early the next morning, I caught a bus back to the Grand Canal Museum to learn more.

It unfolded like a Chinese fan across Grand Canal Cultural Square, a near semicircle of grey stone. A magnificent frieze swathed one wall in bronze, where slaves strained to haul Emperor Yang's dragon boats. In the lobby a line of lights snaked across a great map of China. The world's other great canals were stretched out beside it, even the longest of them a poor second; the Suez and Panama canals combined were less than one-seventh of its length. Then came the text of the *Hangzhou Declaration*, drawn up by a select group of cadres, academics and dignitaries. It proudly summed up the importance of the canal in Chinese eyes.

"The Grand Canal," it began, "is a great engineering project created by our nation's labouring people in ancient times, a precious article of material and spiritual wealth handed down to us by our ancestors, a living, flowing and vital piece of mankind's heritage." From its roots in the Spring and Autumn period, the *Declaration* went on, the canal had become a vital route for waterborne traffic, binding the north to the south and spanning five mighty river systems. Over the course of millennia it had contributed to China's economic development, to national unity, to social progress. It was proof that China's ancient technology had outshone other civilizations.

"With her own milk," another panel waxed lyrical, "the Grand Canal suckles those who dwell on her banks."

"Because of the Grand Canal we get rich!" boasted another.

The reason for the canal's existence revealed itself as I ventured deeper into the museum. At its height as many as 18,000 imperial barges had shuttled 600,000 tons of grain – rice, barley, millet and others – to the capital each and every year.

In fact the Chinese writing system still has a unique character – *cao* – which can only adequately be translated as "the annual transport of grain to the capital by water". It was on that grain that China's emperors relied for their very survival. They parcelled it out to their kinsmen, paid it as wages to their scholar-officials, used it to sate the bellies of their armies and so buy their loyalty, and to fill the Ever Normal Granaries to guard against famine and rebellion. Each of those strong dynasties familiar from the history books – the Tang, Song, Yuan, Ming and Qing – had been made possible by the Grand Canal. When it was functioning well, the grain flowed and the dynasty was secure; when the grain supply was interrupted through natural disaster or by war, decline was inevitable.

To the peasants who had provided the muscle power and grain for the annual *cao*, the Grand Canal was a terrible physical burden. Keeping it supplied with water took priority over the crop still in the ground; farmers had to wait until the barges had passed before their field sluices were reopened, and there were harsh punishments for those who tapped even the smallest spring. For others the canal brought unsurpassed riches. Merchantmen bore cargos from the south – porcelains from Jingdezhen, damasks, satins and silks from the Yangtze delta, ornaments of precious metals, carved ivories, pearls, wines, paper, *tung* oil, ironwares, alum, jadeite and other prized minerals – and the abundance of tropical field and mountain – sugar, liquorice, bananas, areca, tea, hardwoods, bamboo, medicinal herbs, incense. Thousands of tons of Yunnanese copper were delivered each year to the imperial mint. And southward there came in return the produce of temperate northern China, its cotton, wheat, soy, peanuts, sesame oil, pears, jujubes, almonds, melon seeds and walnuts. Like the Londoners who watched the fruits of Empire arrive at their own docks, the Chinese looked on in awe.

"A million *dan* of millet is carried to the capital," wrote one fourteenth-century scholar. "Tribute from southeast China, those hundreds of categories of things presented to the emperor which yearly number in the billions, all must cross the Yangtze, the Huai and the Yellow. How innumerable are the objects the people rely on for their daily lives! Goods come and go, nowhere else under Heaven in such numbers. From across the seas come the exotic treasures of distant peoples, their divine horses and strange wares. Some are more than a year on their passage, all flowing along the Grand Canal to arrive beneath the palace watchtowers. This is truly a feat unknown in the annals through all the ages." With those cargoes travelled ideas, customs, and dialects. Just as importantly as all the grain and silk, the Grand Canal was a force for unifying Chinese culture.

And in the twenty-first century? It is the Grand Canal that is bringing cheap coal to the power stations of the Yangtze delta, the sand, cement and bricks behind the futuristic skyline of Pudong, the tarmac that covers the motorways of wealthy Jiangnan, south of the Yangtze River. If its course dried up overnight, the building sites would be silenced and the lights would soon go out. The roads would be overwhelmed with the task of supplying the essentials of life to Shanghai – overwhelmed, that is, until tanks ran dry and there were no more barges bringing precious fuel. A permanent blockage in the canal would strike the local economy like a heart attack, and its effects would quickly be felt across China and eventually the world. It would be hard to exaggerate its importance to the economic life of the People's Republic.

In the museum's final room was hung a summary of its message:

If the Great Wall was the shield that defended our peaceful agricultural civilization, then the Grand Canal made possible the flow of traffic that poured forth into it an exhuberant vitality. Though born of military and political considerations, the Grand Canal has tenaciously manifested an independence of will, playing an immense role in the economic and cultural development of the Chinese people. With so many cities rising up on its banks, how can we see it other than as the Mother River of the Eastern Plains? The rich and profound connotations which it holds for the Chinese people will continue to stir us, to be for our cultural lives an inexhaustible wellspring.

The coming thousand miles would show how true those sentiments were.

The next morning I flung open the door of a taxi to escape the torrential rain. It was Cong Bian from the previous day who greeted me with a smile.

"Lin Jie, I knew it was you standing by the road as soon as I saw you. I told you yesterday that we were both to be found under this same corner of the sky. We've got *yuanfen*." In a city whose nucleus alone was home to 3,000,000 people and 8,000 taxis, it did seem that we had *yuanfen* – fate – bringing us together. I told him of my plan to sail to Tangqi, a town a few miles to the northward: there could be no better way to understand the canal and the people who lived upon it. Did he know where I might find a barge? He did.

"Last night I told a friend you were travelling the Grand Canal," he ventured as we drove through miles of suburban industry, past compounds of boxy concrete. "We talked about you. He said that it's 1,800 kilometres long. *'Ta you bing ma?'* he said to me. 'Is he crazy?'"

Cong Bian did his best to dissuade, to make me stay in Hangzhou and meet his wife, to drink the finest Longjing tea from Lion Peak and eat West Lake fried shrimp. He looked me in the eye. "It's not as simple as you imagine," he impressed. "My friend understands these things."

Sorely tempted by an easy life of tea and seafood, still I jabbed determinedly at the map. Cong Bian shrugged and chuckled. "You foreigners are very curious," he conceded. "Let's find you a boat."

At a lonely wharf, a vessel was taking aboard fuel. She was tied fast to the filling station, itself a retired barge with steel plates welded over its hold. A gangplank gave ungainly access from the quay. Stretched over a frame of rusting pipework was a tarpaulin, and underneath this stood a pump. A mechanism watched as the counter clicked over, and a man in a grubby two-piece suit squatted on the deck. Cong Bian edged nervously along the gangplank and addressed them. After their greetings I lost the sense of what they were saying: Cong Bian's adopted dialect was better than he claimed. The bargeman weighed me up.

"Tangqi? Two hundred *kuai*," he said decisively. It was no small sum, 40 or 50 times the bus fare, but there was no other barge tied up within sight. "Pay now, before we cast off."

"We're a freighter, not a passenger boat," the woman added. "And you haven't a sailor's permit. If the harbour supervisors see we're carrying passengers we'll be fined."

My *renminbi* went toward the cost of the fuel, and then the hawsers were unhitched and tossed onto the deck. Two engines spluttered into life, the bargeman teased the wheel and opened the throttle, and a satisfying splashing from the stern told that the propellers were tearing at the water. Already ten miles from that scarlet pavilion on the Qiantang River, ahead of me stretched 1,105 more. My landsman's stomach lurched as the barge swung into the stream.

"*Aya*, the price of fuel's higher now than ever," the woman muttered as she squeezed down the narrow gangway. How high? I asked, when they had both finished sucking their teeth in annoyance.

"It's more than five *kuai* a litre now," the bargeman complained. "And now and again there's rationing at the pump." Then he whistled softly at my quick calculation of the price back in England, where a litre of diesel was more than three times what he had just paid. "How do your scrap-metal bargemen make any money?" he asked innocently.

The *021 Cargo* – this is all I remember of her name – was typical of the rusty tubs which busied themselves like restless scavengers, foraging at the bottom of the food chain for loads to shuttle from here to there. Try to imagine the antithesis of a brightly painted English narrowboat. Technically speaking she was a welded-steel self-propelled barge, flat-bottomed and double-hulled, most of her deck taken up by a cavernous rectangular hold. Ropes held car tyres close to her flanks, but despite them her ironwork was beaten and sunk from years of minor collisions, her hull so battered that her bulkheads showed through like the ribs of some starving creature. Her wheelhouse was just a makeshift shelter where Mr Yao and his wife took turns on a wooden stool. This faced a tarnished wheel, a throttle, and a few greasy buttons which remained untouched, their purposes obscure. Window panes and doors had been salvaged from somewhere or other and crudely nailed together to keep out the elements. The roof was of chipboard, oilskin-swaddled and lashed down to cleats, and with its bamboo pike-poles, its ropes, mops and buckets the *021 Cargo* looked not unlike a scrapyard animated and set afloat. In flowerpots grew an emerald thatch of chives and some bolted garlic, a diminutive vegetable garden for a couple who lived on water. Aft of the wheelhouse a hatch led into a tiny compartment where the Yaos might snatch some sleep. A thin mattress ran the width of that lightless nook. Behind this, inimical to rest, the barge's twin engines were exposed on the deck. Their bodies had oxidized to white with the heat, their exhausts to a livid red. Cooling water spat with their vibrations, and a pair of hefty flywheels span frantically, transmitting their powerful torque to the propellers.

Miles from that first listless shiplock on the Qiantang the

day was growing busy. The other traffic that morning was mostly barge trains, floating convoys lashed together stern-to-bow with steel ropes and pulled by hardy tugs. The *021 Cargo* came level with one.

"*Yi, er, san, si, wu*...." The rest trailed off uncountable into the distance.

"*Shi'er sou*," interrupted Mr Yao, guessing what I was doing. "Twelve. They're from the coalfields of Shandong province, carrying fuel for Hangzhou. There are normally twelve to a train." Just as he had predicted, a dozen barges slowly passed us by. Their holds were swathed in taut tarpaulin, and traces of coal lingered on their russet decks. "These twelve barges, perhaps 4,000 tons of coal. How many lorries would you need to carry 4,000 tons of coal? Two hundred? It costs perhaps one tenth of the price of road haulage to carry coal by barge to the power stations where it's needed, perhaps ten or twenty *kuai* per ton less than transporting it by rail. That makes the electricity cheaper, and the economy more competitive."

"These must be the very biggest barges?" I commented. He smiled at my naivety.

"*Bu, bu, bu*. Others carry 1,000 tons each and more...." He talked impassively, as though it were a mere trifle. Before this, my only other experience of canals had been visits to beer gardens set beside rural English locks, of narrowboats designed to carry 30 tons of the Duke of Bridgewater's coal. These behemoths were a world away from the slim vessels on the Grand Union Canal back home.

The convoy was approaching its distant power station at walking pace, but still the tug's wake stretched back to envelop the first three barges in a skirt of white. On the barges' decks the crews smoked, walked back and forth watching the other traffic, or mopped the gangways to pass the time. Children in life jackets played games. The smaller ones, some barely toddlers, were anchored to hitching posts. Mongrels stood sentinel, barking warnings at other vessels.

"You save fuel by buying in to a barge train," said Mr Yao. "One tug can pull many barges, more slowly than travelling alone, of course, but they're not in a hurry."

Like the tiny *021 Cargo*, some larger barges too chose to sail alone. Unladen they towered yards above the stream, the waves slapping on their bow rakes as they rode over them, their flat hulls drawing scarcely a foot of water. Others though were dangerously overloaded, their decks submerged and with water lapping against the coamings which protected their holds. A large wave, a glancing collision, might easily swamp them.

"They shouldn't be sitting that low," observed Mr Yao in a concerned tone. "Barges like that sometimes sink. People drown. In shallow stretches they can ground and block the way for days." He steered a course along the right-hand lane, just as he would on a Chinese road. The bank rose beside us like a vertical mosaic, its irregular chunks of granite rough-hewn, now well-pointed, now a confusion prised apart by roots. Mrs Yao returned from the bow where she had stood watching the world go by.

"How many knots are we doing?" I asked, hoping to impress by using the Chinese for "knot" (it is *jie*, the character for the knuckles on a bamboo stem).

"We don't talk about 'knots' on inland waterways," she corrected. "We use kilometres per hour. We're doing about fifteen. We're limited to seventeen, you see, else the wake damages the banks...." On cue our wake struck the bank and slooshed into the cracks. "... But at this speed we'll still be in Tangqi in less than two hours."

For those two hours I sat hypnotized by the grey ribbon unfolding ahead. The city of Hangzhou seemed never to come to a conclusive end but continued in an unbroken sprawl that escorted us north. Factories and homes had unfurled like tendrils colonizing the margins of an endless source of nourishment. In the three decades since Deng Xiaoping had launched China's economic reforms, this corner of the country had been transformed. The canal pulsated with life, here the narrow channel of Hangzhou, there a broad river wider than the Thames in central London. At such a distance, even the near bank became a blur through the morning drizzle....

"Lin Jie!" Mr Yao called me into the anonymity of the wheelhouse.

"*Gangjian*," he explained nervously. We passed a squat watchtower. The *Gangjian*, Harbour Supervisors, were on the lookout for illegal cargoes, he said, and dangerous loads. We watched the cargoes drift past, all of them heavy but low in value, the kind of freight that made road transport uneconomic: scrap metal, coal, diesel, rolls of steel wire, dredged mud, heaps of sand, gravel and ballast, and orange bricks stacked so neat and so high that they looked from a distance like approaching buildings. They all bore well their rough handling, did not spoil when dumped without ceremony into a gaping hold. There were no more porcelains, no silks or cottons, no tropical fruits and fish for the emperor.

It had been a long time since such exotic cargoes were last carried. At the time of Liberation in 1949 the Grand Canal had been redundant for almost 50 years, superceded by locomotives and ocean-going ships. But what the fragile government of the new People's Republic needed was not the tax grain, the luxuries and the gewgaws that had propped up old, feudal China, but instead coal to power a command economy, and materials to rebuild a war-ravaged country. The Grand Canal became a priority. Up and down its length, thousands were soon shovelling out the silt of decades, removing sunken boats and tree trunks, uprooting reedbeds. Timeless stone arches were replaced with pre-stressed concrete spans; primeval oxbows were recut and straightened. The Grand Canal faded with the imperial system it had made possible, but it was swiftly resurrected as a life-giving artery of what will soon be the world's largest economy.

The *021 Cargo* hove to outside town, where the chimneys of Tangqi became visible around a sweeping bend. Mr Yao could go no further upon the narrow old canal, and set off instead along a wide, new bypass.

"If I see you again, I'll cry out," he promised. After the reunion with Cong Bian the taxi driver, I half suspected we would meet once more.

The rain had stopped. In the centre of town the old canal was empty and unruffled, a mirror for the seamless white of the sky. The Good Works Bridge linked its two banks, hunchbacked, a dark rhombus pierced by seven circles of light. Its age merged into whispers of legends, already old when the English were defending their distant kingdom against Viking invasion. It had withstood the collapse of dynasties, Japanese occupation, civil war, even the vandalism of the Cultural Revolution. Then lumbering barges had struck it and its demolition had been discussed in high places. To the credit of the local Party Committee a bypass had been dug and the bridge spared, renovated as a civic centrepiece. Swallows brushed its marble cheek, swooping and veering to catch mosquitoes. An elderly couple sat in the day's weak sunshine. Their home was humble, of whitewashed plaster crowned by a sagging jumble of black pottery, a style called *fenqiang daiwa* – white-powder walls and mascara tiles – as though each like a sing-song girl were presenting a carefully made-up face to the world. This was how I remembered Hangzhou, before urban planners had set about raising the city's living standards. The only vessel on the canal was a blunt-nosed sampan from which a hunched figure spooned at the water with an oar. Now and then it would reach out with a sieve on a pole to fish a plastic bottle from the ripples. Every twenty would fetch more than enough for a bowl of rice.

A modest hotel on the town square had rooms to spare. Outside, a crowd had stood about laughing and offering advice as two men in leather jackets – bruisers with bull necks, gold chains and pork-pie hats – encouraged their dogs to mate. Any relief at being inside was momentary: there was a rap on the door; two plainclothes policemen were standing in the corridor.

"Mr Lin Jie?" said one. "We need to ask why you're in Tangqi."

御河

Tangqi lay only fifteen miles from the luxury hotels that encircled the West Lake, yet it felt as though it might not see a foreign face from year to year. In small towns like this, officialdom still required unexpected visitors to explain their business and register their presence. The owner of this hotel had no licence to accept foreigners and had put in a call to the nearby police station before word got to them by some other route.

The officers arrived in polyester suits and slip-on shoes, the everyday uniform of provincial detective constables. Cigarettes were surgically attached to their fingers. They made themselves comfortable on the bed and drank tea. One produced a sheet of questions: where had I come from? Where was I going next? The answers intrigued him. Why Chongfu? I told them of my plan and, not reflecting on the folly of truthfulness, about the *021 Cargo*.

"Your Aliens' Travel Permit, please." He held out a hand. "There are no passenger services to Tangqi, you understand. Mr Lin, you can't undertake a trip like this without first arranging it with the correct work unit and obtaining an Aliens' Travel Permit. From the visas in your passport you've been to China many times before; you ought to know this."

Of course I knew this: I had criss-crossed much of China with a rucksack and a notepad over the past sixteen years, had travelled to its islands and deserts and to its four most far-flung points. But I had only seldom informed the authorities:

making such arrangements was complex, and their forced itineraries were often a suffocating blanket of handshakes and stupefying toasts in hard liquor.

"It's dangerous to ride these barges. You might be robbed, or drowned. I'll put 'bus' here in this box for your travel to Chongfu, *hao ma?*" I gave a forced smile of consent, and my immediate itinerary became set. "When you reach Chongfu, remember to register with the police."

They closed the door behind them. There had been plenty of police launches tied up on the banks that day, and news of a foreigner would quickly filter through. I consoled myself that there were still more than a thousand miles left, only... what if in Chongfu, in Jiaxing, and in every place I wanted to see between here and Beijing it was already being decided in smoke-filled rooms how I could travel? Perhaps I should have done something about this before ever leaving home.

But I was here now, and so in that spartan room I set about planning the progress I hoped to make day by day. The task left the six provincial atlases I had brought along covered in scribbled notes. Along the length of the Grand Canal itself, an unbroken strip of sky blue from Hangzhou to Beijing, I scored lines of daily aspirations, destinations to aim for at fifteen-mile intervals. This done, I turned my attention to what had already been written by travellers who had gone before me.

By the very nature of a canal, millions of men had passed this way. Most were nameless, but amongst them was a handful who had recorded their experiences, and copies of their writings were squeezed into my rucksack. The oldest of them was a scholar-official named Lou Yue. In 1169, with China divided between Jurchen tribesmen in the north and the Southern Song dynasty in the south, the Chinese emperor sent a delegation to the Jurchen to wish their ruler well for the New Year. Lou Yue, secretary to the delegation, submitted his *Diary of a Journey to the North* to the emperor on his return. Part travelogue, part gazetteer, part espionage, it was rich with detail on conditions under Jurchen rule. Returning south, Lou Yue recorded his experience of the Grand Canal. This though was familiar territory to him and he wrote now as though mindful of the price of ink.

Next came Ch'oe Pu. In 1487 this 33-year-old Korean official had set sail from the island of Jeju for the Korean mainland to bury his late father. Instead, his ship had been tossed onto the coast of Ming China by a storm. Soon he was being escorted northward on the Grand Canal toward the Korean border. His family, he thought, must have assumed him long drowned.

"The sky and the sea are boundless," he lamented, "the wild geese are high, the fish are deep. My mother must think I am buried in a fish's belly. No-one has been as unfilial as I, no-one has so broken his mother's heart." When Ch'oe Pu at last made it back home to mourn his father, he found the strength to set down his experiences in *A Record of Drifting across the Sea*.

Now Lou Yue had been a native, Ch'oe Pu a punctilious Korean saturated with Confucian ethics, and their writings took for granted a deep knowledge of Chinese culture. European travellers saw China in quite a different light. In 1792 a British flotilla would set sail with an embassy from the Court of Saint James. At its head was Lord Macartney, tasked by King George III with establishing ties with the Dragon Throne. The mutual incomprehension which bedevilled him would bear its malign fruit a lifetime later in the Opium War, the Treaty of Nanjing, and the collapse of China's last imperial dynasty. Though his mission failed, Lord Macartney, his deputy Sir George Staunton, and valet Aeneas Anderson all left memoirs that rang with descriptions of a canal which had made a deep impression on them. To my knowledge, I was now the first Westerner since Macartney's embassy to attempt this journey.

That evening ended with me staring out of the window. I gazed northward into the blackness, beyond the children with their shuttlecocks, beyond the couples waltzing to the music from a beaten loudspeaker. One thousand miles away, if the capital was anything like the last time I had seen it, Beijingers were probably doing just the same.

A presence roused me in the depth of that night, and I raised myself onto one elbow to squint at it. These night-time imaginings were something Rebecca had grown to live with. She was used to being woken by garbled monologues that at the time had sounded like eloquent dialogue inside my head. Especially when travelling for months on end and spending each night in a new room, I would regularly sleepwalk in the small hours or conjure people from the unfamiliar shadows. This presence sat at the end of the bed, its circular cap a smudge against the dim light of the curtains. Mumbling, I asked Lou Yue why he had written parts of *Diary of a Journey to the North* so sparsely – his observations were not as copious as Ch'oe Pu's or the rest.

"Sparse? I was travelling through familiar lands, and I only wrote what was new to me. The *qi* of the heavens was new each day, each town another stage toward an end. Indeed, when the unexpected occurred I wrote at length: 'On the sixth day there were showers, but by evening the sky had brightened. The previous night, the barge carrying gifts struck another on the stern. A puntsman was crushed to death. When we reached Shaobo we paid for his funeral. Tonight the same barge struck a sunken stake and sprang a leak. Nobody noticed, and the barge sank.' This is not sparse!"

In later life Lou Yue was to earn a reputation as a blunt talker – even the Guangzong Emperor once admitted that he shrank from him – and in this waking dream he was just as argumentative as the emperor had described. He had been five years my junior when he made the trip north to the Jurchen capital, but my imagination had summoned up a man much older than myself, a white-bearded Confucian.

"What about 'on the third day we passed Baoying'?" I

pressed him. "This tells me nothing about what you saw. Ch'oe Pu goes on and on and on about the minutest details of city walls, bridges, the height of pagodas...."

"Those details were all novel to that foreigner, that Korean. I was travelling through our Song lands, and I wrote for the benefit of the emperor, who already knew all these things, not for you. Why have you dressed me in the clothes of a Manchu general?"

"I don't know anything about the clothes of a twelfth-century mandarin. How do know what a Manchu general wore, anyway? You died long before the Qing dynasty began!"

"I know what you know, nothing more."

"I need you to know more than that. Why has only Bowing to the Emperor Bridge been spared in Hangzhou, and the Good Works Bridge in Tangqi and those houses beside it? Why build Grand Canal Cultural Square now, after decades of silence? Nothing happens in China for no reason. Tell me what I'm not seeing."

"China hasn't changed. The emperor still commands his subjects and demands their loyalty. The Grand Canal is one of the greatest achievements of my people. If the Chinese are proud of themselves, they are proud of their emperor. Surely you'd noticed that the emperor tells many different stories to his people?"

"Now we're making no sense!" I slumped back onto the pillow, vaguely aware at last that those final words had been addressed in a loud voice to an empty room. The next morning the water heater still loomed at the foot of the bed where Lou Yue had sat. Downstairs, the hotel's receptionist was absorbed in a soap opera. She located a slip of paper with an officious red stamp upon it. Without taking her eyes off the TV she handed it over, the Aliens' Temporary Residence Permit that had allowed me to stay overnight in Tangqi. It had been made out in the name of Liam Jams. I could always deny any knowledge of him, I thought, and set out to find the bus to Chongfu.

A Culture to be Proud of

杭州

北京

across northern Zhejiang province

Reaching Chongfu meant first heading away from the
Grand Canal and riding the highway to the town of
Linping. The workshops which stitched the world's
clothing were to be found in Canton's Pearl River delta, but
the mills through whose gates roll the bolts of cloth they relied
on seemed to line that long road. The muggy climate of this
region long ago made it the home of China's textile industry.
The mulberry thrived here, its tender leaves almost the only
food fussy silkworm larvae would eat before entombing
themselves in their milky cocoons. Villagers no longer raised
silkworms in their own homes; instead for two decades
an inexhaustible rural labour force and a thirst for cheap
clothing overseas had brought in billions of *renminbi* of foreign
investment. Smooth new roads like Route 320 had been driven
across the plains. Whitewashed weaving sheds were strung out
along the way, steel barriers and guards' boxes dividing them
from tumbledown villages like Cold War borders. Where no
building yet stood, plots of paddy had been earmarked and
cleared, and billboards announced the arrival of the next plant.
Sketches of factories and accommodation blocks in sterile ranks
looked like the components of a printed circuit board. Despite
the first intimations that orders were slowing down as Western
consumers reined in their spending, fortunes were being made
where just a few years ago farmers were growing grain.

A last outcrop of granite hills hung in the sky before the

tower blocks of Linping hid them from view and, penetrating deeper into the plain, we left behind Greater Hangzhou. On the back seat a young couple held hands and shouted sweet nothings to each other over the unmuffled exhaust and the radio's clamour.

"You're half good, half bad," the girl told her boyfriend. "That's why I like you!" The other passengers, odd-jobbers carrying their lives in fertilizer sacks, ignored them and smoked. The bus was slow; the *021 Cargo* could not have taken longer.

Chongfu proved to be larger and wealthier than Tangqi. Amongst the usual restaurants and foot spas, the florists, the brothels masquerading as hair salons, were sprinkled gleaming proofs that its ever-richer townsfolk wanted a better life. Inside China Mobile, display cases were packed with wafer-thin handsets. Shopfronts were piled high with computer hardware, with household electrics, washing machines, fridges, freezers, air-conditioning units; the pavements were thick with foodstalls, and with bicycle carts from which were hawked an endless list of consumables. In the backstreets, where slouching houses waited to be swept away, each had given over its outermost room to the pursuit of wealth. Since 1978 and increasingly with each year that passed, by and by every family had become a *getihu*, a small private business, be they noodle makers, acupuncturists, hairdressers, or just an old man hanging up a hopeful sign offering his telephone for public use.

Yet Chongfu was for wealthy eastern China no very remarkable town, and neither was its pollution extraordinary. One odour in particular hung above the car fumes, a volatile ester that smelt of pear drops, inescapably strong, burning the sinuses. It was in places like this, too small for the legal regulations and urban planning that had cleaned up Hangzhou, that the environment was at its worst. It was amongst those tainted backstreets that I refound the canal. It had arrived in Chongfu much the same as it had left Tangqi, choppier now, but still bearing that familiar wet-dog-and-petrol scent. A man was leaning on the cabin of a barge. I called to him with an attempt at a friendly smile.

"*Wei, shifu!* Hey, boss! What's your cargo?" He gave a non-committal grunt, shot a suspicious eye, and slunk back into the shadows of the wheelhouse.

On the assumption that Chongfu's policemen were already expecting me, it made sense to arrange a temporary residence permit before there came another knock on the door. So I flagged down a bicycle trishaw and headed for the police station. In the fashion typical of small-town China, its cyclist wore a Western suit over a white shirt, his sleeves rucked up over his elbows, his shirtfront hitched up and tucked under to let the air cool his smooth belly.

"I'm Shen Jiugao," he said, twisting his upper body about. His skin was unlined and youthful, his face round, with wide, expressive eyes below a high brow which concertinaed neatly when he smiled. "I've never taken a foreigner in my *sanlunche* before. After you've spoken to the police, let's have some fun!" Bouncing about in the seat, staring at the back of Jiugao's head, it was not easy to imagine quite what form that fun might take.

Chongfu's cliffs of dense housing crumbled within a mile to vestigial fields, squares of earth trapped within half-finished building sites. Jiugao turned his head to comment on the passing scene between breaths.

"These fields here... will be new apartments and offices... later this year." Then, further on, where we passed a terrace of vacant shops: "People will open restaurants here... supermarkets... to bring life to our development zone.... *Hen mei, dui ma?* Beautiful, isn't it?"

It was hardly beautiful in any sense that I understood. The shops were of bare concrete, some streaked with water where their downpipes had failed, and they stood marooned in mud. Depressions had filled with the rain of recent days, and algae were blooming bright red on their surface. But Jiugao had lived his life in Chongfu, and if the beauty he saw was invisible to me then I must have been looking at things the wrong way. "Beautiful" is a visually demanding word with little of the moral overtone, the inner gratification that the Mandarin word *mei* carries with it – those hints of admiration, comeliness, praiseworthiness. It would take many more weeks before my eye could filter all the visual noise from such a scene as that construction site to leave what to Jiugao was the self-evident beauty of progress.

The police station too proved to be a beautiful new building amongst the brown of unsown paddy. Its doorway was brightened by a golden Tian'anmen Gate surmounted by the five stars that symbolized the unity of the Chinese people and the Communist Party. Today was a Sunday, a day of rest even in secular China, and only one desk was open. A man had come to register his father's passing. He wore a black armband bearing the Chinese character for "filial piety", and semicircles of sackcloth were sewn onto his plimsolls. He spoke sparingly. The female duty officer nodded understandingly and commiserated, and he handed over his father's identity card and death certificate. She found a name on her computer screen and tapped a few keys. A machine hissed out a notice of cremation. A second certificate followed, and she handed over this confirmation of the death. The man held it up and stared into his late father's face, streaked across with the failing lines of a dying printer. Such was the everyday work of the all-powerful Public Security Bureau. She told us that she knew nothing about registering aliens. Come back tomorrow afternoon, she suggested, and turned to registering a birth. I would be leaving the next morning, and had no intention of returning. Jiugao, when we had left, explained his idea of fun.

"If you've come to study our Grand Canal, you can't leave without seeing the Prefect's Bridge." He yanked bulldog clips from his handlebars and secured his trouser legs.

The ride took us back into the bustle of the town and

through its back alleys, narrow lanes which turned doglegs every few yards where ancient boundaries imposed. Away from the noise and peril of traffic, Jiugao's voice was clearer. He coasted along without the breathy urgency of our earlier ride. He was over 50 (that was as much as he would admit) and had been self-employed for fifteen years. Like Cong Bian the taxi driver he had been laid off from a factory that had failed to keep pace with the demands of a market economy. When next he tugged his brake handle we found ourselves at a flight of steps whose flags were polished smooth by footfall. They rose sharply above a single arch, high enough to allow junks in full sail to pass beneath.

"This is the only old bridge left in Chongfu," he declared with a tone of regret. "In the 1970s, you see, the government here set about a campaign called 'seeking straightness from the three bends'. They widened one of the crooked old cuts through the town centre and made it navigable for big barges, but at the same time they demolished all but this bridge. Chongfu's economy really took off from that time, but we can never replace that heritage." He sighed heavily. "Ah, Lin Jie, I must go home. But we two have *yuanfen* – fate has brought us together. We will meet tomorrow. I'll take you to a temple. Here are my name and number." He took pen and paper and wrote his name slowly, apologizing for the time it took, though his handwriting was pleasingly formed. "I didn't get a good education, you see, so I don't write too fluently. These Nokia phones are good, though," he added, taking his cellphone from a pocket. "I can key in the sound of a word and then choose the characters I want. I don't need to remember how to write them anymore."

He typed a simple message: 林杰你好! Hello, Lin Jie! He had had his youth sacrificed to the Cultural Revolution, his school closed and his teachers sent down to the farms to be re-educated. Thirty years later, the arrival of cellphones had made a technophile of this middle-aged man who might otherwise have struggled through life semi-literate.

御河

My hotel's lobby was dreary in the twilight despite its owner's best efforts. An array of clocks claimed implausible times for New York, London, Tokyo and Rome. The room smelt faintly of ammonia, the pillows of petrol. Around a mah-jong table the carpet was burned by cigarettes and stained with spilt drink. On the wall above the bed a Western woman posed naked, her skin shimmering in metallic pink. Rather than spend a frightful sum on a bland corporate hotel I had opted for this, the kind of cheap place frequented by men looking to pass the night in smoking, drinking and illegal gambling. Opening a bottle of whiskey brought from Hangzhou, I turned on the TV.

On a satellite channel broadcasting from Fujian province, a talent show called *No Ding, No Stop!* had begun. Contestants performed before a panel of judges, earning ¥10 for every second on stage until the panel had all pressed their buttons and a collective "ding" had sounded. Criticism was accepted graciously and with polite bows. The acts were not as polished as their counterparts on shows like *The X Factor*, or even the slickly produced *Super Girl* (it had run on Hunan Satellite TV for three series before being accused of poisoning China's youth), but then again no face was lost, no dreams were crushed.

But the most interesting aspect of *No Ding, No Stop!* was the contestants' choice of material: every act dripped with national pride, a reaction perhaps to criticism that *Super Girl* had ignored traditional culture. The first, a pair of teenage boys from Shandong, danced to a rap they had written about being Chinese.

"Thirteen times one hundred million people, with a culture to be proud of," they sang, while a stagehand held aloft disparate images: the Great Wall, the cartoon *Fuwa* mascots of the Beijing Olympics, the *Shenzhou* spacecraft which had already carried three astronauts into orbit, and China's 2002 World Cup soccer team draped in the red flag (though they had fallen at the group stages without scoring a goal). Next up, a woman played a soft tune on a *guqin* harp, the instrument of the ancient sages. Then a small boy dressed like a terracotta warrior trilled his way through a song about the central plains, his cultural homeland. All were dinged off after a minute or so, but not so the final contestant, a 79-year-old former political cadre who sang about the Chinese countryside. When she had finished her song, the panel wished her blessings as bounteous as the Eastern Sea and ten thousand things according to her wishes.

Was China still too respectful of its Communist past to criticize it and shake off its grip, I wondered? Or were the panel simply doing what anybody would do when faced with a great-grandmother singing folksongs? In a culture which still has a deep respect for its elders it would have been hard to treat her like the others. What *would* it have meant to ding that old Party member off after just a few bars? It would have sent a clear message that her generation could not compete in a new China of TV game shows and cash prizes, and that the Party that had led the Revolution no longer had anything to say about Chinese culture. No game-show panel was ready to do that.

And that set me thinking. What was it that Lou Yue had said in that waking dream the other night? That the Grand Canal was a great achievement, that if the Chinese were proud of themselves then they were proud of their emperor, and that the emperor told stories to his people. The stagehand on *No Ding, No Stop!* had held up a picture of the Great Wall, but it could just as well have been the Grand Canal. All those pictures, all those songs, were elements of the same story, a patriotic tale of China's cultural achievements. When the credits had rolled, the viewers got the chance to vote anonymously. I tried to stay awake, to see whether they would follow the judges' lead, but fell asleep waiting for the result.

When I woke it was light. In half an hour I was in the back of Jiugao's trishaw once more, munching on a steamed pork bun. We agreed to make for the Fuyan Temple, and afterwards to see what opportunities might present themselves for hitching a lift to Jiaxing: Tangqi's policemen would by then be twenty miles behind me, while Chongfu's seemed unaware of my presence.

"I wanted to bring my motorized *sanlunche* today," he apologized. "But my wife insisted you'd prefer to go slowly, see the scenery." So we cycled out past the police station again, stopping occasionally for Jiugao to push his trishaw across the incline of a bridge, for the land was scored back and forth with irrigation ditches. The countryside was closely cropped, carpeted with dense patches of mulberry trees with their flopping, tender leaves. Jiugao called back over his shoulder:

"Life's easy for the peasants here. Jiangnan is never too dry, never flooded. It's a paradise. They only need raise one rice crop each year, the yield's so good. Out of season they raise mulberry saplings to sell for four *mao* apiece." He slowed to a stop and vanished into a thick stand of mulberry. A minute later he reappeared. "Eat these. The peasants don't mind if you take some, so long as you don't take them to sell. We used to make these little parcels when we were children." He had picked the choicest mulberries he could find, and had woven a little basket from a mulberry leaf, held together with its own stalk. The fruit was purple, the length of a child's thumb, made up of drupelets like a raspberry and deliciously sweet. "Most fall to the ground and rot. Just a few trees bear them each season, and they're very delicate, so you rarely see them for sale in the cities. They'll stain your fingers," he chuckled, "and your 'big conveniences', you know, your shit!"

I ate those mulberries as we rode down lanes of high poplars, the only sound the rhythmic squeaking of our axle. Jiugao named the crops growing in the fields – oil-greens, horse-beans, potatoes – and the birds with the prominent eyebrows that darted amongst them. Jumping down from the saddle he tiptoed along a field boundary and returned clutching a leaf. He rubbed it in his hands and held it to my nose. It smelled of camphor.

40

"*Zhang*-tree leaves. We used to boil them up and steep our clothes in the broth to stop insects eating them. Now we buy boxes of chemicals in the market. Most people have forgotten how to do things like that."

We rode on. Soon Jiugao pointed into the middle distance where the barges rode high, empty, as if they were sailing through the fields. Ahead of us, the mustard walls of the Fuyan Temple came into sight above a waving ocean of mulberry.

Legend tells that the Fuyan Temple was founded by a wily Buddhist monk for the tiny sum of three copper cash. One day in AD 503, at the start of the Southern Liang dynasty, the monk arrived at a village begging for alms. After dunning change from some passers-by, he discovered in the village mill a pair of oxen. Going up to one of them, he began to stroke its nose. Before long both ox and monk began to weep, bringing the miller and the other villagers to see what was the matter.

"This ox is the reincarnation of my dead uncle," the monk sobbed. "When he saw me he started to cry. How could I not cry too?"

"You must store up good deeds for yourself," the villagers urged the miller, "by reuniting this monk with his dead uncle." The miller parted with the ox, and the monk led it away. A few weeks later he returned, his pilgrim's scrip over his shoulder. Sitting down, he lit an incense stick and began to chant. At first the villagers ignored him, but after a few days they grew anxious, worried that they had not seen him eat a morsel of food. As time passed, they could not understand how he had not grown hungry. They decided that he must be an immortal come down to earth, and that the spot on which he sat must be sacred. Between themselves they raised enough money to build a temple right there. In their faith they never suspected that the wily monk with the money he had begged had bought three copper cash-worth of ground pepper to rub into the ox's eyes, or that he had butchered it and hidden its dried flesh in his sack to sustain him.

"Without the trick that the monk played on the miller, our temple would not have been here for the bargemen to pray for safe passage," said the temple superintendent. "It was always popular with them." He was a balding man with a stoop, whose arms hung immobile from his shoulders like an elderly *Thunderbirds* puppet. "They came to burn incense and to ask Buddha for a safe voyage. It was one of the biggest in Zhejiang. Then after the 'ten-year turmoil' – this is how we often refer these days to the Cultural Revolution, you understand – there was only one monk left here, and one run-down hall where he lived. All the rest had been razed by the Red Guards."

We stood before the dragon screen whose stone bulk shielded the temple from the bad spirits that roamed the world beyond. An energy company in Shanghai had donated money for its renovation, and their generosity was recorded in a prominent inscription. The Chinese rarely shied away from proclaiming their donations loudly, publicly celebrating good deeds in a way that could seem ostentatious to anybody brought up to believe in anonymous charity. Fortunes earned under the market reforms, the freedom to advertise one's business, and the loosening of controls on religion together have channelled money into these conspicuous displays of piety. Their very public nature is as much a way of obliging a celestial bureaucracy to reciprocate as it is a boast of social status. It is the wider community of lay Buddhists, from widows with their mites to company directors who can afford to donate an entire dragon screen, whose faith has begun slowly to undo the damage done by the atheistic Red Guards.

In the cool darkness of the first temple hall sat the pot-bellied Laughing Buddha. He too was sponsored, this time by a Volkswagen repair shop. The superintendent saw me reading the dedication with a grin. Half deaf, he shouted an explanation though I was only feet away.

"As you see, believers from the big cities have donated

money for us to rebuild the temple, to lay out our garden of Buddhist culture. Come with me, both of you." He led us around the Treasure Hall of the Great Buddha to a courtyard where a bell hung within a wooden frame. He ducked his head beneath its rim and beckoned me to follow. Standing inside the bell, our heads within inches of its bronze, his words drew from it a stifled chime.

"There are 7,000 characters cast onto the surface." His voice rattled excitedly, his face close to mine and his breath warm. "Around the rim it reads 'May the dynasty be stable, may the emperor's path be long and glorious, may Buddha shine more brightly each day, may his wheel of dharma turn eternally'." The Kangxi Emperor's reign had indeed been long and glorious, but his Qing dynasty had eventually fallen all the same.

"The bell was cast," the superintendent went on, "but during the casting the foundrymen ran out of bronze. They used pieces of granite to fill the holes, and this is why it's called the Stone-Filled Bell." He jabbed at the walls where the surface was in places not of bronze but of stone, smooth, amazingly blended into the metalwork. "You can hear it ten *li* away when it's rung. Now, in the hall over there" (he pointed out past the solid bronze as if he could see through it) "we keep our *yin-yang* mirror. When you look into it, you can see not just the reflection of this *yang* world of ours but also the *yin* world of the dead. And you ought to know *this*, too..." he went on, though the idea of a mirror that showed the world beyond the grave had caught my attention "... our stones were stolen from us!"

"Which stones?!"

"Our Fuyan Temple once owned three stones from Lake Tai, so beautiful they were called 'the three most famous stones south of the Yangtze'. They all possessed the four qualities of the best Lake Tai stones: deeply furrowed they were, tall and slender, pierced with holes, and cleft with channels." To the cognoscenti, Chinese garden rocks are much more than eroded limestones, their contorted outlines and whimsical shapes bringing to mind sacred mountains, or reminding the observer of Nature in that pure form the Daoists call the uncarved block. "There's only one stone left here now. After the ten-year turmoil that lone monk was tricked into parting with the other two, and now they're in big cities. I've spoken to people in positions of power, telling them that the stones should be here and that they're beyond value, but they just say they'll 'research' the question." The Mandarin word for "research" – *yanjiu* – sounds like "cigarettes and alcohol"; these officials were just fobbing him off, as well he knew, doing nothing more productive than smoking and drinking at public expense in endless rounds of banquets. The loss of those stones was still hurting him, the last pangs of a blow struck 30 years before. If they had been stolen in England, solicitors could have been instructed and a case prepared; here in China there was nobody to appeal to but political cadres who would not raise a finger unless there was some personal benefit to be had, some bribe, some debt to call in in the future. Just hearing about the futility of solving what should have been so simple a problem soon gave me an aching feeling of helplessness, a panicky sense of the claustrophobic world that hundreds of millions of powerless Chinese must navigate. Then the superintendent changed tack again without warning.

"You're English. I learned English when I was a novice, but then came Liberation and my monastery was shut down. I can't write any English but for one single word. I always recall it, because it looked like the number 200." On his palm he traced the word "zoo". "I still remember the phrases I learned, but not their meaning. 'The monk goes out to play', and 'the monk goes to bed at night'. Do you understand?" I translated them for him, saddened that his studies had been cut short by Mao's wariness of both religion and foreign influences; they seemed such kindly, harmless activities. Then, suddenly, his sharp mind was away on another line of thought without wanting sympathy.

"In this county there used to be all kinds of canal boats, each with a different purpose. There were nightsoil barges to take the shit to the fields, funeral barges to float coffins to their burial, marriage barges painted red for new brides, leper boats where the lepers lived in isolation, *likin* boats that carried imperial taxes. There were even 'flower boats', floating whorehouses that could hold a hundred girls."

Jiugao, as though bored of hearing only muffled echoes, rapped on the bell to summon us back into the light. Later, we three stood before the *yin-yang* mirror and tried to peer into the underworld. In its dull bronze it was hard to make out any reflection. There were only our three shadows, like reminders of our inescapable futures. I gave up looking and ran a finger along a crack in the mirror's smooth face.

"The Red Guards tried to smash it," said the superintendent. "But its strength was too much for them."

We rode on. What had Jiugao meant the day before, when he had said that fate had brought us together? Along with Cong Bian, he was the second person who had said this. He contorted his head over one shoulder.

"We're all born on a certain year, month, day and hour. The Chinese characters which govern the point we were born reflect cycles of nature. There are times when our own birth characters are in harmony with nature, and times when they are not." The imparting of this idea took several minutes of checking and rechecking what Jiugao was saying. I began to feel awkward, aware that he was growing exasperated, disappointed perhaps that my Mandarin was not quite up to the task of discussing metaphysics. "When I said we had *yuanfen*," he explained, "I meant that both of us were predestined to meet, that there was a bond of fate between us – that's the *yuan* – and that when we both arrived at the same place yesterday then we saw the crossing of our paths, the *fen*. Some people might have the *yuan* but lack the *fen*, and so their personal relationship never really begins. Now that we've been brought together, it's my responsibility to make our friendship as good as possible, to put our *yuanfen* into effect."

But I had not even been born when Jiugao's life was mapped out by nature's machinations to include mine. "Do you really believe in predestination?" I asked.

He turned the tables: "Why do *you* think we met, then?"

"Creation's too chaotic for everybody's futures to be set out from birth, isn't it? If we're all governed by *yuanfen*, then what about freedom to choose our own actions? How can you choose to be good or bad if it's already been decided? Don't Chinese pop singers sing about 'walking your own path' these days?" The idea of walking your own path had been raised by Deng Xiaoping himself when he famously launched China on the road to economic reform. Since then it had been adopted as a slogan of youthful independence, especially on Taiwan where people talked of the day when they might step out of the mainland's shadow.

"Lots of people say they want to walk their own path, but they might still believe in *yuanfen*. There's something bigger than us controlling our destinies. Didn't you just say at the temple that you wouldn't burn incense and kowtow, that you believed in your own god, not in Buddha? Doesn't he control the world just the same? Isn't it the same thing?"

I gave a non-committal mumble and settled back into the seat. The idea of an omniscient God wasn't the same thing as the reciprocating nature of the cosmos in Chinese thought, but Jiugao had made a perfectly reasonable point in observing that if one God controlled the world then this ostensibly left just as little room for freedom of action. My understanding of divine omnipotence did not mean that our every action was being controlled, but my Mandarin – not to mention my cod theology – was by now far outside its comfort zone. I was frustratingly aware of how China still confounded me despite my years spent there. The vacuum left by the retreat of communism from every aspect of life was being filled with the individualism of walking one's own path, by the nihilism of fate, the consolation of money, the balm of religion. The Chinese had always been able to hold to different tenets at the same moment, a kind of constructive doublethink long before George Orwell. Religions had generally co-existed well, with a man able to offer Confucian sacrifices to his ancestors' ghosts in return for immunity from harm while accepting that Buddhism taught they had been reincarnated and that Daoism taught of an afterlife which could be improved by priestly intervention. It was the present generation's casting off of society and walking its own path that was truly revolutionary. Materialism and the secular individualism it was founded upon seemed to be wrenching the Chinese from the social structures that had long subsumed them. When last that had happened, in the tumultuous decades that followed the fall of the imperial system in 1911, it had been Marxism-Leninism that had eventually triumphed.

My thoughts wandered as Jiugao rode on, wondering where the Chinese might end up this time. Would they tend toward democracy here just as Chiang Kai-shek's Kuomintang eventually had in Taiwan? A return to the bad old days of hardline communism was impossible: there were precious few who still believed that Marxism-Leninism was the answer. What about a stalemate, with people agreeing to keep out of politics so long as the Party left them alone and kept delivering better living standards? Perhaps, but the very structure of power meant that people were not left alone. Those in authority were unaccountable and corrupt. Every single citizen had their own sad story. As for better living standards, they could only be expected to rise so far, and then, as they began to plateau and perhaps fall, would middle-class China watch news of elections in other once-autocratic states and still accept that its children's futures were being sacrificed for an ideology nobody believed in? Perhaps for a time, but in the long run they would not. It was an unsatisfying conclusion, uncertain as to when and how things would change, but then the best-informed political scientists were no nearer to agreeing about China's future.

In silence we reached the Grand Canal. Doing what he could to help both me and fate on our way, Jiugao negotiated a ride on a barge. It took him an hour and frequent refusals, but this time there was no exchange of money, only a gruff call in heavy Wu dialect to scramble aboard. He stood by his trishaw until the barge's four engines spluttered soot into the damp air and she turned her nose into the stream.

御河

Larger than the *021 Cargo*, the *Jiaxing River Cargo 0312* could carry 500 tons in her gaping hold, but she sailed empty that day. It was by now early afternoon, and the family was preparing lunch. The bargeman's wife carried a stove out onto the deck and into it dropped a pair of honeycomb coals, pierced briquettes of compacted coal dust bound with paraffin wax and heavy oil. Their sulphurous tang had always brought to mind my first autumnal visit to a grey-green Beijing. We squatted beside the stove and ate garlic bolts fried with shreds of pork, and slices of salty mustard root squeezed from a sachet. Then the bargeman ate while his wife took the wheel. He showed off his binoculars, a powerful pair with orange lenses which brought the most distant barges to the tip of one's nose. The banks, die-straight lines on the map, swayed in the long, easy curves of age-long erosion. Their vanishing point lay always several miles ahead of us, the binoculars foreshortening the world to a wall of rusty metal and splashing bows below a fluttering red canopy of Chinese flags. The breathy phut-phut of the engines counted off the quarter seconds like a racing metronome as each new sight appeared, passed us by, and vanished astern – coal barges snuggled beneath the canopies of filling stations; rubbish barges gathered flotsam; tank barges drank deep draughts from refineries; cement barges ploughed their way from upcountry lime works to the construction sites of the city. The starchy aroma of steamed dumplings wafted out from teahouses. The Grand Canal was a world to itself, a noisy, spray-soaked strip of China, a country within a country where every convenience was provided for its inhabitants.

Uneducated beyond junior middle school, Mr Guan spoke Mandarin poorly. His wife seemed to speak none. My Wu was even worse. After a few attempts to get through we all gave up. There was a strong crosswind that day, and using their hands to play the part of barges the two acted out a strange puppet show to bring home how hard it was to keep a high-sided vessel on a straight course. The task enlivened them. Then Mr Guan led me to their living space and bade me sit in a chair. The cabin was roomy, with table and chairs, a long, upholstered seat, and cupboards into which life had been tidied away. The oak-effect floor was of the kind that China's land-lubberly middle classes were now buying in chains like B&Q and Home Depot. It was swept immaculately clean.

"Rest," he urged, and switched on the TV. His son, a quiet little boy rendered quieter by shyness, sat to watch a cartoon version of *Journey to the West*. Monkeys leapt across mountaintops and did battle with demons. Soon he grew bored, overcame his reticence, and motioned to me to see the rest of his home.

It was a surprise to find it better furnished than much of China's population yet enjoyed. Where the *021 Cargo* had been cramped and dirty, here there was a tiled bathroom with a sit-down toilet and a shower. A small galley had enough room to prepare food, and for sleeping there was a colourful quilt spread across a mattress in the bedroom. At the very stern, behind the pounding engines, a row of potted herbs brought freshness to the shipshape frugality. Mrs Guan was there, leaning over the rail to hoist a bucket on a rope. She poured water over the gangway and mopped it.

"Jiaxing... two... hours." She enunciated the words with care and smiled sympathetically when I understood. Even before those two hours were up, Mr Guan throttled back. From the shore I turned to see his wife waving over the stern rail.

御河

The centre of Jiaxing is an island ringed by canals, the very oldest of them dug in prehistory. The city has 1,200 miles of navigable waterways (Birmingham in England's industrial Midlands has scarcely 100, Venice just 26), from which seemingly infinite channels subdivide to irrigate the fields around like arterioles and capillaries pervading their living tissue. Seen from the air the whole world sparkles as the sun catches each strand of water, as though an immense, dew-heavy cobweb were set down across the plain.

Jiaxing's very name began as "flourishing grain", its hinterland a great producer of rice, and of sea salt boiled up in iron pans on the Qiantang estuary. By the Tang dynasty it was the biggest rice producer on the eastern seaboard: "If Jiaxing has one year's good harvest, then many districts may forget hunger", they said. Its grain was shipped across the province and the nation.

But now Jiaxing had turned its back on the canals which gave it life. It seemed the entire city had turned to look at what lay over its shoulder and, as if captivated, had turned to face the other way. The canals were still there, like cast-off childhood playthings, but they had been overtaken now by roads. Only in the last few years had the internal combustion engine finally ousted the sail. Canalside homes had been demolished, replaced by the gated communities of an urban middle class. The landing stages had been filled in, and lives lived on the water's edge lived on only in the memory of an ageing generation and in the picture postcards hawked on street corners.

Divorced now from the countryside, shorn of the trees that had provided a sense of natural proportion, the Grand Canal here looked minuscule, out of scale with the city shooting up around it. Arched bridges built for foot traffic (only recently had the porters finally laid down their yokes) had survived long enough to be an inconvenience to motor cars. They had become relics, like hunchbacked old men unable to move with the times. Jiaxing's urban planners had preserved them as the centrepieces to landscaped parks where people were relaxing on a quiet afternoon.

Suddenly a police launch interrupted the silence, roaring along the empty channel at full throttle like a joyrider on a backstreet. Its wake crashed against the embankment, slooshed up into the air, fell back into the waves. The canal chuckled with memories as it recalled the sensation of life in its water.

Jiaxing held two particular attractions for me. One was the Pavilion for Lowering Sails, the other the city's new Museum of Boat Culture. The museum was closer, a short walk along the towpath from my hotel. There was a lot to learn: Joseph Needham's all-encompassing *Science & Civilization in China* had given me a grounding in maritime theory, but my first-hand knowledge of Chinese seafaring was limited to the sight of junks in Hong Kong harbour. So I was grateful when the museum's curator, a garrulous man with a lifetime of knowledge, attached himself to this rare foreign visitor. We stood before a large scale model labelled as a *caofang*, a grain barge. He pointed first to the ground.

"Our museum was built in 2003, on the site of an ancient shipyard. Barges like this were once built right here." A mischievous smile played about his lips. "Now, Mr Lin, do you notice anything strange about this grain barge?" Her superstructure was all carved screens and living rooms, with no sign of a hold, nowhere for grain to be stored despite her name. "Exactly! This is a mandarin's barge, for the mandarins who managed the transport of grain to the capital. She would have been painted, lacquered, very comfortable, but she did not carry grain." Even to an untrained eye this vessel was quite unlike a Western boat. Most obviously, she had no keel. "Quite right, it has no 'dragon bone'. You call this kind of boat a 'junk', isn't that so? In China we did not use keels. Our boats had flat bottoms that curved up at the bow and stern, with external walls like a house and dividing walls inside for strength and buoyancy." He conjured the hull of a junk in the air with his hands and finished off her blunt profile with a chop. "They were shaped like a length of split bamboo and were just as strong. When you Europeans first came to China, you saw how our junks had dividing walls and you used the idea in your own ships. *We* had been using bulkheads since before the Han dynasty." We walked on, to a diorama of the junks which had once sailed out from the shipyard buried beneath our feet.

"From the fourteenth century, grain barges looked like so...." He indicated one of the models. She had an open hold, an arched cabin of bamboo matting, a single mast. The similarity between her and the barges upon today's canal was remarkable. Chestnut and fir had hardened into steel, and lacquered paper windows had become glass, but otherwise little had really changed in 600 years. She had the same flat bottom and square ends, a bow which swept upwards to ride the waves, a stern-post rudder, coamings around her hold, covered quarters to the rear. An anchor of heavy ironwood hung from her prow. Her mast and sail alone had been rendered redundant by the propeller.

"Under the early Ming emperors, barges could carry just a few tons of rice, no more than six, but by the late Qing each carried 35 tons." He gave his explanation with unconcealed enthusiasm. "They were sixteen metres long, three in the beam. The locks were less than four metres wide, so they could be no bigger." He pointed out models of other shapes and sizes as we walked through his galleries.

"This tiny thing is a snail boat. People used them to gather winkles. Over there is a fishing junk, and there were others for carrying salt, silk or sand. There were merchant junks full of commercial goods, and tribute junks bringing presents for the emperor. There were 'junks for offering the fresh', which sailed as fast as they could to take perishable food to the imperial court. The canal locks were opened without question when one of these arrived, so that it could whisk fresh fruit to the Son of Heaven without needing to wait its turn. Duck boats were painted green above and red below, with planks let down into the water for the ducks to waddle aboard on. Actors performed plays on floating stages while the audience watched from little boats. If you were a mandarin carrying important documents you would travel in a vessel called a 'fast junk, rapid as a horse'. Others carried building materials, bricks, timbers, roof tiles, just like today." Their sails were all of heavy matting, made rigid with laths of bamboo. They were what mariners called lugsails, wider toward the stern than the bow, and held taut like a vertical wing. For the task, they were unsurpassed in efficiency. Their profile is still with us, a visual shorthand for timeless China on a thousand glossy tourist brochures.

"With sails like these, junks could sail into the wind. In Europe, Mr Lin, your square-rigged ships found this difficult to achieve. But a canal is narrow, and the wind could blow a junk sideways into the bank. Remember, they had no keel to stop this." The curator made a lugsail with one hand and blew on it as it came toward him. He let it drift leeward. "Chinese bargemen hung boards over the side to counteract wind drift." And thus the leeboard was invented, some 800 years before it was copied by the Portuguese. The curator was well into his stride now, brimming with pride at China's achievements. He traced a character on a palm; it meant "rudder".

"Our junks used stern-post rudders long before your ships. By the fifth century, our junks had more than one mast. You did not have this for another thousand years! The compass, too, was being used by Chinese sailors by the twelfth century!" He counted off each point on his fingers, making of maritime technology a game, as though by racking up a high score early on China should by rights have had an unassailable lead. But then China had been caught out by the arrival of the Royal Navy and the subsequent Opium Wars. Under the pressures of conflict and trade Europe had raced ahead, and junk design gradually lost ground to Western shipbuilding with its curving hulls and pointed bows. The curator was quite right, though: without the compass, the watertight bulkhead, multiple masts and the stern-post rudder (not to mention gunpowder) the Royal Navy would never have painted the map of the world red. The British Empire was won with discoveries made on the far side of the globe.

A crocodile of primary schoolchildren in the red neckerchiefs of the Young Pioneers filed into the museum. They squealed when they spotted a foreign face, and it was with difficulty that their pretty young teacher quietened them down and got them to focus on the day's outing. The curator excused himself and began to explain his exhibits to his new charges. "Now, children," he began, "do you notice anything strange about this grain barge?"

Free to wander the halls, I came across a display of canal locks. In this respect, too, the Chinese had for most of recorded history been far ahead of Europe. They had observed the world around them and reasoned that the earth was alive and suffered illness just like their own bodies. The *yin* and *yang* of rivers, earth's arteries, could become unbalanced, and the *qi* energy that flowed in them could become blocked and cause disease – floods and droughts, shallows and rapids. These could be cured by canalizing a river, turning it into a flight of manageable stretches using simple weirs of rock and bamboo. Yet weirs were too inflexible a structure to allow boats to pass. The Chinese had solved that problem before the time of Christ with the invention of the flash lock, wooden boards slotted into grooves on opposite banks to form a temporary dam. Boats needed only to gather above the closed lock, then at a signal the boards would be hoisted and the sudden flush of water escaping would carry them downstream. Then with time those crude flash locks were superceded by the double slipway, two shallow inclines rising from the water to meet in a peak. Boats were hauled up one slope, would balance precariously upon the cusp, then career down the other side. Though their crews directed them as best they could, it was perilous work, and wreckings were common. As dynasties came and went there were other innovations – pound locks that allowed the rise of vessels of immense burthen, and side ponds that made staircases of locks possible. It was not until the dawn of the Industrial Revolution that British engineers would hit upon the same ideas. But by the 1950s the last of the canal's old flash locks and slipways had been supplanted by Western imports, and within a single lifetime another strand of Chinese self-reliance had been broken.

On the long walk across town to the Pavilion for Lowering Sails there was plenty of time to think. Jiaxing was writing another sentence into the story that China was telling itself about the Grand Canal. That story told of how China had achieved so much so early, of how it had created the canal with no outside help and under the rule of strong leaders, and of how foreigners had learned technology from China rather than the other way around. The ideas were disjointed, but I had begun to piece their meaning together.

As for the Pavilion for Lowering Sails (so named because

barges would drop their masts to ride the Green Pine Lock that lay alongside), I had been looking forward to seeing it since reading in the castaway Ch'oe Pu's diary that he had spent time there in the spring of 1488. A place for travellers to rest while their boats passed the lock, my imagination had sketched a pavilion set amongst trees and lotus ponds. I had uncovered no illustrations, only passing mentions: "By sandy banks and willows, at the setting of the sun; the evening mist curls about the masts, as it has always done," one Ming poet had written (the Ming was not the high point of Chinese verse). But its tiny garden proved unequal to my imagination, a knot of belvederes set upon artful crags, shaded by trees but trapped within a graffitied wall. Only a portion had survived, on the edge of some ramshackle homes in the shadow of a road bridge. Walkways led between patches of weed, up stone steps to gazebos and balconies. Doors were closed, padlocks rusted shut. Where steps had rambled through limestone grottoes, fig trees had seeded themselves and now blocked the way. I peered over the wall hoping to see the Green Pine Lock, but it had been dredged away. Two men were taking measurements with a ranging rod and theodolite, and a trio of elderly women sat upon a bench eating bowls of rice.

"The Qianlong Emperor once came here," announced one. "Now a park is being built to restore the pavilion to how it used to be." The surveyors, hearing her talk, stopped their work and came over to listen. She eyed their yellow jackets and hard hats with equanimity. "Our houses will be demolished to make room," she said. "But this is where I've lived for most of my life." She pressed a hand against a wall that stood hard against her seat. She showed no animosity toward the surveyors and they no awkwardness that their work was sealing her home's fate, all three united now in curiosity toward a stranger.

"Where will you live when your home has gone?" I asked.

"It hasn't been decided yet. An apartment block, perhaps. I'll likely just be given social housing, poor housing...." She trailed off into Wu dialect to make a comment to her friends.

The surveyors went back to calling out numbers, preparing to scratch out another sentence in an old story that China no longer wanted to hear. The woman's home told only of the poverty of the pre-reform era. A new generation of urbanites did not want to live in draughty shacks with no sanitation, and a new generation of pragmatic leaders like Premier Wen Jiabao was expected to provide them with better. Once the migrant workers had swarmed over this site and carted the rubble away, once these crags and belvederes had been cleaned and restored, the clock could be turned back to an age the people of Jiaxing could be proud of, when the Son of Heaven himself had visited the Green Pine Lock.

御河

The drizzly leading edge of a distant tropical cyclone arrived that same day. The pollution already had me at a low ebb, and now the chill brought out a trio of painful mouth ulcers. As the day grew dark I sat down in a branch of McDonald's: the thought of eating anything too flavoursome held no excitement. Outside, a little girl, her pigtails held in place by extravagant ribbons, was dancing to the pop music leaking from the restaurant's doorway. As she danced, a bland tune segued into one I recognized, *Don't Wanna Grow Up* by the Taiwanese girl band S.H.E. Its catchy riff had been stolen note for note from the opening bars of Mozart's Great Symphony.

"Why can't I find a pure rose?" S.H.E. sang. "Why are my princes not princes enough? I'm not expecting a glass slipper and a white charger, just surprised that sweet nothings can turn out to be lies. Don't wanna grow up. Once you grow up the flowers all go. Don't wanna grow up. I'd rather stay simple and slow."

That little girl was blithely happy. She knew nothing of what China had been like before it began to open up to the world in 1978. Even her mother who stood watching over her must have been too young to remember the start of Deng Xiaoping's reforms. A whole generation had been born, raised, wed, and had itself given birth since the advent of the Four Modernizations. In that short time, urban China had been transfigured. As the economy had boomed, and as cities had modernized their dilapidated old housing stock, streetscapes that would have been familiar to Confucius himself had become unrecognizable. In the last few years the country had crossed a watershed, and it was now a pleasant exception to find a single building of any real age in the big cities. I fished out a notebook. How best to describe the landscape this girl would grow up into? Her mother had been born into a utilitarian world of blues, greens and greys, but today's Jiaxing was gloriously colourful. Everywhere it shouted "buy things!" at you. That simple message was unrelenting, no respecter of space or moderation. Without moving I could see advertisements pasted onto taxis, rickshaws and buses, on litter bins and lampposts, smothering buildings from the risers of their steps to the hoardings of their skylines and, above these, even on their aerial masts. Adverts were glued to the very pavements, below rows of sponsored parasols. Banners were trailed across roads and had even colonized the space between earth and sky, suspended vertically beneath red helium balloons. The buses that day had had adverts sandwiched between the clear plastic of their handstraps, on the back of their tickets, on their windows, on their flatscreen TVs that ran promotions for sexual health clinics....

To my notes I added the question "loss of innocence?", as if my mind had performed a simplistic leap from material possessions to some unwitting fall from grace. After a moment's reflection I struck out those words: so many millions had suffered and died before the start of Deng's reforms that "innocence" was obviously wrong. Perhaps I had meant artlessness, or unaffectedness? I was uncertain; they all sounded patronizing. Then, as that little girl carried on dancing to *Don't Wanna Grow Up*, my eyes began to well up with tears. I blinked them away and gave an embarrassed laugh: the cold and the rain had put me at a lower ebb than I had thought. In the dead of that night something woke me. Lou Yue was a shadowy figure in a corner of the hotel room once again.

"You almost wept today," he said accusingly.

"It saddened me that China has changed so much, and that she'd never see the simple China I saw when I first came here. The song was stupid, but its words made me feel like that."

"*Simple?*" Lou Yue's voice rose as if in disbelief. "You think you know China? You have only known it these few years. You did not see it before the reforms, only read about it later in books. These people have lived their whole lives here. China was never *simple*. Life was far harsher when I travelled here, especially under the Jurchen who ruled the north. I saw Chinese being beaten by foreigners. *You* are comforted by what you think are the certainties of the past, critical of the present, afraid of the future, not wanting to grow up. You smelled the sulphur of honeycomb coals burning today and felt nostalgia for the China of your youth. To the bargewoman that smell was of the only fuel she could afford, nothing more."

"The future can look brighter than it is," I heard myself say. "The things that China thinks it wants will just turn out to be disappointing."

"You think China shouldn't find that out for itself? It doesn't need your protection, your sympathy. You can leave this place whenever you want. Who are you to tell China that it is losing its innocence through these reforms?"

"I'm angry because they're demolishing *my* China!" My voice was raised now. "And I miss it."

"*Your* China?! It was never *your* China – you just passed through when you were young and carefree. You had the money and the status to ignore the realities of life here before all these things came along that you think you dislike. The people you met weren't carefree like you, they were worn down. The little girl will grow up far happier than she ever would have. Why shouldn't she have what you already have?"

"In China these days there's nothing *but* the search for money and status driving people, nothing deeper. At least people had something to believe in under Mao."

"Ah! Now you romanticize that butcher! Mr Lin, you cannot reduce the entire Chinese people to a search for money and status."

I seemed to lie in a half sleep until dawn, thinking. What was it that troubled me so much about the gradual demolition of old China? By the time a grey daylight lit the room, I had come to an answer of sorts: once the physical buildings were gone, all the vulnerable memories and emotions that attached to them would be liable to dissolve like gossamer with the passing years. Already it was becoming harder to recall the scenes. The private, everyday places had almost all gone. The tangled Shanghai streets where I kissed my girlfriend from my university days had become the open acres of People's Square; the wood-fronted restaurant where my wife and I had shared that special meal had vanished beneath office blocks. On turning each familiar corner with a breast full of memories, only to find that they had been bulldozed away, it was as much a feeling of dread as of sadness that wrenched the insides – dread that as time went by there would be no touchstone to test my memories upon. Nor was I alone. The old woman at the Pavilion for Lowering Sails would be losing a lifetime of memories in the rubble of her home, and there were hundreds of millions just like her.

御河

Six hundred miles to the southwest, the cyclone that had been dominating the weather made landfall the next morning. It had been strong enough to take life in the Philippines, but up here in Zhejiang it was felt as just a low, leaden sky from which water fell in perpetual torrents. The rain was so heavy that the barge looked as though it might sink before ever the heavens were exhausted.

"Does the weather ever get so bad that you have to stop?" I asked the skipper.

"When there's a heavy fog, so thick you can't see where the banks are, then we tie up. It's very dangerous if you see another barge so late that you can't avoid it." What about when it grew dark? "We still work at night!" he gasped: he was a *getihu* – an entrepreneur – and was surprised, insulted almost, to be asked such a question. "It's a little more dangerous, and whoever's steering needs to be attentive, but we must make money, isn't that right?"

His mate nodded his agreement: "We say that 'an inch of passing shadow is worth a foot of jade'."

Three rain-soaked hours had been wasted trying to hitch a ride. Wangjiangjing was only eight miles from Jiaxing, a two-hour walk were it not for the fences and inlets that now made an impossible assault course of the towpath. The skipper knew why I had waited so long – there was an old bridge up ahead, too small for barge trains to navigate, and so there was scant traffic. This stretch of the Grand Canal had been relegated to the status of "ancient", a little-used museum piece. Most bargemen rode the New Grand Canal, he said, dug a decade before as a spacious shortcut. Then there were the harbour supervisors; without warning they boarded barges to check they were not overloaded, and there was a fine if you were caught with passengers. We were inexorably nearing Jiangsu province, where regulations were more strictly enforced than in easy-going Zhejiang. The news was both unwelcome and prophetic.

The rain was still lashing down when we tied up beside the sprawling cement works on the outside of town. The skipper went to ask about taking a load back to Jiaxing. I set off on foot, heading for a distant bridge. The towpath to Wangjiangjing ran beside acres of waste ground, fields churned for the moment into a Passchendaele of mud. The plain beyond was a water-sodden grey-green, flecked over with smokestacks and pylons. A file of rusty barges nuzzled the bank, their sterns stuck out into the flow like a flock of ducks dabbling. Their engines were shrouded in sheeting, their windows unseen behind tarpaulins. Bent almost double against the weather, my ulcers a painful distraction, at first the Rainbow Bridge did not strike me as special. It soared high above the quaking water, in essence a near-perfect copy of the Bowing to the Emperor Bridge in Hangzhou. Here, though, its footings had been bound around and around with ropes which drooped like swags of dirty bunting. Tyres had been woven into that mess to fend off barge strikes. Saplings grew from cracks in the stonework, and rainwater ran down the bridge's face like tears. It was the only arched bridge left in this county, 400 years old, too precious a symbol of the town to demolish yet too narrow to be convenient. In it, Wangjiangjing had already given up the sole sight I had come to see, but the skipper of one of the rusty barges did not hold out much hope of me finding a ride further north that same day.

"If we get caught with an unlicensed crewman it's a 2,000-*kuai* fine, more if we can't 'walk through the back door' to pull strings. The harbour supervisors are corrupt like all cadres, you understand. They make up their own rules to benefit themselves. If you don't fly the national flag, a fine. If they can't make out your registration, a fine. If you're overloaded, a fine." With so many officials using their authority to line their pockets, it was understandable that bargemen were not welcoming me with open arms. "You'd do better to take the bus, friend," he suggested.

"Do you think I might have more success tomorrow morning?"

"*Ye keneng,*" he opined with a shrug. "It's *possible....*"

Graffiti

杭州

北京

across southern Jiangsu province to the Yangtze

The rain shows off some places to their advantage, teasing from them an extra layer of romance or interest which passes unseen in the dry. Wangjiangjing will never rank among them. The town was scarcely more than grids of apartment blocks on half-finished streets. Its drains could not swallow the rain which had fallen that day and sheets of water stood calf-deep, turning even the shortest walk into a long march. A banner had been strung above the main road: "Wangjiangjing, a pilot town for the national comprehensive reforms of small towns and cities, welcomes you!" It had once been named "the town which clothed all under heaven", so many of its inhabitants wove silk and cotton on their household looms. Now the textile industry had been mechanized, and the taint of chlorine hung heavy, persistent even through the lashing rain.

The only hotel I could reach without wading through water was cheap, only half finished, and unconcerned with police regulations. The receptionist did not want to look at my passport, as though the less she knew the better. Her voice grunted from under a pile of quilts, and a disembodied hand tossed a key. The room was on the first floor; the stairway beyond led to where construction work had halted in midair. The doorjamb had been splintered, and screws held in place what was left. A bolt had been positioned too high to meet its clasp, but a chair wedged beneath the handle achieved much the same effect. The walls were stained brown where mosquitoes had been swatted. Others threw leggy shadows, lured out by the carbon dioxide from the beer which helped pass the time.

China Central TV was screening a documentary about the ethnic minorities of Yunnan province. There were the once matriarchal Naxi, the Buddhist Dai whose forests pushed down into Burma and Laos, the Va who saw powerful deities in natural phenomena, the tattooed and turbaned Blang, the animist Derung whose entire population could squeeze into any one of the apartment blocks going up in Wangjiangjing, and many others. In all my years in China I had never been to Yunnan, and these peoples and their cultures were a mystery. So why the hell was I lying here wrapped in an unlaundered quilt when I could have been sat in the tropical sun drinking Pu'er tea and eating fresh pineapples? There was an obvious answer: it was the workers of towns like Wangjiangjing who were refining cement for the skyscrapers of Shanghai; it was they, not the hill tribes of Xishuang Banna, who would build China's future. But there was something deeper too, a bloody-mindedness, a one-downmanship that would rather seek out places that nobody could find lovely than follow the crowds to the popular destinations. And there must have been a persistent streak of masochism, too, or perhaps it was inverted snobbery or simple miserliness, that had me eating instant noodles when my wallet would have stretched to much better. Yet in some perverse way I was happy like that. Hadn't somebody once grumbled about going on holiday but inadvertently bringing himself along? With me it was quite the opposite: China was always an escape. Back home I was the anxious first-born child of textbook psychology; here in China I was eight hours ahead of those neuroses, half a world away from myself. As for Lou Yue's appearance the previous night, he had struck a nerve about being comforted by China's past, but he had been right. Soon the beer lulled me to sleep, and by morning the rainclouds had receded to the horizon and the sun had come out. Warming myself at the window, gradually the chill of the night left my bones. I coughed, like everybody coughed: the chlorine had worked its way into our lungs as we slept.

The barges beside the Rainbow Bridge had dispersed under cover of darkness. A wasted hour on the towpath proved that the skipper had been right: those few barges that used this narrow channel could not simply pull over on demand when a landsman hailed them. Instead the clattering rural bus to Pingwang crossed within a mile from Zhejiang into Jiangsu, the long, coastal province that swept up from the Roman nose of Shanghai to the outstretched arm of Shandong. A new province demanded a new atlas. Just like the last it promised discrete villages, tiny red circles separated by white farmland. In truth the land, scornful of this cartographic fancy, was an endless building site, a ribbon development of factories and sideroads that led as yet to nowhere. The jasmine bushes by the wayside were dusted with grime, yet tiny white flowers still bloomed on them. Wild roses blossomed, and poppies swayed in the traffic's wake. Overhead, birds sang above the engines' roar. Those little intimations of welcome did much to lift tired spirits.

A westerly breeze carried sweet air from above Lake Tai. Pingwang was the hub of southern Jiangsu's waterway network, and there I stood in the sunshine to survey the vast, glistening crossroads at the heart of the town. Here again were those sinuous barge trains, too long to have risked the bottleneck at the Rainbow Bridge. In broad arcs they glided gracefully away to Shanghai, to Zhejiang, and northward ever deeper into Jiangsu. The name Pingwang signified the Flat Prospect of these lands: the view had once been of unending reedbeds and lakes. Then the Chinese had brought civilization, had tamed nature just as Cong Bian had boasted in his taxi. I wished now that Jiugao the rickshawman could have been there too: through his smiling eyes the shining steel of Pingwang's new factories would have been beautiful.

Beneath a signpost pointing out the way by water to Suzhou, a barge was tied up to a bollard. She carried scrap in her hold – offcuts of sheet metal, curls of coarse swarf looking like the shorn hair of some gleaming giant, and waste punchings which stuck vertically from the heap like monstrous stencils. A woman squatted to wash clothes. I asked where she was headed, and she gave a blunt reply.

"Huzhou. *Gan ma wen wo*? Wotcha doin' askin' me?"

"I want to go to Wujiang."

She looked me up and down. "You don't have a sailor's licence, do you? Nobody will take passengers, especially not a *laowai* like you. *Mei banfa*. No way." It was said with hostility as she backed into the wheelhouse, though there was a defensiveness in her face. She had made it plain for all to see that she did not accept stowaways. A young woman in the crowd caught my attention:

"Sir, this is going to Wujiang." And she stepped out to flag down a roaring minibus. The conductress squeezed down the aisle. As I folded my change I saw that one banknote had characters written upon it, a neat hand in blue ink across the undulations of the Great Wall. They read "The Great Law of the Falun Gong is the True Law". Instinctively realizing the seditious nature of that tiny graffito, I slipped it into a pocket before anybody noticed, then wondered whether in my tiredness I had imagined it.

御河

On a V-shaped plot at the edge of Wujiang stood a hotel garnished in such Graeco-Roman opulence that it would not have looked out of place on the Las Vegas Strip. Opposite, on the forecourt of Dio Coffee, were parked rows of black limousines. A uniformed youth in white gloves guided each new arrival into ever tighter spaces. Dio Coffee, serene oases of dark wood and velveteen, is China's riposte to Starbucks and Costa. It has a studiously European air that, as was clear from the cars and their occupants, China's new rich loved to soak up. Even its carefully chosen Italian name means something close to "follow the European path" in Mandarin. The customers that afternoon sank back into the plush seating, drinking in the cosmopolitan atmosphere as they relaxed. Dressed alike in suits and ties, it was impossible to guess their business, difficult to tell from just looking at them whether they had earned their money as *getihu* or as political cadres.

A girl in a pinafore and mob cap took the order and brought a glass of lemon-scented water. Unsure whether to drink it or wash my fingers in it, I took a sip. She watched with fascination. A barista ground the coffee beans by hand and brewed them in their own tiny percolator. The girl left a plastic tub of coffee whitener. I chuckled, comfortable and relaxed like the other customers, and settled down to read more of Lou Yue's *Diary of a Journey to the North*. It happened that he had run aground on shoals right there at Wujiang in February of 1170.

"*Huanying guanglin!*" The waitresses chorused their welcome as the door opened and another customer entered. He walked to my table, stood by my shoulder, cast an eye over the *Diary*'s woodblock characters and read them aloud:

"Then a great wind drove the waters of Lake Tai into the canal. Spreading our sail, we travelled on...." Lou Yue's style was concise, his writing still comprehensible after 800 years to anybody educated in modern Chinese. It brought the distant past vividly into the present. The man asked if he might join me. His name was Hu Zhixiong, he said, and he hailed from Confucius' birthplace, Qufu in Shandong province, some 600 miles away. He wore a black leather jacket (an unnecessary layer given that the weather was in the nineties) and thick glasses which squeezed deep furrows into his temples. Qufu was not far from the summit of the Grand Canal. Had he himself seen it?

"I've seen it, but there's no traffic there anymore." This news was unexpected. Mr Hu could see that his offhand remark had come as a surprise. "There were big floods at the end of the Qing dynasty, you know," he offered by way of explanation, "and the canal was severed by the Yellow River. Soon after Liberation it was redug, but there's really too little water up there."

"It's dry?!"

"Not dry, but too shallow to carry a boat."

Yet the atlases in my bag showed the canal as an unchanging blue line, and the map in the lobby of the Grand Canal Museum had linked Hangzhou to Beijing in an uninterrupted string of bulbs. Mr Hu was contradicting what both these were telling me about the canal's course, yet there seemed no reason to disbelieve him. I made a mental note to discover more about the floods and their effect.

I asked instead: "Why are you so far from your home?"

"I'm a furrier. I sell the fur trimmings on clothes. They don't have these animals in Jiangnan."

"Have the animals all been killed by hunters in Jiangnan?" Nothing bigger than a rat had ever crossed my path in all my years in China, and I suspected that any wild mammal more palatable had long since been driven to extinction.

"Well, we don't *hunt* them in Shandong anymore, though they still do that in Heilongjiang, in the northern forests. We farm them – arctic fox, red fox, mink, rabbit...." He counted off the species on his fingers, leaving his thumb proud as though to indicate the quality of his pelts.

"And cats and dogs?" I grinned mischievously.

He spoke with evident pride in his work, pushing forward a substantial stomach as oblique proof of his success: "Some cats and dogs, but not many. We mainly breed foxes. They're fully grown by spring, and then we kill them and sell the skins to the clothing industry. They export them to Europe. You're European – some of your clothes could have my fur in them." There was little chance of that – I invariably wore jeans and a T-shirt and owned nothing with a fur trim. Besides, the trade was a little cruel. "Not cruel!" he exclaimed with a look of childlike hurt. "We feed them good food to get good skins, and we kill them humanely. If you mistreat them they damage their own fur. Worthless."

Animal rights groups had compiled many reports on China's notorious fur farms, all filth and overcrowding and animals being skinned alive, still I shied away from arguing. I had never visited Mr Hu's farm and he had a right to be believed. Besides, his Mandarin was immeasurably better than mine and he would only have felt more superior after shooting down clumsily worded arguments. Travelling widely enough in China, too, had tempered my views: the living conditions of humans there were rarely the topic of high-street petitions back home. In China, where as late as the 1960s tens of millions were dying of famine, the ethical boundaries of what was cruel to mere animals were evolving only slowly. I changed the subject. Was it Mr Hu's first time in Wujiang?

"Not at all. I've been doing business here for thirteen years." He stared out of the window and mused. "Jiangnan is rich, Mr Lin. No-one begs on the streets. Just look outside. People have electric scooters and motorbikes, but they never get stolen. The price of one wouldn't even buy you a meal in that restaurant." He pointed at the lightshow playing on the stucco of the Graeco-Roman hotel. "It's *mei*, isn't it? How do you say *mei* in English?"

"Beautiful." That seemingly simple word was having to work hard. The only aspect that this hotel and Jiugao's new shops shared was how different they were to what had gone before, how alien their architecture to traditional forms. Two girls in red cheongsams held open the hotel's doors as a pair of drunken businessmen stumbled out. They forced cigarettes upon one another, each refusing to accept with such vehemence that they seemed to come to blows.

"The Party had a campaign a few years back to get people speaking English in preparation for the Beijing Olympics," I said, turning back to look at Mr Hu. "Did you learn any?"

He slapped his knees with both hands and wagged a finger. "You're very humorous, Mr Lin! I like you! No, no, I didn't learn English like the Party suggested I might, just interested in hearing a word or two." He paused to think. "The Party has its reasons for these campaigns, you understand. They know what's best for China. Still, they couldn't have predicted what was going to happen when they started to open up after Mao died. Nobody thought that the economy would take off like it did. Premier Wen Jiabao is one of Old Hundred Surnames just like me. Grandpa Wen understands what motivates us Chinese, how we *think*." He tapped at his temple. "Tell me, Mr Lin," he went on. "How do you British see China?"

The banal reality would have disappointed him: most people's interest in his culture did not extend beyond takeaway food, and most would have trouble spotting the differences between China and Japan. But I did want to tell something of the truth, if only to see his reaction.

"In England, when many people hear the word 'China' they think first of your food, and then..." I lowered my voice, "... of the human rights question."

"*Human rights?!*" he squawked, making a mockery of my whisper. "China's population is too big, too chaotic, for us to worry about human rights! I tell you, Mr Lin, there are thirteen times one hundred million people in China, and the Party cannot keep society harmonious without being firm. In the future, perhaps, but for now it's not possible." He sank back in his chair and huffed.

Remembering the banknote with the Falun Gong graffiti, I took it out to show him. The Falun Gong's popular *qigong* meditation practices had been very publicly outlawed in 1999 after thousands of adherents had appealed for legal recognition outside the Communist Party's Beijing compound. That had been less than ten years since the Tian'anmen Square crackdown, and things had still been tense. The Party at the time had accused Falun Gong of being an alternative power base – that it was counterrevolutionary – and of being superstitious, fallacious, a danger to China's stability. It was arguably some of those things, depending on one's view of religion, though whether it was a threat to one-party rule was quite another matter. Looking at history from the Party's perspective, the suppression of Falun Gong was understandable: millions had died in insurrections sparked by mystical cults like the Yellow Turbans, the Jesus-inspired Taiping, the shadow-fighting Boxers. China's rulers had always had a rational, if ultimately selfish, mistrust of alternative centres of moral authority. The campaign to portray Falun Gong as a brainwashing cult had been thorough, but there were still people willing to risk imprisonment to pass graffitied banknotes into circulation. Mr Hu looked taken aback when he saw it.

"I've never seen anything like this before. This kind of 'black organization' is very damaging to society." He handed the note back and changed the subject, nervous perhaps of discussing Falun Gong in public, more likely simply because this pragmatic businessman did not care for such troublemakers and their pseudo-science. "Ignore this. Ninety-five, no, ninety-*nine* percent of Chinese support the Party. There's no-one in China who hasn't a place to sleep and food to eat. Compare that with India, like you see on the TV, and look what's become of the Soviet Union – a laughing stock. Even in our poorest provinces the Party has given everybody the chance to work for their own future. Here in Jiangnan," (he nodded to the limousines beyond the window), "people aren't content with small change – they want to earn big money." Then he squawked once more as another thought came to him: "Why do the Americans want to say terrible things about us?"

"I think the Americans fear you, Mr Hu. They're like the hegemon kings who once ruled China's warring states. China will soon have the biggest economy on earth, and the Americans are afraid."

Mr Hu grinned. "They're *afraid*, are they? Well, if they want to fight, we're prepared to fight." Nobody had mentioned fighting. "The status of Taiwan is a big question for us Chinese," he said firmly.

The Taiwan question was 60 years old, but there were few issues that engendered more intense feelings. After the retreat of Chiang Kai-shek's Kuomintang forces to Taiwan and the end of the Chinese civil war, the Communist Party had claimed to be the rightful rulers of that island, though they had never in fact controlled it. The Kuomintang in turn had claimed to be the rightful rulers of the mainland, though such a state of affairs was a pipe dream. The US meanwhile, wartime allies of the Kuomintang, had sent its 7th Fleet into the Taiwan straits to forestall a communist invasion, and since then Washington had treated Taiwan as its "unsinkable aircraft carrier in the Western Pacific". Only in recent years had Taiwan and the mainland even grudgingly admitted that the other was a *de facto* – if not a *de jure* – government. At the 2008 Olympic Games both had agreed that Taiwan would compete as "Chinese Taipei" to save face on both sides. Proposals that the People's Republic of China and the Republic of China on Taiwan be politically united under a policy called "One country, two systems" had been raised by Deng Xiaoping in the 1980s but had been scoffed at in Taiwan, a first-world democracy with nothing to gain from subordinating itself to the communist mainland. A sabre-rattling stalemate had ensued, as certain Taiwanese politicians had advocated full independence and a renunciation of any claim over the benighted mainland. In 2000 the election for the first time in Taiwan's short history of a non-Kuomintang leader, Chen Shui-bian of the Democratic People's Party, had only deepened the animosity: the Kuomintang at least had continued with the gentlemanly pretence that China had never been divided after the civil war. Chen though was a Taiwanese nationalist, leaning towards severing ties with the old country. Only fearful pragmatism had stayed his hand: the People's Republic had made it an article of law that a declaration of independence by Taiwan would immediately bring down upon it a full-scale invasion. Since Washington had always maintained that an invasion of Taiwan would provoke a military response, the US now found itself in the uncomfortable position of supporting an island whose independence would have brought it into armed conflict with Beijing. America's position, the Communist Party reasoned, was one of interference in domestic Chinese politics, and it became a stick with which to beat the US all the more roughly.

But now tensions had eased, thankfully, with the election of Ma Ying-jeou to the presidency of Taiwan. Ma had immediately taken a position of pragmatic reserve, walking a tightrope between supporting the ideal of unification while refusing to be drawn on details. At least independence seemed no longer to be on the cards. Ma's stance had been enough to convince the Communist Party that it would not find itself needing to explain to thirteen times one hundred million people why it had not prevented the disintegration of their country. Now commercial aircraft were flying between Taiwan and the mainland without stopping off in Hong Kong, cargo ships were sailing from Kaohsiung to Xiamen without breaking their voyage in Japan, and for the first time since 1949 it was possible to post a simple letter from Taibei to Beijing. Still, this was an amicable ceasefire rather than a long-term solution to the question of Taiwan's status.

"We Chinese are peaceful," said Mr Hu. "But if the Americans want to fight us over Taiwan, let's have a war. We will win." Before I had reached Beijing, others would have said the same, and worse.

The Emperor's River

御河

The sun beat down the next day upon the amputated stumps of Wujiang's Long Bridge. It had once been well named, the longest pre-modern bridge in China, one-third of a mile long, but just twelve of its seventy-two arches were left standing. What had been done here one spring evening could only be hinted at on a stone tablet: "In May 1967, most of the Long Bridge collapsed." Overnight, stones well-mortared for 600 years had fallen into the canal. Countless thousands of temples and pagodas from Harbin to Hainan had fallen down around the same time. To this day, a century and a half after the Second Opium War, Beijing's tour guides are right to remind visitors of how the British and the French razed the Old Summer Palace; the irreplaceable murals stolen by German archaeologists are still mourned in the Silk Road grottoes of Bezeklik (they were eventually turned to dust by Allied bombs in the ruins of Berlin). But though the Communist Party carries an even greater burden of blame, rarely is the vandalism wrought by its own Red Guards openly admitted. Those ardent teenagers had grown up now, were living normal lives as bargemen, policemen, rickshawmen, fur farmers, and few wished to rake over the past. The apocalyptic zeal they had channelled into Mao's call to "Smash the four olds!" had been turned outward by some into the infinite possibilities for private enterprise, inward into regrets about a wasted youth by most. Despite the number of books on Western bookshelves telling the experiences of educated Chinese in the late 1960s, there was a conspicuous absence in the very country affected by the events of those years. Forty years on, that decade was still too momentous to grasp. Yes, the Cultural Revolution had officially been acknowledged as a mistake, but that very acknowledgment had forestalled a wider catharsis which might have led to questions about the Party's culpability. Perhaps when the Red Guard generation has passed on and democracy has come to China things will be different, a new generation of Chinese historians will publicly and without fear begin to tackle the despoilation of their heritage, and the atmosphere of sad loss that haunts the Long Bridge will gradually fade.

As the unfamiliar sunlight bathed me, that violent episode which had taken place within my own lifetime felt remote. Red Guards had brandished their little red books and their sledgehammers here in the name of perpetual revolution, but theirs had been an alien cause born of a foreign ideology, and ultimately it had failed. It was Wujiang's new cultural revolution that was truly Chinese, now that the Party had admitted that the best way to raise living standards was to allow people the freedom to do what the Chinese diaspora had shown them to be especially skilled at – making big money, just like Mr Hu the fur trader had said. In the town centre, the gleaming storefronts of Sun Yat-sen Road all bore Chinese brand names. People's Square had its counterpart in a People's Shopping Mall. *Huanying guanglin!* rang out like an anthem each time a customer stepped into a shop – We welcome your presence! Loudspeakers in every doorway blared out at such an amplification that their music became an inaudible roar. Wujiang had been ranked amongst the top ten most developed of China's small cities, and it wanted to shout about it.

But that same shouting had also awakened people to the pernicious damage the reforms were bringing. Of China's 750,000 towns and villages, 251 had been declared unscathed enough by modernity to be worth preserving. They had been recorded, catalogued, and listed at the Bureau of Cultural Relics. A handful had survived hidden away amongst southern Jiangsu's marshes, a labyrinthine world where life and death once turned on the health of the waterways. The inexorable demolition of their old buildings had been halted, cordons thrown up, ticket booths erected. One of them was Tongli, a tumbledown village upon a clutch of islands close by the Grand Canal.

There was no music blasting from the doorways there, the only noise the guides' loudhailers sharp and tinny above a hubbub of voices. The old courtyards seemed to let out a sigh of relief once each tour party had chattered its way to the next. The Chinese had come in their thousands to visit Tongli just as the English might spend time in the Cotswolds, come to reminisce over things they had never experienced, to eat the hundred-fruit honey cake their grandparents had told them about. They delighted in the atmosphere of traditional China just as they had soaked up the European flavour of Dio Coffee. Old women sculled boatfuls of them on circuits of the village, but the boats shone with fresh varnish and they never rowed out any more with fishing nets and crab pots. A few decades ago, every dot on this map had been a Tongli. Now its fading heritage had been cleaned and packaged for easy consumption, like the roasted water-caltrops that were sold on the streets. Fishing and rice growing had become less profitable than the story of Tongli itself and had withered away. The heritage industry was Tongli's biggest employer now, a way for the villagers to make money without becoming just another marginal note in the story of China's economic miracle.

I stood beside a bridge at the village's heart and waited while lunch, a skewerful of stinky tofu, was deep fried. Beside me, a guide bawled needlessly – her party stood within feet – into her loudhailer.

"The locals," she bellowed, "have a tradition called 'walking the three bridges'." The tourists, elderly women from Nanjing, nodded: this custom was well-known in China. "They say that walking across the Peace Bridge brings you good health through the four seasons, across the Luck Bridge a flourishing business, and the Celebration Bridge eternal youthfulness."

The tofu fryer, a short man with a wispy moustache and a string vest, fished my lunch from the oil. Its crisp skin parted between my teeth, its innards curd-like and musty like a young Stilton cheese. A pennant behind him read *Three Bridges Stinky Tofu*.

"You can look me up on the internet," he said. "A writer came here and loved my tofu so much he wrote about me."

"Is the story of the bridges true?" I asked. "Do you really do all that walking, or is it just something you tell the tourists?"

"Walking the three bridges? Yes, traditions like this are growing strong again. When a child reaches his first month, his parents come to carry him across all three so he'll have a long, healthy life and earn big money. People from outside Tongli, newlyweds from Suzhou and Shanghai, come to be photographed on all three for the luck it will bring."

"I got married before I left England," I confided. "If I walk across the bridges alone do my wife and I both get all those things?"

His eyes wide open in admiration, he stuck out his chest and held up a thumb. "Friend, you told your wife to look after your home while you came to China? Now that's what a *real* man would do, not worried about what the women think!" We shared a manly laugh, though the humour for me lay more in the gulf between how he imagined our relationship and the reality. Far from being left to pine for her absent master, Rebecca was doubtless spending her days, as always, working full time as a university lecturer and her evenings in a whirl of social engagements. If anything, she was having the better honeymoon. That realization alone lightened the guilty feeling I had been carrying since Heathrow at leaving her staunching a nosebleed. I congratulated the tofu fryer on his excellent stinky tofu and sauntered away in good spirits; he quickly caught up.

"Friend, walk with me.... This is my house. You see these bricks?" He poked at the wall where the plaster had flaked away to reveal an unyielding petrol-blue underneath. "Three hundred and fifty years old. These ones, a different shade, are 250 years old. But *these* ones, they're new, repaired after Tongli became famous." He prodded at the spalling red bricks and a layer came away on his fingers. "The old ways are the best, isn't that right?" Brushing his hand clean he ushered me into a dark corridor. It turned doglegs into the heart of Tongli's buildings.

"It's so cool in here," he observed. "Like natural air-conditioning."

We entered onto a courtyard where bamboo baskets were piled high upon racks, each filled with slices of ivory tofu speckled with mould. A trio of women sat on stools, chatting away animatedly as they knitted baby clothes. Outnumbering the tofu fryer three to one, they looked self-confident.

"You're back, husband!" observed one with an indulgent smile. "Sold out?"

"That's right, back for more," he replied, then, turning to me: "Here are my mother, my wife, my daughter. They make the tofu just like we've always done here. We press the soy-milk whey ourselves, and leave it to grow mouldy. We sell three squares for one *kuai*. Every basket has hundreds of squares, and we have many baskets. We all share in the work, and the harder we work the more we earn. Life is very good for us right now." The retelling of the Grand Canal story might have condemned one old woman's home in Jiaxing, but here it was guaranteeing a family's future.

御河

By night the headlamps are dimmed to bright smudges in halos of exhaust fumes. The dark mass of the Long Bridge broods in silence; its wrecking has at least freed it from the traffic and brought it these moments of utter tranquillity each night. The tall pagoda beyond is lit from within by a soft white glow. Reflected in the black pool it is bewitching. Its perfect symmetry and hushed radiance leave me spellbound. The passers-by say it is beautiful, too, and for once we agree on the meaning of beauty. This glowing vision follows me around

Wujiang's streets, forever appearing from behind hoardings and neon until I find my hotel.

By morning the glowing pagoda has turned to a grey rod upon the skyline, like the cold ash of temple incense. On the road once more, the bargeman's prediction for Jiangsu – that its hard-pressed skippers will be unwilling to take passengers aboard – seems to be coming true.

"I was born and raised in Suzhou, and I've worked there all my life," says the taxi driver. He has waited patiently until, frustrated by the impossibility of finding a barge, I have accepted his offer. "But I've never been asked to drive to the Precious Belt Bridge. People who want to see the bridge always go to the far bank, where there's a good view." It is only when he says this, well into Suzhou's industrial sprawl, that it strikes me that by standing upon the Precious Belt Bridge I will have found the sole place where it will be invisible.

The Precious Belt Bridge, built so that merchants of the Tang dynasty might more easily cross a broad lagoon, is the most photographed spot on the entire thousand miles of the Grand Canal. There is a picture of it upon my map. Its broad granite causeway runs dead straight for two furlongs. Its roadway is flat, with no parapet to stop skittish horses from plunging into the water. It has survived intact the percussion of Hirohito's bombs, the predations of the Red Guards, and the schemes of the modernizers who thrice planned to dismantle it. At last it has been made a national monument. The driver, confounded at each wrong turn by dead ends and impassable ditches, finds it with difficulty. At its end is an islet. The sun is setting in an orange glow over the fishing nets, making the oil tanks gleam like copper and the windows of her factories glow like squares of amber. The water sparkles, and the splashing bow waves of the barge trains bear fleeting rainbows. The calm of the lagoon reflects the dusk-lit face of the bridge. Its arches merge into their reflections to create a chain of dark, round jewels set in shining bronze – a precious belt. As the sun sinks and a pale shadow rises in its place, I sit in the mute company of two stone lions. A delighted chatter in accents I recognize from home drifts across from the tour boats. The buoys' warning lamps burn, and soon an arc of white stars traces the span of a road bridge. Tall smokestacks wink with sparse fairy lights, and the running lamps of the barges come and go in red and green.

御河

It had been the need to communicate with the farthest parts of his new empire which prompted the First Emperor to push highways out to the corners of China, across the borders of the warring states he had unified. Wide and tree-shaded, until the arrival of the telegram and the railway they were the arteries of a nation, radiating from the capital to the very edges of the Chinese world, taking emperors' commands to distant mandarins and bringing news back to court. Despatch riders, a bamboo box strapped to their backs, might cover 200 miles in a day if the weightiness of its contents demanded it. Every three miles along the Grand Canal post route they would find a rude, thatched booth where they could find fresh horses. At each town they passed they would find a postal relay station. In scarlet halls the arrival and departure of letters amidst the clatter of hooves was recorded in duplicate and stamped with a chop. When the postal system reached its apogee in the Qing, a wooden board accompanied each document from its starting point to its destination. In cobalt characters it faithfully recorded the time of departure, the speed of its rider, and each stop he made, proof of its provenance down to the last minute.

Even encroaching upon the horizon of living memory, mandarins on official business had been lodged in those postal relay stations, had been given good food, entertainment, a soft bed. The Chinese gave them the name *yi* 驛, a character which required 23 strokes of the brush to write. For the brazen disparity between its elaborate form and austere sound it had long been a favourite character of mine, and visiting the reality it embodied an ambition. Suzhou, ever a populous and sophisticated city of scholars, had been blessed with fully half a dozen such *yì*. The local map promised that on the Grand Canal there stood the very last of them.

It had been built upon open fields buried now beneath flyovers and car repair shops. Under the dead-eyed stare of factory compounds ran a clinker towpath. Porters scuttled along under a burden of bamboo yokes, carrying hodfuls of bricks to the barges. A small pavilion was squeezed onto a taper of land. A plaque bore its name apologetically, as though the presence of this mere room needed to justify the effort of finding it. A man in blue overalls sat smoking a cigarette.

"Is this all that's left of the postal station?" I could hear the disappointment in my own voice.

"*Duile*, just this entrance gate." He nodded at a memorial set into the wall. "The station was renovated at first, but then after the ten-year turmoil only this was left." He took in my features for the briefest of moments and asked coolly if people in my country collected plastic bottles for a living. Travelling in China there would be the occasional person like this, and often from amongst those least likely ever to have spoken to a foreigner, who unlike the rest would not turn a hair at my sudden appearance and address me as though this were the most natural thing in the world. England did not have bottle collectors like they had in China: it was impossible to make a wage from it. Is that what he did for a living? He lit another cigarette as if to avoid answering. "I come here to sit and watch the barges go by when I've free time."

The engines on a tug moored beside our pavilion coughed into life as if to confirm his point. He quizzed me about home: how many *kuai* were there to the pound? he asked. Did I have a pound he might look at? I gave him a coin to keep. How many hours' flight was England from China? How much was a ticket? How much did refuse collectors earn? How much did a house cost? It had been a few days since Lou Yue had accused me of having no concept of how the Chinese really lived. Deep down I was awkwardly aware of how true that was. Here was a man one or two rungs up the ladder from the illiterates who raked over the garbage heaps looking for scraps. He had no health insurance, no savings to speak of, just a bedroll and a space on the floor of a shared lean-to. Despite that, the topics that interested him were scarcely different from those of an English dinner party. Anywhere, money and prices are a lubricant to conversation, things that transcend language and place, their Arabic numerals universally understood, a shorthand for greater differences. But their limitations are telling. Once on a Chinese train I had been required to put a value to my clothes. A pair of Chinese cotton sandals bought in London had elicited gasps: they had cost me the equivalent of their maker's weekly wages. From those few garments the carriage had extrapolated a picture of what England was like, talking amongst themselves and occasionally shooting off another question for clarification. In the end, though, any number of questions about prices could not have painted for them a true picture, just as questions asked of a bottle collector from Suzhou said more about this one outsider's vague impression of the challenges in his life than his answers could ever truly reveal.

御河

In 1979, with the onset of Deng Xiaoping's reforms, the Suzhou Steamship Company bought four passenger ships and began to sell tickets to travellers looking to sail between Suzhou and Hangzhou. Long before a six-lane motorway linked the two cities, a night-time passage was a comfortable alternative to a bumpy bus ride, with the added bonus of saving the cost of a night's accommodation. Soon almost 1,000,000 journeys were being made each year. There were others, too: in Jiangsu province alone, by the time Mao died in 1976 there were 240 scheduled canal routes serving 1,500 destinations. But then came German-built coaches with their roll-pitch control, independent suspension and air-conditioning, and of the dozens of passenger ferries which had once shuttled up and down the Grand Canal the *Blue Wave* was now the sole survivor, the only people to sail her the tourists willing to pay for the romance of an overnight cruise. I had missed enough on the way north to justify a trip back to Hangzhou; albeit in the dark, the *Blue Wave* ought to cover the stretches I had travelled by road.

I was to share a cabin with two Chinese beauties, as the captain put it. Lanlan and Meigui (their names meant Orchid and Rose) were both attractive, with big brown eyes and the high noses and sculpted cheekbones of Central Asia. They sat amid a mountain range of luggage like travellers in a caravanserai. They were from Urumchi in China's far west, but despite their features they were both Han Chinese, their parents from Sichuan and Hubei. Their Mandarin had the crisp perfection of those who have grown up in a land where every immigrant speaks a different dialect and relies on China's lingua franca. After the staccato babble of Wu, it was a delight just to listen to them chat and to understand each word.

"If you're travelling from Hangzhou to Beijing, how can you have so little with you?" Lanlan made a suspicious face while she weighed my shoulder bag – my only luggage – in her hand.

"My make-up's bigger than that!" exclaimed Meigui, holding up a flowery flannel bag and laughing. She laughed unaffectedly, without raising a coy hand to cover her mouth as most Chinese women might. "And our cases are *full* of souvenirs." So, what were they doing on the *Blue Wave*?

"We'd both seen the adverts on TV by the Suzhou tourist board, you know the ones? They call it the Venice of the Orient, and they say 'above there's paradise, below there's Suzhou and Hangzhou'. The TV pictures are all of canals in the mist, cormorant fishermen, gardens...."

"... weeping willows, pagodas," interjected Meigui. "Well, we flew into Shanghai and took a train to Suzhou. As soon as we left Suzhou's railway station we realized that Jiangnan was just as *zang luan cha* as anywhere else in China." The phrase meant "dirty, chaotic and substandard", a way some Chinese had of describing what had become of the urban environment. For Lanlan and Meigui, reality had fallen short of expectation. I sympathized with their disappointment. My first visit to Suzhou had been back in 1993. Over the years it had changed from a relaxed provincial city of tree-lined streets to a cosmopolitan hub of glass-and-steel office blocks. The visual displacement that has gone with those changes can only be compared to an English market town becoming overnight like the high-rise City of London.

"The scholars' gardens were beautiful," said Meigui. "But there were so many tourists we could hardly see them. There was an English girl on our boat trip around the city moat, but she only photographed the rickety houses they hadn't demolished yet."

"The only place that looked like the adverts was Tongli," added Lanlan, "but Tongli felt like a museum. The foreigners there took pictures of an old woman washing her clothes. Why do you foreigners do that? You never photograph the beautiful things."

"They're photographs we couldn't have taken back home, that's all, just like I imagine you two take photographs of scholars' gardens but not deserts."

"Xinjiang's deserts are *frightful*," said Lanlan with feeling. At that moment our boat passed the Precious Belt Bridge and we paused to peer through the window. There was not a soul upon it. It looked lonely and vulnerable, unvisited alongside the hurly-burly of shipping, like it was not meant to be there.

"You two are a long way from home," I commented, turning back. "Do you feel safe? Most Chinese women think that travelling outside a tour party will get them robbed or murdered." They shrugged in unison.

"We're not 'most Chinese women'." Lanlan smiled widely. Was that why they had not simply taken the coach to Hangzhou? It took just a few hours and was far cheaper. There were plenty of coaches in Urumchi, she answered, but only one Grand Canal in China. Besides, they could afford it. They would not say what they did for a living, only that they earned big money. They intrigued me, these two confident women who talked like sisters and who thought nothing of flying 2,000 miles to see places they had dreamed of visiting since their childhood in the deserts of Xinjiang.

Sloping away discreetly while they prepared for bed, I found the door to the bridge open. The captain sat in the dark upon a high chair, one hand on the silvery ship's wheel. He patted the stool beside him. In the blackness ahead there was nothing to be made out but the running lights of the barges.

"Are you using radar?"

"Radar, eh?" he chuckled, as if amused to hear a technical word from the mouth of a foreign passenger. "This isn't the Yangtze, mister – we use our eyes."

As my sight recovered from the tungsten brightness of the cabin, the sky slowly resolved into a light black smudge, if such a colour could be said to exist. The banks though remained formless, as thick and as black as tar.

I muttered: "I see nothing."

"Look at the margin." He pointed at the near bank. "The sky's reflected in the water, our running lights too. The ripples have a different texture to the earth. If the moon's up it's even easier."

"And if the weather's bad?"

"If it rains at night, if it's misty, we often need to stop. If you can't see the bank it's dangerous to carry on."

"Why don't you just use your searchlight?" There had been a lamp of considerable size mounted upon the bridge. He reached up over his head and flicked a switch, and for an instant an intense whiteness shone out from above, lighting our way like daylight but blinding anybody sailing towards us. As the light died, so did the shades of meaning my eyes had gleaned from the thick veil. Only slowly did they recover, and the world reverted to four triangles of black, two of them dark and two a shade lighter, all meeting in the distant centre of my vision. Red and green spots floated into view and then vanished. Remembering what Mr Hu the furrier had said about the state of the canal in Shandong, I asked the captain if he knew anything about the floods that had supposedly severed it there. He nodded.

"The Yellow River, our Mother River, has two paths to the sea – one north of the Shandong mountains, one south – but she is always unsure which she prefers to take. Before 1855 she flowed south of Shandong, but then the dikes upriver at Kaifeng burst, and when the water subsided we saw she had swept away the canal and was flowing in her northern bed. Thousands were drowned, but it's the same every time the Yellow changes her course." If the Yellow really was China's Mother River, then she appeared more in the guise of a filicidal Medea than a devoted Demeter.

We sat in silence while the captain navigated the centre of Pingwang. Then, as the *Blue Wave* straightened up, he spotted something in the darkness ahead and flashed on the lamp for the briefest of moments. The barges of a train travelling north unladen were dragging in midstream only a hundred yards away. He barked at me to leave the bridge, and I slid out onto the gangway. Through an unseen loudspeaker his voice bellowed, echoing around the barges and dissipating into the blackness. The train closed on us, its rusty freeboards towering over our deck, until the water between us became too little, we were both sucked together and, soft and dream-like, we struck each other a glancing blow. Our loudspeaker roared again, and a tough-looking woman on the rearmost barge shouted back with a petulant grimace as she passed.

"They were on the wrong side," the captain explained. "Not paying attention, you understand. It took me twenty years to qualify as Number One, but some pilots aren't so experienced." I could only take his word for it.

Lanlan and Meigui were sitting up in bed talking when I got back, oblivious to the drama. The cabin smelled of cologne. Lanlan saw me sniff the air and held out a bottle of green liquid.

"It's called Fragrant Dew. It stops mosquitoes biting." She dabbed a little more onto her wrists. "Mosquitoes love to bite us. Everybody's blood has one of the five flavours – sour, bitter, sweet, pungent or salty – isn't that right? We must taste sweet to them."

"We think they should be given little punishments for biting people," added Meigui. "Can't they fine them?" They both laughed at the thought. They examined my insect repellent, far more effective than their citronella, but in the end they turned it down – the Chinese used Chinese ways to stop mosquitoes, they said. I shrugged and sprayed DEET over myself, and in the morning awoke to see Lanlan scratching her bites and muttering.

A dawn mist was rising when the *Blue Wave* tied up in Hangzhou and a line of sleepy tourists filed across the gangplank. The city was already wide awake, scurrying to its cool offices before the sun grew too hot. Lanlan and Meigui hailed a taxi and set off alone. At the bus station I bought a ticket back to the same Suzhou I had left only twelve hours earlier. It was half the price of a berth on the *Blue Wave*, offered complimentary food and drink, and took just three air-conditioned hours. It was no wonder that the *Blue Wave* was the last of its kind.

The annual Dragon Boat festival was approaching, and Suzhou's streets were full of stalls selling traditional *zongzi*, patties of sticky rice steamed in bamboo leaves. I ate one and contemplated how to get to Wuxi. The tactic of engaging a taxi driver astute and mercenary enough to smooth the way onto a barge had worked before, and the first I hailed was willing to risk an arbitrary fine to take my money.

"Wuxi?" He had asked, unsure of my meaning. "There aren't any passenger boats to Wuxi. You mean you want to go to *Hangzhou*?" A ¥100 note drawn from a pocket had made my illicit intent clearer.

Half a dozen container cranes stood hunched over a wharf. Beneath, barges were unloading sand. Their moorings were black, and oily rainbows played upon the surface. The driver approached a boatman, offered him a cigarette, and they talked out of earshot. The boatman lifted his hands in clear refusal and pointed to another barge. A mound of sand hid the driver from view, but he returned with a broad grin on his face. The *Suzhou Cargo 026* had just sold a load of yellow sand, dredged from the Yangtze her skipper said and needed for construction. He was sailing back that way and I could travel with him to Wuxi on condition that I hid. I was steadily nearing the Yangtze now, and the urban sprawl was growing denser. In the twenty miles between Suzhou and Wuxi the open countryside scarcely once impinged on the scene, as though buildings had shouldered their way like buffalo down to the prime watering spots until no space was left. Plumes of steam trailed from the apparatus of factories like the breath of great metal monsters. Demolition crews swarmed across the few farmsteads that dared remain, stripping their tiles and reducing them through skeletons to patches of rubble. The raw ingredients for what would replace them – the sand, gravel and gypsum that go to make up roads and factories – were heaped in cones upon the shore like giant limpets exposed by the tide. And everywhere there were barges, three, four, five or more deep by wharves bristling with cranes. The skipper called through the hatch:

"This is Wuxi's wholesale grain market." He pointed to the bank, where barges were disgorging bellyfuls of sacks. "They buy and sell rice, wheat, soy, maize, flour.... I've carried rice for them in the past. There, behind the granaries, they have their own railway station." The granaries, like vast aircraft hangars, peered down imperiously at the clamour around their feet.

Rather comically, Wuxi means "There's no Tin!", a name that was given to the city after the ore deposits in the mountains ran out, to dissuade more prospecters from arriving. Once that had happened, the Grand Canal became the city's saviour, a highway for shipping its produce across China. On a straight mile of wharves outside the north gate, some 80 merchants once kept warehouses in one of the largest grain exchanges in the country. At the Hibiscus Lake Teahouse they had conducted their business over pastries. In 1911, the year that Sun Yat-sen's revolution toppled the Qing, Wuxi still handled the better part of 500,000 tons of grain entirely by water. Now railway trains dozens of wagons long rolled through the suburbs with plaintive, drawn out wails that seemed like a lament for the past.

御河

"We say that these houses are 'as tightly packed as fishes' scales, as close as the teeth of a comb'," an old man told me as we gazed along the water. Roofs and walls contorted with age clung desperately onto both banks, drawing as close as they dared to the edge without actually falling in. We stood on Purest Reputation Bridge, the narrowest point now of the Grand Canal, where the stones pinched together until there were scarcely a dozen yards between them. Designed for narrow, unhurried junks, before a bypass had been dug this bridge had been an impossible bottleneck, a bar to the advances that Deng Xiaoping's Four Modernizations had planned. "Protect Wuxi's Grand Canal heritage for future generations!" urged a sentence painted in enormous characters onto one embankment. How exactly were the people who saw that slogan expected to comply? It was not the kind of task that the average citizen could accomplish alone! The old man chuckled at my misplaced indignation.

"The authorities enjoy painting slogans like that. *We* can't protect it, of course, but we know that a decision has been taken on the subject."

We stared down together at the water. It was a greenish brown, immobile and unused. I asked him: "Do you remember when this was the only route for barges, before the bypass was dug?" He answered with pronounced satisfaction.

"*Dangran*, of course – I'm 80 years old. I can remember before Liberation, when fishermen used to work here by night with lamps to attract the fish, and with cormorants trained to catch them in their beaks." Were there any fish here now? He shook his head: the tradition of catching fish with birds clung on only in remote villages, and in the tourist towns along the Li River in distant Guangxi. "I remember the old lantern festivals. We hung globe lanterns lit with candles from all the bridges, along the banks, over all the temples. Others were painted to look like fish, and people would set off strings of firecrackers." The fish had symbolized plenteousness, and the firecrackers had scared away demons with their noise: *peng peng peng peng peng!*

On a map of Wuxi I had jotted the name of a temple reputed to have been a centre of worship of a guardian deity of canal travellers; I knew of no others that were left. The old man studied the characters – *Shuishen Miao*, Temple of the Water God. He knew of it but could not place its whereabouts. It had once been a focus for the communist underground, he said, reaching deep into his memory. It was this connection that had saved it from demolition. Others knew where it was to be found. It proved to be a building unmemorable amongst the façades. By its doorway was a plaque announcing in a suitably quiet voice that this was the home of the Wuxi Daoist Society.

If the Fuyan Temple in Chongfu had been full of the incense and vivid colour of ebullient Buddhism, then this Daoist temple was its antithesis. There was nobody in its small gatehouse, and the courtyards were empty. The halls were in gloom, and in their atmosphere of sombre silence could be felt the dark presence of shawled figures, statues of men who had transcended life and death and become ethereal immortals. The organized practice of Daoism had all but died out in the People's Republic during the ten-year turmoil, when priests who had been the living repositories of tradition were persecuted and their monasteries destroyed. Now a new generation of Daoists was rediscovering their scattered beliefs. Pervading the temple were proofs of Daoism's ancient knowledge of astrology, of its deification of the stars as controllers of human destiny. In one hall, row upon row of statuettes represented the 60 years of the Chinese astrological cycle. 1970, the year of my birth, was presided over by the dog-headed Grand General Ni Mi. Nearby, the carved animals of the Chinese zodiac had become deformed versions of themselves, scarcely recognizable as their species. Daoism was often counterintuitive like that, but these names seemed almost intended to baffle the uninitiated: a rabbit, almost the only animal I could identify, bore the unfathomable name "Celestial Palace of the Scorpion Worthy Spirit Ox Perfected Green". Other statues sat behind tablets bearing equally abstruse titles: the Southern Extreme Great Emperor of Longevity, the Wealth Spirit of the Five Directions and Five Roads, the Mysterious Dark Perfected Man, King of Medicine Sun Simiao. In another hall, the Star Lord of the Plough held deserted court upon a decorated throne. In a tradition called the Way of Highest Clarity, Daoism has it that adepts might make an astral voyage to meet the deities that dwell within the stars of the Plough which revolves around Polaris, the very hub of the cosmos. Those star lords, refined beings who fed on light itself, could be presented with petitions and persuaded to intervene in the fate of relatives who had entered the underworld.

Elsewhere, the temple priests had rekindled an ancient ritual called the *jiao*, where astral spirits were invited down to commune with humans. The detritus of that communion lay scattered about – half-burned candles, decapitated soda cans full of ash. The walls were pasted with join-the-dots star charts and scraps of paper covered in scrawled cacography. The priests had consulted the secret registers of the celestial bureaucrats presented to them at their ordination, had followed those star charts, undertaken trance-like voyages to the heavens. They had taken with them talismans, proof of their priestly credentials, written in contorted forms of Chinese characters that invoked authority in the spirit world just as in this world their orthodoxy invoked respect. Their spidery shapes were menacing and eerie, like something one might have glimpsed through the *yin-yang* mirror in the Fuyan Temple.

A carpenter, the only other living soul, was busy marking up wood. His workshop was carpeted with golden shavings and smelled of scorched pine, its freshness and industry a world away from the unearthly prayer halls. He saw me leaning on the doorpost to inhale the scent of resin, and indicated a trestle. His band-saw squealed, pitching sawdust into the air until the tiny space was thick with it. A flaxen grit settled on damp clothes. The carpenter took up his pencil and marked the wood against the tenon of a second beam. With a chisel he slowly hollowed out a mortise, then clouted the joint together and hammered home a peg.

"No nails, you see." He carried his work out across the yard to a side chapel, and there he hoisted the timbers like a gibbet beside a wooden figure which dominated one wall.

A mercury vapour lamp filled that chapel with a harsh light which stripped from the god all his mystery. Only when the curtains were drawn and the lights extinguished would the shadows make this chapel a place of worship.

"Who is this god?" I asked. The carpenter shrugged.

"*Bu zhidao*. Dunno." He marked the gibbet against the wall and mumbled a measurement. His work was painstaking, I told him. "You must see the work I've finished in the big hall."

In its centre, a deity wrapped in silks and satins was enframed within a sculpted cage towering up to a high ceiling. He had chased the wood with scrolls and flowers, had smoothed on gold leaf that shone through the gloom. The work was only months old, yet it might have been aeons. Dust had collected deep in its folds; a candle flickered; a thimble-glass of spirit had marked the passage of time in its rings as it evaporated a little more with each day's heat; silver-paper ingots had warped and discoloured.

"Who is it?"

Again he shrugged: "*Bu zhidao.*"

"What about the Southern Extreme Great Emperor of Longevity, or Grand General Ni Mi? Do you know anything of them?"

"I don't understand Daoism."

If asked to name the saints in a Roman Catholic church and comment on their significance, I could have done no better. But it was he who was carving these gods, unaware of who they were, unconcerned, his interest merely businesslike: "I enjoy working with wood," he admitted, "and these days the temples have money and need rebuilding."

By a doorway I found the god I had come in search of, and his story. The late Ming had seen Japanese pirates despoiling the lands around Wuxi. The district magistrate, a young scholar named Wang, had led his people in building a defensive wall. Indebted, they had erected a shrine in Wang's honour so that they could forever offer him sacrifices. Facing out over the water it was soon a popular stopping place for others, too. Soldiers escorting the imperial grain barges north, the mandarins who oversaw them, fishermen, boatmen and merchants all came to pray for safe passage. Wang reciprocated, watching over them in return for their offerings, and so they returned and prayed again. By and by this local official had taken on the mantle of Wuxi's water god, a Chinese Saint Christopher to protect pious supplicants. His statue sat behind glass now, and before it the spirit tablet that embodied his soul. I lit a stick of incense, suspecting that these days few others felt the need to ask for his protection.

御河

The next day I take a walk along the towpath, hoping to negotiate a ride. A skipper calls out when he spies me hovering by his bow: "Take a seat, have some tea!" He pulls up a tricorn stool, as small as a child's, and hitches his trouser legs up around his knees to cool himself. I mimic him – it is a habit I have learnt from the working Chinese – and reveal pale shins.

"Mr Lin, the Grand Canal isn't a route, it's a *concept*." He taps at his temple. "I hold the maps in my head. There are at least five or six ways of getting here from Hangzhou. I know them in the dark." He gives me the impression he could navigate blindfold, by smell. "Some of them are fourth class, some fifth. It depends on the size of your barge which one you take." He is well informed; the knowledge which determines how much he earns and where he earns it has made him obsessive about the canal's classification. The entire Beijing to Hangzhou Grand Canal is divided into seven sections, he explains: there is not only this Jiangnan Grand Canal, but others north of the Yangtze – the Inner Grand Canal, the Central, the Shandong, the Southern, the Northern, the Tonghui. Across the Yangtze it is third class, he says, designed for 1,000-ton barges. Beyond Yangzhou it is wider and deeper still, all the way to Xuzhou at the farthest reaches of this province. The canal is vital to the economic prospects of Jiangnan's cities, he stresses: each was gradually getting around to upgrading its own section as demand for cargoes grew and as traffic got heavier. How far beyond Xuzhou is it navigable? I press him: a fur trader had said that there was little water at the summit.

He ponders the question. "Depending on the season, I'd guess to the Weishan Lakes." The Weishan Lakes, four interconnected bodies of water some 80 miles long, straddle Jiangsu's border with Shandong. This means that none of the canal within Shandong or Hebei, Tianjin or Beijing, is passable. We trace the long, dry section with our forefingers in the atlases I produce, and the skipper catches my look of despondency. "The government is planning to use the Grand Canal to carry water from the Yangtze to the north, where there are droughts. When it's finished there ought to be a lot more water in the canal. Perhaps some day you'll be able to sail to Tianjin," he consoles.

I am rueful. "I don't plan to do all this again. What's the situation beyond the Weishan Lakes?"

"The water level's too low. It flows, but there's not enough water to float a barge." Everybody on the canal, it seems, agrees with Mr Hu. We sip our tea thoughtfully.

"I like your spring couplets." The subject turns to the red paper strips pasted onto his cabin. They have been stuck there since Chinese New Year and read "May the five lakes and the four seas be calm," and "May each bend in the river be safely negotiated." "Do they protect your barge?" He does not answer, but leads me into his living space, where upon a ledge is a porcelain statue of the god of wealth with his flowing black beard. Fairy bulbs wink on plastic candles which do untiring service for real incense. Guan Yin the goddess of mercy stands in serene stillness. "Do you burn incense to the water god as well?" I ask, but he has not realized that Wuxi has a water god. He shakes his head too when I ask to ride with him to Changzhou: with a full load of chemical fertilizer he is likely to be inspected. But he says he will help, and together we walk along the towpath. The trees on the Emperor's Pier Mound, a temple-topped islet, are in broad leaf. The city around us is noisy; the Qing emperor Qianlong loved to spend his nights on that quiet spot. The skipper sees a face he recognizes, another Yangtze bargeman returning home unladen, and arranges a ride.

Now the canal wanders back and forth for a while before striking out in a straight line toward Changzhou. Except for a few moments where the green of the fields seems at last to be holding back the inexorable drift of industry, there is nothing new in the scenery. In my notebook I try new ways to describe coal dumps and factories, but give up. For three hours we pass one after another, a monotony broken fleetingly by rarer sights that hold the attention: a waste-oil depot where barges can empty their tanks rather than flush them into the water, a shipbuilder's yard.

"How much did this barge cost?" I ask, seeing the flash of arc welding.

He seems embarrassed to tell me. "Four hundred thousand *yuan* to build new, split between me and a partner. Now we've a huge loan to repay." This is an enormous debt, perhaps twenty years' salary for an urbanite in a state-run work unit. Is it worthwhile? "If I carry gravel I can deliver 500 tons from a depot and earn 10,000 *yuan* profit. Of that I get a half share. But there's the cost of insurance, a certificate of seaworthiness, port registration. You pay 250 *yuan* to pass through the shiplock into the Yangtze, and you sometimes queue for days. Everybody takes another slice until there's only 2,000 *yuan* left, and from that I make the repayments. Private bargemen like me can squeeze our margins, take whatever's going, but factories are closing and building projects are being put on hold. There's still profit, but not much."

Youshui, the word he chooses to express "profit", means "oily water". It conjures up images of the glossy sheen on wet fruit, or of the cream on milk. High diesel prices are making his oily water thinner than ever, I suggest. He harrumphs at the mention: "Sometimes it's scarcely worth doing this job."

御河

West of Wuxi, the Grand Canal began its imperceptible rise into the low hills that herald the Yangtze. That slight elevation had always made this stretch difficult to keep full: engineers had forever struggled to stop the water from simply running away. The task had proved to be a balancing act between slowing the stream with locks and so allowing silt to settle and choke the bed, or else wasting precious water through the scouring action of a swifter current. Dredgers fitted with counterbalanced beams and grappling buckets scraped up silt from the depths while the canal went on working, but dredging could only achieve so much, and when the canal was not being used to transport grain it was dammed in sections and its bed recut. In the winter of 1076, just one year out of the many hundreds when these immense undertakings took place, the Grand Canal at Yangzhou alone was recut by over 4,000,000 labourers. Technology has not solved the problem, and hundreds of thousands of cubic yards of silt are still dredged up each year.

"Downtown Changzhou was always a real nuisance for us," the skipper complained, pointing out the wide mouth of a new bypass that would circumvent the city's strangulated heart. In a thickset font that brought to mind the "big character" campaigns of the 1970s, a colossal billboard announced the completion of the Changzhou Route Change Project. But instead of caricatures of political enemies it bore an artist's impression of the sparkling new cut. In that idealized world, leisure yachts coasted up and down between landscaped banks, and happy families leant on the balustrades to watch them. There was no sign of the grimy barges which made up its real traffic, or of the furtive lovers who sat upon the benches.

"Ten million tons of freight pass through here each year, but it was always so underdeveloped that we used to say 'the Grand Canal is 1,000 miles long, and Changzhou is the first bottleneck'. Back in Luoshe there was a boat jam not long ago. A barge train grounded, and by the next day there was a queue fifteen kilometres long. You see, the problem is that this canal is shallow from the silt, but bigger and bigger barges are using it to reach cities like Shanghai."

The problem would be solved, he prayed, now that the bypass had opened. Within just three years work had begun and finished. It was sixteen miles long, 100 yards wide, eight deep; eleven major bridges had been built; its two new docks could handle 12,000,000 tons of freight each year; US$375,000,000 had been spent. If future economists require an explanation for China's astronomical growth in the first decade of our century, they need only consider that Changzhou was just one small city that even most Chinese could not place squarely on a map.

御河

In Changzhou the day's grime left a tidemark on the washroom basin of a small restaurant. The girl at my side wore clothes that caught the attention: high-heeled boots, a miniskirt, a halter-necked top. A line of inky black flowed from the soiled material she was rinsing.

"They're silk stencils, for tattoos," she explained. "Our boss has an understanding with Old Wooden Planks who runs this restaurant. We all get along down here."

"Old Wooden Planks" is the name the Chinese give to the boss of anything from a street stall to a multi-million-dollar company. He had set up shop in an underground mall, a common sight in China's cities, a way of making public squares pay for themselves in rent without building upon them. Shop units are squeezed tightly together, legitimate stalls are set up in the passageways, and the unlicensed traders occupy what plots they can. Every now and again this last genus will bundle its stock up in its kerchiefs and sprint for the exit when *Chengguan* are spotted. *Chengguan* – the men of the Urban Management Administration – are resented by the millions who scrape a living hawking goods on China's pavements. Officially they are responsible for keeping the streets orderly, seeing that people do not block footpaths, and other such minor matters. In practice they are feared for abusing their power and for running what amount to protection rackets. Often no better than thugs given uniforms, stab vests and batons, they have been implicated in the murders of people who have been brave enough to stand up to them. Even without those venal and violent *Chengguan* strutting about, underground malls like this one had always provoked in me a sense of claustrophobic threat, a consequence of their low ceilings and maze-like floorplans. I had only ended up there after following the signs for the toilets.

"*Gen wo lai,*" said the girl simply. "Follow me."

The unadorned concrete of the corridor leading to *Tiger's Tattoo Parlour* only deepened the incongruity of the room it opened on to. Women lay supine on beautician's tables, their faces spread with face packs and their eyes blinkered. The high-heeled girl pegged her stencils to a clothes line to drip-dry and pointed me through a door. Tiger himself was there, young and gym-toned, in jeans and an unbuttoned Hawaiian shirt. I had passed the occasional tattoo parlour already but, apprehensive, had never once ventured inside: in China, tattoos had long been reserved as a visible punishment for criminals. Now snakehead gangs and triads wore them as proof of their standing. Tiger held out a hand.

"You look – it takes years of work to get terrible hands like these." His fingers were stained black, calloused from where the needle-gun rubbed against them all day. He showed them off as a badge of honour, confirmation that the decision to leave Shandong had been right. Jobs were few back there, and he had moved down to the delta five years ago. Now he owned several tattoo parlours, shuttling between them as customers arrived.

"In traditional China," I sidled toward the reason for my apprehension, "only certain kinds of people had tattoos...." Tiger understood, but laughed it off.

"Criminals? No, China has opened up these days. Having a tattoo is nothing special. It's not just the 'black societies' that want them. Men or women, young or old, I tattoo everybody."

"Women? Really?" There was scepticism in my voice, but he produced a thick ring binder, photos of his past clients. Their skin was still red raw, freshly tattooed, but his artwork was clear and bright. There were dragons, tigers, mountain ranges, buddhas, the famous profile of Chairman Mao that had once graced the lapel badges of an older generation, swirling patterns from Zhou-dynasty bronzes that looked almost Celtic in their intertwined abstraction. Half of the tattoos were set against the pale, flawless skin of women. They seemed to prefer roses, Christian crosses or flying swallows to the sweeping works of art which covered their boyfriends' flesh. They were secreted away on the nape of a neck, in the small of a back, on an ankle, a breast. Not a single person had chosen to have a Chinese character etched into their skin: surrounded by the mundane reality of Chinese writing all day, it did not hold the mystical charm that attached to it in foreign eyes. Despite the evidence of Tiger's photos, the prejudices of decades were not so easily adjusted. I still suspected that "walking your own path" in directions like this must have its limits.

"Don't these women regret it when they want to marry? I've

heard stories of girls being dumped once boyfriends discover they have a tattoo, and stories about employers refusing to give work to people who have them." Tiger was insistent, a little irritated even at my disbelief.

"China has *changed*. It was like that a decade ago perhaps, but now young people want their body to be different to everybody else's. It's a fashion, yes, something we see pop stars wearing, but it's also a very ancient art. Have you ever noticed that the word 'tattoo' in Chinese is related to the word 'civilization'? In the Shang and Zhou dynasties we Chinese thought we were *superior* to other races because we wore them. You could say we're rediscovering some pride in our Chinese culture, *dui ma?*"

At that moment a boy walked in. Barely in his teens, with spiky hair and a white vest, he told Tiger that he wanted a coiled dragon tattooed on his shoulder. Tiger offered him a pattern book, and the boy picked out a design. The needle worked fast. The three of us sat in near silence for an hour, Tiger occasionally shifting his balance, the boy rhythmically chain-smoking as if to hypnotize himself, myself watching as the tattoo grew and became a recognizable creature. When the work was done Tiger whipped out a camera and took another snap for the album. As the boy left another arrived, dressed in a basketball jersey and baggy shorts as though he had just walked off the streets of South Central Los Angeles. Already a dragon writhed across his tanned back and down one arm. He introduced himself as Tiger's bodyguard. This only convinced me further that tattoos were more linked to criminality than Tiger would admit, but he just laughed the issue aside again.

"He's my best friend. I just *call* him my bodyguard, that's all. He's African, aren't you?" The bodyguard smiled weakly at what must have been a constant joke at his expense.

"They all say I'm African because my skin's so dark...."

As I left, I stopped to talk to the high-heeled girl. Had she had a tattoo, working so closely as she did with Tiger? She raised a coy hand to her mouth and laughed.

"Oh, no! I wouldn't dare!" On the back of her hand was tattooed a blossoming rose, small but indelible. "This? This is nothing...." She looked embarrassed and, turning to greet a customer, cut short our conversation. Whether she really was so comfortable with the idea of having a tattoo that she had forgotten it was there, it was impossible to tell from our few words. Tiger, his bodyguard, the young boy with his freshly coiled dragon, the high-heeled girl with her tiny rose seemed only to want to make their bodies unique just like teenagers in America and Taiwan, their richest sources of youth culture. All that day I went on trying to shoehorn the evidence of my eyes into one more fragile assumption long held about the Chinese. But those assumptions were no longer valid: their country was changing in unsuspected ways.

御河

Emperor Yang's Grand Canal had been dug by hand from virgin soil and rice paddy – "a million men with teaspoons", the process has been likened to – and reading so many historical texts that was the impression I had formed, quite unreflectively, of how canals were still dug. Of course, a moment's consideration and I would have realized that these days they were dug mechanically, and perforce more often than not through the dense housing of an existing city. That simple fact had not occurred to me, and so the reality came as a shock. Changzhou's bypass canal had scythed through its suburbs to leave a ravaged arc sixteen miles in length and a full quarter of a mile wide. One million square metres of housing had vanished as though vaporized, leaving just the chalky smudges of their foundations. Yellow-helmeted labourers wandered like dazed survivors.

"Were the people who lived here compensated when their

homes were demolished?" I asked the passenger who stood beside me on the bus. He shrugged.

"Of course not. There are always promises but the money never comes. The city must have its new canal. These people, *mei banfa* – there's nothing they can do."

Beyond that scar, the shops and homes gathered themselves warily together as if they went in fear of a similar fate. When the skyline dropped for a final time it was to signal the very edge of the city. It was there that 160 acres of farmland had been ring-fenced and spared the pile-drivers and the bulldozers' blades.

Yancheng, the Drowned City, was a time capsule from the Spring and Autumn period of China's history, half a millennium before Christ, long before even the First Emperor's terracotta army was interred. Its triple concentric moats were wide and tranquil, bolstered by earthen walls that still stood yards high. Archaeologists brought to this place in the 1950s to uncover their young nation's ancient past had unearthed wooden canoes. "The first boats under Heaven" they were proudly hailed, and taken to the National Museum of Chinese History on Tian'anmen Square. From Yancheng they had once sailed out on now long-vanished waterways. Today the moats that once protected King Fu Chai's palaces are connected to the Grand Canal just as a whorl on a fingertip might trace its tiny folds to the lifeline of a palm. Tracing them vicariously on the map I rode the buses one by one toward Danyang. Changzhou's bargemen seemed painfully wary of foreigners and moved me on from one wharf to the next. Only at a safe distance from the city, in an undistinguished township called Benniu, was I invited to sit and talk.

"Yes, boat jams really are a problem," agreed the skipper when he heard what a previous bargeman had said. "In winter, when there's less water in the Yangtze and in Lake Tai, the water in the canal is lower too. This is only natural. In February a coal barge grounded right here – it was 300 tons overweight – and the canal was blocked. Then a week later the same thing, and a week later again. In March a barge sank in Wuxi. Overloaded. We had to wait two weeks for the traffic to flow properly. Then the same in Suzhou, and Tongxiang...." He counted off each boat jam on the fingers of one hand, slapping them exasperatedly into the other palm. "Thousands of barges stuck. I had bricks in my hold but the building sites couldn't get any. This stretch between Suzhou and the Yangtze is the most congested in China – it carries almost as much freight as the main shipping channel of the river itself."

"What can anybody do about it?"

"The canal must be upgraded. You see that?" He pointed at some towering sand-dunes on the bank. Rootstocks had begun to colonize their lower margins, as though drawing them greedily back into the earth. "Silt. They've been doing more dredging this year."

Amongst my papers was a poem by an otherwise unknown writer who at some time in the twelfth century had watched the dredging close to where we now sat. The bargeman read it.

> *Though an inch at the sluices raises the water by a foot,*
> *By Chengting it has leaked away to the eye of the sea.*
> *The Qin levied ochre-clad criminals to dig this canal,*
> *Emperor Yang had it widened for his dissolute pleasures.*
> *Untended for years, it is choked now with silt,*
> *Along its length I see only mud.*

While Huns, Goths and Vandals were fighting over the distant remains of the Roman Empire, the great windlasses at Benniu, each turned by 40 oxen, were peacefully hauling merchant vessels across a sophisticated canal lock. Those "Hurrying Oxen" had even given the town its name. But that ancient lock had been gouged away when the engineers of the People's Republic had recut the canal. The bargeman explained what was in those neck-craning hoppers that now dominated the banks – rock powder, fine gravel and coarse gravel, coarse sand, yellow sand, foundation sand. Each had its uses. Through his eyes Benniu became an endless line of builders' yards, his main source of cargoes, like a periodic table of the elements of progress. The stone was quarried in Huzhou, he said, from its bamboo-clothed granite, then shipped to holding depots like these where men like him might make a little oily water selling it on. He was no different to the pedlars who bought cigarettes wholesale and hawked them in bars for a profit, he reasoned, or to the speculators who bought low and sold high on the Shanghai stock market. With a smile he refused me a ride with his bright orange bricks. By now I understood why.

The day was growing hotter, the dust swirling about inside the bus to Danyang. On its outskirts, faced with unyielding hills dead ahead, the barges bore north toward the Yangtze to wander instead through their rolling margins. In Danyang a tiny hotel looked out over a road lined with booths selling engine parts. Here too the doorjamb had been shattered with a blow, mended more than once. The mosquitoes seemed not to notice a shuffling new arrival. A coil of insecticide would deal with them. As it went to work, I walked the streets in search of Danyang's speciality, a liquor called sealed-jar wine. It was cheap even for China, only pennies a bottle.

"The water god of Lake Lian gave this wine to the people of Danyang in exchange for the hand of a beautiful woman." The shopkeeper's accent was harsh. "She'd been bound for the capital to be Emperor Yang's concubine."

A man at the counter chimed in. "It's made from glutinous rice and spring water. It's very sweet, very fragrant."

The shopkeeper read aloud from the bottle. "A flavour as light as dew upon a flower, a colour like spring in a cave."

"Ah, then you must go to see the Wanshan pagoda," said the other man thoughtfully when he heard about my itinerary. "We Danyang folk call it 'the first pagoda on the banks of the canal'." Early European travellers had mentioned a tower seven stories high here, a landmark for barges approaching Danyang. It was news to me that it was still standing.

But the Wanshan pagoda had grown pallid, a confusion of old plasterwork and new repairs. The park it stood in was empty, its children's playground consisting of disused Ferris wheels and dodgems, and of rusting train rides whose stuffed-animal drivers were soggy and sad. Then dusk fell, and outside the park gates Danyang's shopping streets were soon ablaze with neon. This was small-town Jiangsu, barely a dozen miles now from the lifeblood of the Yangtze, and the noise was like a barrage assailing the ears. Above the pop music that roared from the doorways and the hand-clapping of the sales staff who called out to attract passers-by, the *"Good news! Good news!"* which blared from the loudspeakers was of discounted cosmetics and cheap clothes rather than of Mao Zedong thought. Lou Yue had not appeared for some days now, but our argument over China's apparent loss of innocence had played on my mind. Which was really the more innocent – the price of this lipstick, or the sloganeering of violent class warfare? When looked at like that, China was more innocent now than it had been for decades, my reaction to its changed cityscapes unwarranted. As the voice on the tape kept insisting, it really was good news that there was cheap lipstick for sale on New People's Road.

Whiling away the tail of the day in an internet café, I sent an email to Rebecca reviewing our first month of married life. Looking on the bright side, not a single bad word had passed between us since our wedding. Back at the hotel the booths were in darkness, their shutters pulled down. The loudspeakers had been hushed, and the only light came from the lanterns which threw out red halos in welcome. The mosquito coil had collapsed into ash, and a haze hung about the room. The canal barges rumbled a deep bass accompaniment to the drone of the cars. I opened the sealed-jar wine and poured myself a generous measure. It was luscious, caramely like a cheap sherry, sweet like muscovado sugar. Old Wooden Planks here was a woman in late middle age and a jacket of scarlet nylon. She was sitting up at reception to watch TV with her husband, and they nodded at the bottle. We talked into the night, putting the world to rights about crime and punishment, and together we drained the dregs.

"They really ought to renovate the Wanshan pagoda," said the taxi driver late the next morning. "It's falling down. The park's dirty. Nobody visits except for the newly-weds who come to be photographed beside the flowers." I regretted listening to the man in the shop: it had cost the price of a day's food to enter the park, and there had been little to justify the expense. My real reason for stopping in Danyang had been to visit the remnants of an early water-conservation project that lay just to the north of the town. It had begun life as a broad but shallow lake, a depression fed by the streams that drained the low hills. Amidst the fighting that marked the long decline and fall of the Han dynasty, the brilliant strategist-general Zhou Yu had staged mock naval battles on that miniature inland sea before doing battle with Cao Cao at the Red Cliffs. Local legend still has it that the people of Danyang, looking on in wonder, had named it Lake Lian – the Lake for Manoeuvres. Later, the accomplished engineers of the Tang dynasty had built sluices into its shore and through them had drawn water to top up the nearby canal. Like the poet had said, every inch of lake water benefited the canal by one foot, and for centuries the reservoir at Lake Lian had continued to feed its water into that high section. Then, slowly, silt had turned it to a mere marsh.

Though this was the highest point I had yet reached, the rise from Hangzhou had been gradual. The old lakebed was just a few yards higher than the Qiantang shiplock, a difference indiscernible over 180 miles. Only unquestioning water, obeying its natural instinct to fall, could betray the true lie of the land. We stopped the taxi and peered through shrubs and wire fencing. The landscape was flat, parcelled into long plots for rice growing and aquaculture. The sparse green of seedlings poked up through the still water of nursery beds.

"This is a state farm," said Mrs Lu. "They grow seed-stock to sell to farmers, and fruit, and seafood – prawns, crabs, oysters. Very wealthy." She rubbed forefingers and thumb together. We gazed into the farm and watched a crane stooping for food amongst the drowned roots; only a handful of historians now remembered that this place had once been a marvel of hydrology.

The land began to crumple and jade-blue daubs appeared on the skyline, the last, low hills before the flatlands north of the river. The road wound through villages clothed in the yellows of ripe wheat and drying rape, the bright emerald blades of young sweetcorn, the ochre of the soil. The late morning was proving fearfully hot, and the car windows were down. It was winnowing time, and a fine dust of chaff settled on my sleeping face. I woke to find Mrs Lu staring back at me, her voice offering to drop me at the big bridge in Xinfeng. There the canal had found its ease, slung deep between terraces of market-gardens thickly sown with vegetables. It yawed from side to side for the first time since Hangzhou, seeking out an even path to the Yangtze like a serpent meandering through the land's gentle undulations. To both north and south it bent out of sight, leaving twin horizons of pale trees and fading smokestacks. By the austere walls of a farm, set sentinel upon the terraces, was parked a trishaw just like Jiugao had ridden. At a weirless creek the rickshawman stepped down and vanished through a doorway. He returned with another man.

"You want to go to the Yangtze shiplock, *dui ma*? You're from Xinjiang?" Both men fingered my clothes as though I were a slave they were interested in buying. On searing days like this I had taken to wearing an embroidered skullcap to protect a shaved scalp. With a cheap shirt and faded trousers I flattered myself I might occasionally pass unnoticed as a migrant from the Great Northwest.

"I'm a *laowai*," I countered: many Han Chinese think the Muslims of Xinjiang untrustworthy, and I did not want their possible prejudices to jeopardize the likelihood of a boat ride. I did not wait for him to name a price before offering money; on waking that morning there had been a knot of worry in my belly, an unstructured feeling of disquiet that had slowly formed itself around the possibility that there would be no more willing bargemen in closely watched Jiangsu, no story to tell. His boat offered a straw to clutch at. It was just a sampan, of weathered wood sheltered under plyboard and propelled by an outboard motor. After the exposed lie of the land further south, where crosswinds had whipped the waves into a constant spray, it felt good to ride between towering earth ramparts. Down on the surface of the water, below the level of the surrounding countryside, industrial China shrank away to become just the tip of a chimney, or the span of a bridge appearing out of nowhere. Its hectic modernization felt distant, as if none of it mattered to this quiet place. The boatman nodded thoughtfully when asked how Xinfeng's population passed its time.

"It earns its money in factories that make *zhoucheng*." The *Concise Oxford Chinese Dictionary*, coverless now and thumb-blackened through years of use, translated *zhoucheng* as axle bearings, a prosaic essential for a healthy economy. "You're travelling north of the Yangtze?" he asked. Then he knitted his brow and lowered his voice as if imparting a solemn warning: "*Aya*, the economic conditions there aren't as good as here in Jiangnan. When you reach Shandong you'll see they're very backward. Look after yourself in Hebei. We all know the people there are immoral."

His thrumming sampan needed less than an hour to reach the bowstring bridge that marked the Yangtze shiplocks. These were unmistakable in the distance ahead, a mess of gantries and machine rooms rising above a tableland of barges. The canal, as if forever uncertain how best to approach the skittish river, split now into three, a trinity of incarnations from different ages. The oldest, Emperor Yang's original handiwork, led away west only to be consumed by a landscape of pressure vessels, of tanks and heat exchanges, ducts and pipework leaking fumes of unnatural colours. Their smells hung on the breeze and settled on the tongue – eye-smarting sulphur, the vinegariness of acetic acid, bathroom-cabinet smells of phenol and calamine lotion, and a strange, seaside tang like old-fashioned fishmeal glue. After days of breathing easily, the air here was unhealthy, worse even than in Wangjiangjing where the rain had been unable to cleanse it.

"How can you bear this pollution?" I demanded of a bystander whose gaze had met mine.

"*Yao xiandaihua, yao jieshou,*" he answered with a resigned smile. "If we have to modernize, we have to accept it. The future will be better. Just now, *mei banfa* – there's nothing we can do." He strode off, leaving no chance to press him further. How was I to make sense of what he had said? My first instinct had been to suppose that he was prepared to put up with the pollution in the belief that it would lead to better things, that he approved of the direction in which the Party was taking China. If that had been the case, he would only have been repeating the official line on China's industrialization. But his words had been sparse and ambiguous. In Mandarin he had not needed to add subjects to his verbs, nor even an "if", leaving cause and effect hanging together tentatively: "Have to modernize, have to accept." Who had to modernize, and who to accept? Mandarin tends towards the path of least effort, and parts of speech that English assumes are vital are generally dropped. I had added them in as always, but I'd had to make assumptions. Even that "have to" was double-edged: *yao* also meant "want to", as though the language assumed that if something was possible then it must be desirable, or that if you had to do something then you must also want to. And what about his *"mei banfa"*? Meanings could easily hide behind the façade of that pervasive little phrase that literally meant "have no method". I had added a "we", but in truth it left its subject unexpressed – I? China? The Party? Its indirect object too was missing – there was nothing to be done about what? Perhaps the pollution, but he might just as well have been resigned to the fact that there was nothing he could do about the powers that had decided on modernization. And yes, the future might be better, but how? Had he hoped modernization would be completed, or that it would fail and stop? He might have meant any one of these possibilities, or even all of them at once. As if its very language was a metaphor for this entire country, a seemingly straightforward answer had fragmented into a world of contradictions.

御河

At the start of the Grand Canal weeks before, just one lone barge had passed from the Qiantang River into the Sanbao shiplock. Here at the Yangtze they were moored twelve deep, lashed end-to-end in long trains and sticking to the banks like rafts of bacilli multiplying on a microscope slide. Others swaled back and forth in the shipping channel behind stubby tugboats, steeling themselves to enter the lock chamber. Hydraulic rams forced the gates apart. There was no sound save an unearthly rumble from invisible loudspeakers. The lockmaster's bark echoed angrily, disembodied and directionless. The bargemen obeyed, trimmed their engines, and lined up like schoolchildren. Then they advanced, and the water was churned into a white froth. In a matter of minutes, thousands of tons of gravel were lifted to the level of the Yangtze as effortlessly as if the god of the river had raised them up upon his open palm.

The engineers who installed those modern pound locks could not have predicted how quickly the traffic would outgrow them. The queue to pass through the twin Yangtze shiplocks had grown in tandem with China's economy, and now the waiting barge trains jutted out into the river itself. Entering from that three-mile-wide shipping channel, the sailors said, was like turning off Chang'an Avenue into a Beijing *hutong*. When I tried to see the shiplocks at work close up, a guard escorted me away, a firm hand on my shoulder, uninterested in the letter of introduction which explained my reason for being in China. The Chinese jealously guarded the strategic junction they called China's Crossroads, wary of any outsider who wanted to examine the place where their grandest canal crossed their greatest river. It had been no different when other outsiders had come to this place during that inglorious clash of cultures we call the First Opium War.

By 1839, British merchants had for decades been engaged in a triangular trade between Europe, India and China: opium prepared in British India was shipped to the Chinese port of Canton where it was sold for silver; this silver was used to buy tea from the plantations of Fujian province, which in turn sailed back to English ports to raise capital to buy more Bengali opium. For decades before the triangular route became established, the self-sufficient Chinese had been net beneficiaries of Britain's thirst for tea, there being practically no manufactures that the British could convince them to accept in return. Silver had flowed into China in exchange for chests of *congou* and *bohea*. But the demand for narcotic opium was so high that the British found they could demand cash for it, and soon silver coins and ingots – the medium in which Chinese imperial taxes were paid – were leaving Canton in a torrent. The Chinese emperor, aware that demand for opium was causing troublesome inflation, not to mention making addicts of much of his populace, banned the drug trade and had his commissioner seize and destroy the British merchants' stockpiles. The problem seemed to have been solved. But when news of China's solution reached London there was consternation: the import duty raised on Chinese tea was so great by now that it was to all intents and purposes underwriting the British exchequer. No opium sales meant no silver, no tea, and no tax – an unacceptable situation.

It had long been clear to any military man having even a nodding acquaintance with China that what the Chinese possessed by way of an army or navy was laughably ill-equipped to face the British. Whitehall was in no doubt that just a single Royal Navy man-of-war, well positioned on the Yangtze, could halt China's grain transport in its tracks and starve its emperor into accepting terms. With shipping providing China's Ministry of Revenue with one-third of its customs receipts, the shattering effect of not just one vessel but an entire British squadron dropping anchor squarely upon China's Crossroads can well be imagined. In July of 1842 the British did just that, a few miles from today's Yangtze shiplocks, beside the fortified city of Zhenjiang. Rockets and shells were fired into the city while Her Majesty's infantry landed. The city walls were scaled, the Manchu garrison slaughtered. Those who survived died at their own hands, but not before butchering their wives and children rather than see them violated. Leaving a warship to asphyxiate the Grand Canal, the British sailed on to Nanjing and threatened to destroy this, China's second city, demanding Hong Kong as their ransom. The Chinese could scarcely agree fast enough: that barren island was a small price to pay to have the British release their stranglehold.

While his countrymen were committing murder ashore, a naval surgeon named Edward Cree sat on the deck of HMS *Rattlesnake* to paint a watercolour in his war diary. It was of Golden Island, a dreamlike collection of temples and gardens surmounted by a graceful pagoda. Lord Macartney, King George's ambassador to the Chinese court, seeing the roofs and turrets of that very same island one autumnal morning fifty years before, had likened it to a fairy edifice raised upon the river by the magic of an enchanter.

Now, as then, Golden Island's highest spire is the Pagoda of Merciful Longevity. In the crowded halls at its foot, offerings of small change and food attended mumbled requests to the statuettes of gods. Where prayers were written down, left visible on wooden slips, they were for personal wealth and fame, for worldly success:

"Let me pass my Japanese exams."

"I wish to be a teacher, a celebrity, to excel in all I do."

Graffiti were etched into the walls, too. I climbed the pagoda, the writing growing sparser with each step. On the lower storeys it had been the banal scratchings of furtive moments, all nicknames and love hearts, but the saffron plaster of the topmost was different. Up there, closer to heaven and liberated from the mass of tourists who had turned back with aching thighs, the most committed had communicated their deepest desires to the universal mind. No money had been offered, and no incense, only sincere faith.

"Wang Xiong and Li Su," read one. "If we cannot be together until we are both grey haired, then may our souls at least be joined."

"Chen Lianrong and Tao Ruping, who came to Golden Island. May we have peaceful lives, and everlasting friendship."

"Gu Yuehong. On Mothers' Day. May my mother live a peaceful life."

"I wish only health for my elderly parents."

"Protect Wang Qi. May he never know the tragedy of imprisonment."

Those prayers were like a revelation, something I had encountered nowhere else. One of my strongest impressions of China had long been that years of mutual struggle and suspicion, followed without a pause by the ruthless economics of the reform era, seemed to have left many people with low expectations of others' altruism; social interaction often appeared predicated solely on money and influence; people expressed low expectations of strangers' motives, especially of those in power over them, whispering imprecations over their superiors and even admitting outright that they hated them for their corruption. With no overarching reason for trust, it was easy for people to distrust one another; altruism could often feel distant. Chinese moralists from the time of Confucius on had taught the necessity of *ren*, which might be translated as "humanity's innate benevolence". Only after the 1911 Revolution, and particularly under Mao, had Confucius and his tenets been vilified as feudal and backward. Chinese Marxism had inherited the secular benevolence of "from each according to his ability, to each according to his needs", but then Marx and his failed economics had been cast aside and the Party had offered nothing but materialism in his place. Despite the explosion of faith in recent years, the great majority of Chinese still professed no adherence. When considering that majority, those who had not inherited a tradition of faith through their ethnicity (and China's Muslim population is comparable in size to Saudi Arabia's) or by way of kith and kin whose faith had survived communism, I had often imagined their religious beliefs as indistinct, expressed perhaps in the burning of incense and an improvised prayer for good luck if at all. More times than I cared to recall I had watched people inscribing those wooden slips that decorated Buddhist and Confucian temples, asking always for success and money. For years I had been so blinded by the country's visible preoccupation with material wealth that these scratched glimpses of what was really etched into people's hearts left me chastened. It had been easy to forget that the Chinese were just 1.3 billion individuals, each one still as fearful and hopeful as the rest of us, each carefully trying to navigate a safe path through life for the people they loved.

From the pinnacle of the Pagoda of Merciful Longevity I had

expected to look out over the Yangtze, or at least that was the distinct impression left by the diaries of Lord Macartney and his men who had seen a river so broad they had mistaken it for an inland sea. Instead, where porpoises had once played about the Royal Navy's moorings, the water had stiffened into land. The Yangtze had receded to a buttermilk smear against the horizon, and fields and factories had reclaimed its bed. The breeze cooled the air high above the smog of the city, and a hazy translucency drew the world closer. Alone, enveloped in silence, my mind wandered down on that dreamlike veil as though it might float free from its body and effortlessly cross the river to Guazhou.

I cannot say for how long that reverie enfolded me in stillness. When finally a party of tourists broke the spell I walked back into the city. There Emperor Yang's canal no longer disgorged into the tidal Yangtze but into an artificial basin annexed from the river. The chimneys on the Guazhou shore emerged from the warm mist like a phalanx of ghosts. From a spice market wafted the warm scents of star anise, ground coriander, and ginger. The canal beside it was black, so effervescent from the corruption in its depths that it fizzed like a champagne flute. Happy memorials had once been rushed from this place to Beijing, announcing to the emperor that his grain had successfully passed into the Yangtze. Only the water was lifeless now, running an odd course through the heart of the city, weaving along between deep banks of mosquito willow, bolting back and forth in unnavigable doglegs.

A couple of boards had been thrown out onto a floating pontoon, and there was assembled an armada of pedalos. I propelled one little craft as far as a bridge 200 yards distant. She was built for two, and strong willed when on an uneven keel. I weighed up the cost of the deposit: for just ¥100 I could mutiny and pedal all the way to Hangzhou. The final scenes of *The Great Escape* flashed into my mind, only with my white fibreglass swan gliding between the cargo ships in place of a rowing boat. The mental image made me laugh out loud. The sound rang beneath the bridge and died away, and I pushed the rudder hard about and headed back. Stepping back onto the pontoon, my knees gave way. Old Wooden Planks looked on with amused disappointment: "Your legs haven't enough power in them. Friend, you're no *qianfu!*"

In China, expendable men had often taken the place of valuable draught animals. The *qianfu* were the Grand Canal's trackers, the poor souls who lived and died hauling junks on the stretches where sail became impractical. Each would begin his day's work by strapping a stout towing board to a hawser thrown out from his barge. Placing it flat across his chest, on a signal from a gong he and his comrades (and there might be a hundred or more for a large grain barge) would heave along to a hypnotic work song, a Chinese shanty: *hoyalla hoyu, hoya, hoya, hoy-waudi-hoya, hoyalla hoya, hoya, hoya, hoy-waudi-hoya....* A driver walked behind them, encouraging slackers with a swift lash. When there was water enough, it might take two dozen *qianfu* to keep a barge moving at just one mile every hour against the current; when there was not, they were expected to work even harder. In places where the water grew so shallow that boats grounded, they were dragged by main force along the bed.

"Do you remember the *qianfu?*" I asked. The pedalo seller was in late middle age, and there was a possibility he had seen them in his youth, that he might be my vicarious witness. He shook his head.

"My grandfather used to tell me stories about them. He said he would come as a boy to watch them pull the boats over the lock into the Yangtze. That would have been around the time of the Xinhai Revolution of 1911. They went almost naked, very muscular, he told me, and they sang all the time."

They were not singing for joy. Though stretches were of stone or wood, the towpaths were mostly of mud, frequently submerged, and *qianfu* often worked chest-deep in water.

Their diet was monotonous: rice or millet with now and again some vegetables fried in rancid oil and seasoned with soy. Offal would be a rare luxury. Lord Macartney's valet Aeneas Anderson had watched in disgust as some even picked and ate the lice from their clothes. Yet people agreed they were comely and well-built. In summer, when they worked half-naked, their skin was like copper. When they stripped off to swim, Europeans saw that their natural colour was remarkably fair. The pigtails which during the Qing dynasty all men were required to wear were a nuisance, and so they coiled them around their shaved heads and tucked in the extremity. They might be given auspicious red caps with red buttons on them when hauling an important barge, and jackets likewise fringed with red. Otherwise, they would be in the blue cotton rags of the peasantry from which they sprang. On their feet, if they wore anything at all, were straw sandals. When they at last became too old or sick to work, they would fade away and die without orisons. Such a death was often the best the *qianfu* could hope for: they could rejoice that they had not been crushed or drowned. The Korean Ch'oe Pu had even witnessed a eunuch official shooting at them for sport from his barge. Their six copper cash in daily wages for such hardships sounds as paltry an amount as it actually was.

That evening I sat until even the topmost branches of the mosquito willows were in shadow, sipping from a bottle of cold beer and listening hard for the echoes of the *qianfu*: *hoyalla hoya, hoya, hoya, hoy-waudi-hoya, hoyalla hoya, hoya, hoya, hoy-waudi-hoya....* But they had long gone.

Life's Bitterness

杭州

北京

from the Yangtze to the Huai River

"Would you please speak with Old Wooden Planks, Mr Lin?" suggests the concierge on the morning of a third day in Zhenjiang. More than 200 miles now from Hangzhou, finding a room in this busy port has been harder than elsewhere, and I have opted in desperation for a *zhaodaisuo*, a hostel on the bottom rung of the accommodation ladder. Old Wooden Planks has been happy to take my money until the police lean on him. It clearly annoys him to wave goodbye to so many *renminbi*. "If, a myriad-to-one, something unexpected happened to you, the police would shave my whiskers for me. I feel embarrassed." He knows he is dissembling, and that personal safety is less an issue than police control. He has no reason to feel embarrassed: the city's Public Security Bureau seems not to welcome outsiders, and his disregard for his lack of a permit to accept foreign guests has done me a great favour these last two days. Those words of thanks console him. He goes on stirring his lunch, a pork and marrow stew, and his one foreign guest walks down to the Yangtze.

With the inexorable shifting of sandbanks, the Grand Canal on the river's northern shore has slowly migrated downstream as it tries to keep a mouth free of silt. There is no hope of following its modern incarnation, an isolated stretch opposite the Yangtze shiplocks: there would be huge fines for smuggling a foreign landsman across the river. But at Yizheng,

119

a little farther west, there is an older branch, less frequented, and less likely to be supervised, and so it is Yizheng that I choose.

The town marks the southern terminus of the 100-mile Inner Grand Canal, its oldest surviving section, which can trace its antiquity back to 483 BC and to a waterway dug to connect the Yangtze to the Huai River. On it the armies of King Fu Chai of Wu sailed north to conquer an enemy. The following year a triumphant Fu Chai was lauded as hegemon king, the most powerful man under the Chinese heaven. A decade later he was dead: left open to the threat of invasion from the south, his kingdom had fallen. With Fu Chai's death there ended the relative peace of the Spring and Autumn period, and the Chinese world began its tumble into the mutual annihilation of the Warring States.

Fu Chai's canal was but a fraction the length of Emperor Yang's a millennium later, but it was revolutionary in the way it linked north and south in a country dominated by rivers running from west to east. Joining the Yangtze to the Huai had profound consequences for China, for it engendered a mindset that took for granted the simplicity of carrying men, goods and ideas across the grain of the nation's geography. In the centuries that followed, that one act shrank China just like the Pacific Railroad would one day shrink the United States.

御河

Any last vestige of the 1,000-year-old pound lock at Yizheng, one of the world's first, had vanished: nature treats China's archaeology with casual indifference. Its site had been entombed beneath the shifting Yangtze and the breakers' yards. Yizheng was a town in transition. Its old heart, though sclerotic and congested, was beating still, a knot of roads lined by trees that throbbed with cicadas. Its proud centrepiece, a tall pagoda pockmarked with age, was inaccessible behind railings. The last of the day, a glow which permeated the sky from the western horizon to its zenith, bathed it in a tapering, amber light. To the eastward, the air had that peculiarly Chinese crepuscular quality, a grey-green dustiness that seems to shine softly from somewhere within itself, as though the world were embedded in dusky emerald.

It was a short walk to the edge of town where the ship chandlers had set up shop. The roadway before them, oil-stained tarry black, was a jumble of cables and fenders, shiny brass propellers, odds and ends of nauticalia. One shopkeeper had bought a refrigerator whose profits might defray slow days. It was filled with Zhenjiang Beer, its thermostat so high it scarcely chilled them. He broke open a bottle then stood and wafted away the mosquitoes as I drank. A bargeman asked him for lubricating oil and squatted to wait. He was heading toward Yangzhou, he said, leaving the next morning, the earliest he could hope to pass through the Yizheng shiplock.

"There are jams at the shiplock every day, you understand, because it has just a single chamber. Barges can only pass through in one direction at a time, and there are so many waiting near the gates that it's difficult to steer through them...." He made his rough Mandarin understood with chapped hands that did service for both the lock and its barges. The chandler interrupted him.

"Not long ago a barge sank beside the lock gates. Overloaded with gravel. Pressed up to the gates by the other barges. The water from the lock swamped her. It took four days to suck the gravel up. You remember?" The bargeman nodded and offered his cigarettes around.

"If you don't overload your barge these days," he shrugged, "there's no oily water to be made." He pulled a wad of dirty banknotes from his pocket and counted out the price of the oil.

"The economic conditions here are better than they used to be," the chandler commented as the bargeman walked away.

"We don't have any natural resources, but the towns fifty kilometres north and south of the Yangtze are rich because of the river. In China we say that if a town has no mountains and no river then it will be poor. We have no mountains, but the river keeps us wealthy enough."

Yizheng did seem wealthy enough, a comfortable place to live. The day had been pleasantly wasted, strolling the town's narrow streets in the shade of mature plane trees, a delight all but gone now that most towns had lopped them down for road widening. Yizheng felt more relaxed than brash Jiangnan, less polluted, less *zang luan cha*, as Meigui aboard the *Blue Wave* had put it.

"If it hadn't been for the ten-year turmoil then ours would be a big city by now," he went on. "In the newspaper was the story of a businessman from Harbin who went to Shanghai looking to build a factory. He didn't enjoy the noise and chaos, but he happened across us and liked our atmosphere, and so he stayed."

"The young people, do *they* stay?"

"If they're unmarried, perhaps eight in ten head south of the river to find work. Half of them end up marrying there, but many return. Life here is more pleasant, even if the opportunities to earn big money are fewer. My daughter, she graduated from university in Suzhou, and now she's living there, earning money. She'll come back, though. Her *jia* is here." *Jia* – home – ever a prize beyond value.

The sun dropped behind the ironmongeries, leaving the two of us in shadow. Another Zhenjiang Beer was pulled from the cooler. The chandler swatted at another mosquito and creased his brow in thought. "*Nimen waiguoren*," he volunteered. "You foreigners, if you want to know China, you need to understand that we have three serious social problems." He counted each one off on his fingers as he spoke. "One. Education isn't free. Here it costs 1,000 *kuai* to put a child into school for a year, but if that's half your income then *mei banfa*. If you have no hope of a good income, you have no hope of improving life for your children by schooling them." Talk of hope had stirred a memory.

"What about free schools, Project Hope schools? Isn't there one in Yizheng?" He shot a pitying glance through the gloom.

"Project Hope is for rural counties, backward places – Qinghai, Gansu, Guizhou. We live on the Yangtze, millionaires in comparison." He left this Chinese Catch-22 hanging in midair as a party of schoolchildren walked past, each slurping at a tub of KFC ice cream. "Children like these have never tasted bitterness like my generation. Old people like me, we still eat rice porridge for breakfast, but the young say it leaves them feeling hungry. They all want to eat stuffed dumplings, something that fills their stomachs and makes them fat. By middle age they'll have problems. We call them 'the illnesses of wealth and status'.

"And that's my second point: medicine isn't free, and what we Chinese most fear is illness. If you need treatment you must pay, and if you can't pay then you don't get treatment. I was once treated in hospital for an inflamed gall bladder, and you wouldn't believe how poor the doctors' and nurses' idea of professional ethics was – all they thought of was money, money, money. They actually demanded to be given 'tips' in red envelopes to do their jobs! There's nothing to choose between them and thieves who loot from a burning house! Three. Housing is expensive. The city has homes for the poorest, but the conditions are unsanitary. If you work for the state they subsidize these things, but such people are growing fewer. *Getihu* like me have to survive on our own now, as though society didn't exist."

His dilemma was what confounded me most about life here. The very first line of the national constitution declared China a socialist state, but that declaration was a glaring falsehood. The Party had long since ceased to avow Marxism by any reasonable definition. By the early 1980s, before ever

I'd opened *Beginning Chinese*, the system of rural communes had been dismantled; now state-owned industry had largely been privatized. A new generation of leaders described their agenda as "socialism with Chinese characteristics", and under that slogan they had created an economic free market. The path to the present day had been littered with such slogans: Deng had told China to "Seek truth from facts", and Premier Wen had gone on to say that "Reform is the driving force, development the goal, stability the prerequisite". In the constitution was enshrined the idea of "To each according to his work", a recognition that the principle of "To each according to his need" was no basis for an economy in the real world. Of course, there was an official explanation for these mental gymnastics.

"You should understand," said the ship chandler, "that what you see around you isn't capitalism: it's a form of socialism adapted to China's situation, by which the Party plans to lead China to true communism. For true communism you first need wealth to distribute, and wealth is generated by free markets, by people like me." Only that argument ignored an inconvenient truth: Chinese socialism was creating a nation where wealth was spectacularly unevenly divided. With the Communist Party in power, much of the population was comparatively worse off than ever – just 0.4% of the people held 70% of China's wealth, while 300 million of the poorest lived on a dollar a day – and yet the Party held out the hope that at some rapturous future date it would simply declare China rich enough for the wealth to be spread fairly. I could not imagine the rich – or even this modest shopkeeper – sharing their wealth with the poor without a revolution. Wasn't that what was meant to have happened in 1949? It was hard for me to believe that the Party was sincere, easier to believe that "socialism with Chinese characteristics" was simply a story told to paper over the cracks in its politics while it clung on to power.

"My own country," I told the ship chandler, "has free healthcare and free schooling, and cheap housing for the poorest. It's strange that socialist China is less socialist than capitalist Britain, don't you agree?"

"Mr Lin," he answered with a sigh, "China has thirteen times one hundred million people, and we are a poor, developing nation. There are many contradictions here. How much is an aeroplane ticket to your home?"

That night I dreamed Lou Yue stood before the window. Shifting my weight onto one elbow to raise my head off the pillow, I remembered the next morning that I had whispered to him: "You can't tell lies forever." Then I had laughed menacingly under my breath to let him know that I had found him out and that I was not afraid of him.

御河

The next morning dawned clear and bright. In the pool below the shiplock the boatman of the previous evening was waiting his turn. His barge proved to be a well-loved vessel with a jungle of herbs growing in pots on her deck. We set out for Yangzhou, the ancient fields of the kingdom of Wu stretching out all the while to a circular horizon. He would carry me as far as the Great Bend, he said: beyond that there were too many eyes. For most of the morning ours was the only vessel in sight, reason enough why this man was willing to have a passenger aboard, even to let me hold the wheel for a moment to keep her steady: with two straight banks, no crosswind, and nothing to crash into, it would have taken a true Jonah to endanger the ship. He unfastened the ropes which held the roof down and heaved it back on its hinges. The windows folded down to hang around the wheelhouse like a glass skirt, and we were open to the fresh air.

As Yangzhou drew closer, plumes of smoke began to rise

from the treeline and our engines echoed beneath bridges. Nervous now, muttering, watching for an opportunity to rid himself of his illicit cargo, the bargeman dropped me unseen beneath a flyover. Ahead the Great Bend was visible, a sudden convulsion of the water into a tight oxbow. This was my first glimpse of the Grand Canal as a living river, as water which, no longer confined by stone banks, had found its own way through the soil. This stretch to the south of Yangzhou had had plenty of time to sink comfortably into the landscape: the Battle of Thermopylae, the one event from Europe's classical history that had stuck in my mind at school, had not even been fought when it was dug. Back in the early 1980s, before mass tourism and cheap air travel, a China that had only just extricated itself from the Cultural Revolution must have seemed so distant to my Classics master, its ancient history doubly so. Now that school trips to the People's Republic had become an affordable prospect, there was a real hope that British children might learn about King Fu Chai of Wu just as I had learned about Leonidas and Xerxes: his achievement had certainly had more effect on the world at large than either of them.

御河

With the completion of Emperor Yang's Grand Canal in AD 610, scarcely a corner of his empire could not be reached by water. Yang's favourite place, Yangzhou, lay at its heart, an advanced city far ahead of its time, famed for the 24 wooden bridges that spanned its waterways and for the brick-built sewers that anticipated Sir Joseph Bazalgette's by a thousand years. Under the outward-looking Tang dynasty that followed Yang's demise, merchants from Japan and Korea, from the kingdoms of Indo-China, from India, Persia and Arabia came and settled in the city. Their coins of gold and silver bore the Islamic *shahada* and Christ's Cross as witnesses to journeys made across Eurasia. In one manuscript of Marco Polo's *Description of the World*, the Venetian is said to have been Kublai Khan's governor in Yangzhou for three years. The Chinese, painstaking archivists of their complex bureaucracy, seemed not to have noticed him, and scholars now doubt his claims. But if Yangzhou's most famous foreign visitor in truth never did walk its tree-lined avenues, there were unquestionably others who had. In 1265, for example, there arrived a man named Puhadin, a descendant of Mohammed, come to spread the simple truths of Allah. We know of more. In 1951 a party of soldiers sent to demolish Yangzhou's city walls discovered the marble gravestone of a Genoese woman named Katerina who had died there in 1342. Soon another stone turned up, and it became clear that Katerina had lived in Yangzhou amongst a community of Italian merchants. They might have known Oderic of Pordenone, a Franciscan friar sent by the Pope to spread Christianity in the East, or the Nestorian Christians who had by that time founded a trio of churches in the city.

To the Chinese, though, Yangzhou was famous above all for salt, a jealously guarded government monopoly since the Han dynasty, when an emperor's nephew had briefly declared independence on the wealth it generated. The city's prime position on the Grand Canal, close to the Yangtze and to the brackish coastal marshes, made it a hub of the salt industry. The merchants to whom the Controller of Salt sold licences to trade were in a position to set the price within their allotted domains, and they became spectacularly rich. Travellers admitted to their mansions returned with wondrous stories. One had placed mechanical nudes in his house to tease his guests; a veritable Croesus scattered gold foil to the winds; an orchid lover had those most valuable of flowers strewn over his floor. Across the city, libraries and colleges were patronized by men eager to win the prestige which lofty Confucianism denied to those who indulged in grubby commerce. The most famous scholars and poets of the day flocked to them, and

Yangzhou quickly acquired a reputation as a seat of learning.

Heaven must have seemed so fickle to the last of those salt merchants. They had provided so much of the Qing dynasty's tax revenue that its emperors looked upon them as an inexhaustible source of income when times were tough. As the dynasty hit crisis after crisis, profits evaporated. The merchants' beautiful edifices came crashing down around them when in the 1850s the Taiping Rebellion saw Yangzhou despoiled. At the same time, those catastrophic Yellow River floods severed the Grand Canal in Shandong province. With the canal impassable to the north, and with its southerly stretches in rebel control, traders began to relocate to foreign-administered Shanghai where cargoes were being loaded onto ships to make the voyage north by sea. The arrival of the People's Liberation Army in 1949 only sealed the fate of Yangzhou's crumbling marketplaces.

But after just three decades of communist austerity, in the late 1970s Yangzhou's businessmen took up where they had left off. Soon their growing city engulfed King Fu Chai's ancient waterway. Now the pale green water flows almost imperceptibly there. A park has been laid out along its banks. Surrounded by lovers and families, I felt far from home: there must have been hotel attendants I had spoken to more often since my wedding day than my own wife. I went to find something to eat, to commune at least with food, and beside the canal found a halal restaurant run by Muslims whose descendants had long ago made their way to Yangzhou and never left.

Orgetlek too, raised on the rolling grasslands of Inner Mongolia, felt alone in Yangzhou. He sat down beside me as I was sieving a bowl of mutton soup through my teeth. With scant companionship this far from his home in Ar Horqin, it seemed that incidental parallels drew him to strangers. The sight of mutton bones on the table drew from him a shy smile of recognition and comradeship. Together we gazed down at the barge trains.

"*Liaobuqi*," he muttered. "Amazing. Before I came to Jiangsu, I had never seen so much water, so many people." Growing up in a rainy Yorkshire city, in many ways I felt more at home in Jiangsu than did Orgetlek, though he was as much a Chinese citizen as any Jiangsunese. In other ways, Jiangsu was equally alien to us: our mother tongues were unrelated to Mandarin, their scripts both alphabetic. At home he spoke only Mongolian and had known no Mandarin before middle school. Its characters were hard for him to remember. When he wrote his name his hand was precise, as if printed, quite like mine but unlike the cursive scribble of the Han who had learned it since early childhood. It reminded me of the way Jiugao the rickshawman wrote, who had lost his education to the ten-year turmoil. Only by looking closely at Orgetlek could one see the traits – the narrow eyes, high cheek bones and flat face – that characterized his ethnicity. They were subtle. Did the residents of Yangzhou look down on him because he was from a minority?

"I don't understand the local dialect at all. Even Mandarin is foreign to me, and they can hear from my accent, tell from my features, that I am not Han. But my Mandarin is good, and I speak it better than the farmers and the migrants who come from the interior. The people of Yangzhou respect education, they always have, and a postgraduate like me is not their inferior." He paused and thought for a minute. "They sometimes become frustrated that I can't understand their answers. I asked directions to a hospital soon after I'd arrived here, but they spoke in such heavy dialect that I understood nothing. Eventually I just said *xiexie* and pretended to know what they had meant. I was late that day." I too had done the same thing more than once.

He felt more of an affinity with the Japanese, he admitted, whose language and culture were easier for him to understand. Jiangsu was just a stepping stone from Inner Mongolia to Honshu, where he wanted to continue studying philosophy. We walked into the gardens of the Islamic missionary Mohammed Puhadin's tomb, full of Arabic script and austere graves.

"I chose Japanese over English at school," he explained. "If I'd applied to a Japanese university from any other college in China I would've had only a one in a hundred chance of a place. Here, though, in a college with connections, it was perhaps seven in ten. I'd thought about studying in England, too, or America, but that would've meant learning a new language. What's England like?"

Compared with the energy of China, England could feel mundane. It had precious little of what the Chinese approvingly called *renao*, the "heat and noise" that made their streets buzz day and night. If one was invigorating, the other was torpefying, but I was aware enough of my own partiality to know that a young man from the Mongolian grasslands would find England in turn an exhilarating barrage of the unfamiliar and the exotic.

"And Japan?" he asked. I shrugged: a fortnight in Hiroshima was more than he had yet enjoyed, but it was not enough to comment with any accuracy. "You see, as a Mongolian I feel a connection with the Japanese. Our cultures are similar, a mixture of polite ceremony and hospitality on the one hand and violence on the other."

"Do you mean the Nanjing Massacre?" It was a safe guess: seventy years on, memories of the bestial rape, torture and murder of tens of thousands of civilians in China's former capital were being kept alive by the Party. The result was a constant undercurrent of anti-Japanese feeling. Orgetlek nodded. He had been exposed to the line his government was pushing about Japanese war crimes, but he had reached a more nuanced conclusion than they might have hoped.

"I mean Nanjing, and all the rest of Japan's war crimes. Yet I've studied Japanese culture for many years now, and I know how peaceful and intelligent it is – the *chado* tea ceremony, Zen Buddhism, *No* theatre. Of course I am heartbroken by

Japan's past behaviour, but I will soon be studying in Japan and I could not go there if I hated the Japanese like I am being encouraged to. My heritage is Mongolian, you see, and the man I most admire is Genghis Khan. He loved honesty and loyalty, but he conquered Asia. Peace and war, hand in hand – we two peoples are very similar."

Orgetlek was a true believer in Genghis Khan, and as we sat in the wooded grove by Puhadin's tomb he related the khan's life story – how his father had been poisoned by a rival tribe, how with his mother he had survived on wild fruit and game and had murdered his own brother, how he had been saved from starvation by wolves. Orgetlek's tales had been learned at his parents' knees, beside the woodstove, just as they had always been told. It was not easy to guess how he might react when he discovered that contemporary Japanese life was unimaginably far from his own steppe upbringing and from the idealized Japan of his imaginings.

"If we were in Ar Horqin," he went on, "I would ask you to my home to eat. I would have no choice: it is a custom." Since we were inescapably a thousand miles distant from Ar Horqin, we walked instead to a restaurant he sometimes visited. It was not expensive, he apologized, but he was a student, with little money. "If we were in Ar Horqin," he began again as he read the menu, "we would eat a whole roast lamb, and roast millet, and drink milk tea with butter, and then *airag*. My family ferments its own *airag* from mare's milk. Do you like to drink? Let's order beer. We Mongolians can really drink, not like the Han. Their faces go red and they shout and laugh after just one bottle, like little children. *Xiaojie!*" The waitress came and Orgetlek ordered unfussy dishes, with little meat, and apologized again. He admitted he had no real understanding of Chinese cuisine, which was quite alien to his Mongolian diet. Before the first plate of bamboo shoots and tree fungus arrived we had each drunk two litres of gassy beer.

"I've been thinking," began Orgetlek, "about what you said,

131

about China's streets being full of people all the time, always hot and noisy. You see this as a good thing, but I disagree. The streets are busy because too many Chinese have nothing to do. Isn't England 'boring' because people all have jobs to go to? China seems lively only because we have a vast population, a backward economy and high unemployment." A dish of Japanese tofu interrupted him, its velvet-soft curd swimming in dark soy sauce, and another of chives cooked with minced pork. "I'll need to find a part-time job when I get to Japan, to help pay my university fees. When I told my family this, they said 'Orgetlek, you can't *dagong*, you must get a proper job!'" For many young Chinese, to do unofficial work – to *dagong* – is their only way of making money. The word implies temporariness, uncertainty, low wages, in contrast to the status and permanence which having a regular appointment always used to bring. Times have changed, and the iron rice bowl has been broken. "When they hear the word *dagong*, they think it's beneath a child of theirs. I should stay in China and find a position in a company, they say. I worked as a translator for Mongolian Milk for a time, and they want me to go back. When I tell them that they are wrong to dislike *dagong*, that I can earn as much money doing *dagong* in Japan in an hour as I can in a week of regular office work in China, they have no reply, *no* reply...." He refilled my glass and pushed across a dish of shredded raw potato swimming in chilli oil. "*Toktoi!*"

"*Toktoi!*" We both drained our glasses and refilled them for each other. By the time some vegetable dumplings had arrived to soak up the alcohol, it was too late. Orgetlek's phone rang and he stared at it red eyed, forgetting for a moment how to answer. It was a photographer calling; his photos were ready to collect, and he needed them for his passport application. We stumbled out into the road and parted in a welter of backslapping. It was late, but still the pavements in that leafy Yangzhou backstreet were crowded. Orgetlek had been right. Their presence might make China hot and noisy day and night, but would I trade places with the palmist squatting on a scrap of cardboard? With the trinket seller who had set out her plastic jewels on a cotton sheet? With the bare-chested rickshawman, or the girl shouting prices from a doorway? Even the life of the well-heeled businessman sitting in the black limousine I would not have swapped for my own as I walked off my drunkenness with no plans for the next day and no concerns as to where it would lead.

御河

For some years before coming to the throne in AD 604, Emperor Yang of the Sui dynasty was Yangzhou's commander-in-chief. He was said to have nurtured a fondness for the city which stayed with him throughout his life. Folk stories tell of how this fondness inspired him to create the Grand Canal.

Listening one day to the singing of his favourite young courtesan (goes one tale), Yang was transfixed by the paintings on his palace walls. Hills and streams, villages and temples were so lifelike that they reminded him of when he had travelled amongst that beautiful countryside for real. He assembled his ministers and told them that he wanted to sail south to see Yangzhou once more, a journey that would require a long voyage around Shandong province.

"But the Meng Ford is almost dry," they protested, "and the azure ocean stormy and deep. We fear some tragedy might befall your majesty!" Yang's brother-in-law had a better suggestion: a channel could be dug from the Yellow River to meet with a tributary of the Huai. This would bring his highness to Yangzhou in no time, and without a dangerous sea voyage.

The barbarous Ma Shumou, he who was soon to acquire a taste for children's flesh, was made Protector-General for Opening the Canal. He forced the work on apace, not allowing his labourers any rest, and by and by the bodies of one and a half million of them littered the countryside. By the time the dams were breached another million were to have perished. Unconcerned by his subjects' plight, Emperor Yang was delighted with the canal and ordered 5,000 ships to be built for his first voyage. Together they stretched over 200 miles, and most magnificent of all were Yang's personal dragon boats, each 200 feet long and 50 in the beam, with painted pavilions and cloisters rising four stories above the water. He bedecked them with jewels, gold and jades, and from the Yangtze delta chose 500 young virgins. Each dragon boat was fitted with ten colourful towropes, each rope pulled by ten virgins and ten goats. From Kaifeng to the Huai the bows and sterns of the armada touched in an unbroken line. Embroidered sails were everywhere to be seen, and the smell of incense hung in the air for miles around.

The true driving force behind the creation of the Grand Canal was not Emperor Yang's lusts or Ma's ghoulish appetites but instead the rising importance of the Yangtze delta. Yang had sound economic reasons in mind. By the time he ascended the throne, the delta had overtaken the old Yellow River heartlands in agricultural output. It was temperate and stable, richly supplied with irrigation channels, less prone to natural disaster than the north. Under the strong government of the Tang dynasty, Yang's canal turned the delta into China's rice basket, shipping hundreds of thousands of tons of grain north each year. In total some 4,700 Chinese *li* long – 1,700 miles, as we would reckon – it rapidly became the greatest of the waterways which covered the Tang empire like the crackle glaze of a celadon bowl.

As for Emperor Yang, he is not celebrated in the People's Republic for his legacy, nor for reunifying China after generations of fracture. Instead, in the cut-and-dried judgement of communist history he is synonymous with harsh rule and with ranking his personal gratification higher than the good of his people. An ill-starred plan to rebuild the Great Wall left many more millions of his subjects dead, but it was with the canal that Yang watered the seed of his own destruction: its northernmost branch allowed him to launch a vast peasant army against the Korean kingdom of Goguryeo. Where his father had already failed before him, Yang threw endless men and resources into those impenetrable mountains. As campaign after campaign was defeated, all China rose against him. Yang was assassinated by his own generals, murdered in his extravagant Yangzhou palace at the age of 50, and the Tang dynasty was founded on the ruins of his dreams.

Today the road to his tomb is long and straight, its tarmac carpeted with drying grain. Tractors bounce past in clouds of soot, and the chaff rises in billows. The farmers of Huaisi Township have moved into the smart, detached homes which line the road, but they have brought their bucolic ways with them. The sky is overcast once more, the day another achingly hot one beneath its pale canopy. A ceremonial gateway stands before the tomb compound, framing its gateway in white marble. The caretaker, thin in his old age and browned by the sun, lies on a bench. Silently I place ten *yuan* in his sleeping lap and push open the door. Beneath a pyramid of earth, Emperor Yang and his wife Xiao are asleep too. I scramble up a slope strewn with couch grass and with the swaying white of ox-eye daisies. Even at its summit, electricity pylons stride past still further overhead, hurrying out from Yangzhou to the villages. This memorial to the architect of the world's longest man-made waterway is tiny compared to the farmers' homes. "If you require a monument, look around you", reads Wren's tomb in Saint Paul's; but the Grand Canal that would be Yang's monument is far from here. His tomb has suffered under what the Chinese call "the wind and rain of history". Erosion had worn it to a stump by the Cultural Revolution, when the Red Guards dug it away to reveal the brick lining of the grave vault. Only the arrival of a respected local official had stopped them from broaching it and desecrating the very corpses.

A voice calls out: *"Wei! Nide ma?"* The caretaker waves Mao's face questioningly at me. "We see very few Chinese tourists here," he explains later. "Yang is an unlucky emperor, and some believe that bad luck will taint them. How do we know that Yang was an unlucky emperor? Well, when he was buried there was a great lightning storm. Heaven was unhappy with his behaviour, you see. Then, two years ago, lightning again struck his grave. When the storm had passed we went outside and saw that the bricks had been smashed to pieces." He points to the mound, where a section of the wall still lies in ruins as a reminder of Heaven's ongoing displeasure at bad rulers. With all around it a forest of tall pylons and telegraph poles, it is easy to believe that some supernatural force had targeted Yang's tomb to make an example of him.

There was a knock on the door that evening. Orgetlek stood outside with a bag held aloft: "I've some presents for you." He took each in turn from the bag, announcing its arrival as though it were attending a soirée – "Butter! Roasted millet! Mongolian vodka!" – but then he looked downcast. "I have no time to stay. These presents are what I would have given you if we had met in Ar Horqin. The Han Chinese do not eat butter. I hope you enjoy it."

When Orgetlek had gone I sat on the edge of the bed with his gifts. The millet, half a pound of tiny brown grains, was in a plastic bag. The butter was in a heavy pouch, a rich liquid yellow that oozed from its snipped corner. It smelled rancid, but not unpleasantly, in fact the smell was somehow comforting after weeks without dairy food. The vodka had travelled in an innocuous bottle. Poured into a glass it smelled of slivovitz and, at 60% alcohol, seemed to evaporate on the tongue. Orgetlek had carried them all from Ar Horqin and had denied himself these reminders of home to show hospitality to me. That painful thought aside, there was no way I could finish what were after all raw ingredients, drink this whole bottle, even carry them all the way to Beijing in what was my tiny bag. Instead I took a symbolic spoonful each of the millet and the butter and a glassful of the vodka, savoured them, but left them behind the next morning with a note for the maid to take what she wanted, even though she would surely not eat what to her were the curious foods of a nomad race.

At a cluster of steelmongers which went by the name of Wantou, the Head of the Bay, the Grand Canal's straight new course met the older stretch that arrived from Yizheng. In the shadow of a power station, houseboats were tied up along the bank. They were of a comfortable size, neither the trim little vessels which zipped back and forth between wharves nor the 1,000-ton behemoths carrying Shandong coal. Their holds had been covered over, and walls of wood and tin nailed together to form cabins. Tarpaulins bearing the logo of China Railways had been ratcheted tight around these living spaces like green fatigues. Television aerials bobbed on poles, and generators swung to and fro seeking out the wind. Today it was just a matter of minutes before a sampan was found.

The canal quickly broadened, and the banks receded. Soon neither trees nor walls were close enough to answer the sound of our motor. Its gentle burr was swallowed into the still air. Our wash became a distant, silent sawtooth. The smoke of burning rice stubble drifted over us, and into that warm haze the banks vanished. Barges slunk deep in the water, hunching their square heads into the shoulders of their sterns like criminals trying to avoid recognition.

"Have to pay attention to these," said the pilot. "Their sightline is very poor when they are sitting so low. In this smoke, it's easy for them not to see us." Yet we landed without incident on the outskirts of a town called Shaobo, a place that had cropped up time and again in my reading. Called "the first great town north of the Yangtze", the earliest known lock on the Grand Canal had been built there in the year 385. In the year that William the Conqueror was born a two-rise pound lock had replaced it, an advance not seen in Europe until the 1700s. In Shaobo too began the Grand Canal dikes that protected the farmland of eastern Jiangsu from inundation. From here they stretched north for 40 miles, protected by magical statues placed on them by an emperor. Before even arriving, Shaobo had been elevated in my mind almost to a place of pilgrimage.

Standing upon the western dike with my back to its fringe of trees, China felt remote. The world melted away into a haze of mist and smoke that bleached the distant shore and distilled the burr of the barge engines into the softest of murmurs. The dike itself, a colossal bulwark of earth and stone had it been set down upon dry land, became just a delicate ribbon that held back the boundless waters of the Jiangsu lakes.

Lakes Shaobo, Gaoyou and Hongze drained a vast swathe of China north of the Yangtze. The Huai that fed them poured its waters into a spongy lakescape that found its only exit through the Grand Canal. The fickle Yellow River, forever fluctuating between a northerly and a southerly path to the sea, had long ago overwhelmed that native Huai, had submerged its bed beneath silt through which it could find no way out. With no easy escape for its waters, the people of this plain feared the Huai and its every mood. Big rain then big flood, they said; small rain then small flood; no rain then drought....

Now the silt has left the Grand Canal and the lakebeds suspended precariously above the farmland to the east, and any breach in their dikes brings terrible suffering. In 1699, after heavy rain, just such a breach opened at Shaobo. The Jiangsu lakes, together 160 times larger than Windermere, surged through the gap, flooding the land fifteen yards deep and drowning thousands. When finally the current had subsided and the breach was plugged, the Kangxi Emperor ordered the casting of twelve bronze animals: nine oxen, two tigers and a rooster. Set upon strengthened dikes, they commanded the water to submit to the power of the Son of Heaven, and for two centuries the water obeyed. Then, like China itself grown disrespectful of emperors, the unseasonable summer storms of 1931 added to the Huai valley's flood season. By mid-August the lakes had risen to within a whisker of overtopping the dikes, and Jiangsu held its breath. On August 26th the wind veered, strengthened, and pushed a westerly storm surge before it. Early that morning the dikes collapsed at a town called Gaoyou, emptying the lakes into 10,000 square miles of densely populated farmland beyond and drowning 200,000 people in their beds. Anne Lindbergh, wife of the famous aviator Charles who publicized the disaster in the Western media, struggled to find words to describe what she saw; she could only liken the scene to Lake Michigan having been dropped onto New York State.

Only once the Japanese and the Kuomintang had been driven from China could the victorious Communists set about building modern flood defences. In 2003 the Jiangsu lakes rose even higher than they had in 1931, yet the dikes, 100 yards wide now and rising high above the water, held firm. It has been science rather than superstition which has finally removed the threat of inundation. Of the twelve animals on whose bronze shoulders the task once rested, only one has survived, a two-ton ox whose nose is burnished from generations of caresses.

It sits these days in a landscaped garden. A podgy child rode it like a hobbyhorse, stretching forward to grasp its horns while her grandfather looked on. Unusual for his age he wore a silken *tangzhuang*, a shirt in the old Chinese style, collarless, and with loop-and-knot fastenings. On my trip there had been many signs that China was reacquainting itself with suppressed traditions, and here was another.

Though few Chinese would have reflected upon it, their clothing had long been a visible sign of a loss of identity. Under the Qing dynasty, the Han had been forced to wear the long *changshan* gowns of the Manchus as a sign of submission; under Mao the blue Sun Yat-sen jacket, a conscious take on German military uniforms, had been enforced as the plebeian norm. Since the start of Deng's reforms people had packed away their Sun Yat-sen jackets and adopted Western styles of dress. They were already familiar with them: most clothes worn in the West were, after all, stitched by Chinese workers. Today they might be ubiquitous, but two-piece suits and T-shirts and jeans were almost unknown as clothing to most mainland Chinese before the 1980s. They owe nothing to traditional Han culture.

And then President Jiang Zemin had presented *tangzhuang* to the foreign delegates at an economic forum in Shanghai, and suddenly everybody wanted one. The very name *tangzhuang* – costume of the Tang – evoked the glory of that dynasty, even if the design was not strictly historical. As interest in China's pre-modern clothing had grown, daring individuals and groups of young friends had started to wear full historical costume in public, as though they had wandered off the set of a period drama. They did it to differentiate themselves from the man on the street, and they did it to assert their pride in Han culture. If China's ethnic minorities could wear their costumes every day, why should the Han, by far China's largest ethnic group, not cast off Western styles and wear their own traditional dress? This grandfather, dressed in a simple *tangzhuang* and black trousers, had the air of an elderly Bruce Lee, urbane and self-confident.

"Sit a while, chat," he invited when he saw me reading the inscription below the bronze ox. We sat on a low wall, sharing a page of his *Yangtze Evening News* to keep our bottoms clean. He watched his granddaughter wriggle her way up the ox's slippery neck. "The situation for women has got a lot better," he mused, as though letting me eavesdrop on an internal conversation he had been having. "These women who end up as prostitutes, what do they expect if they follow the path of money? China decided to walk down that road, they decided to walk their own path, and that is the result."

I nodded, uncertain what to say. In force for 30 years now, the one-child policy had left China with a growing problem: this predominantly agricultural people had always had a preference for sons over daughters, and now for every 100 girls being born there were 117 boys. That number was predicted to rise within a few decades to 125, leaving 40 million men with no wife, no financial safety net in old age, no heirs to carry on their surname and offer sacrifices to their departed souls. Already there were many millions of men taken far from home by the demands of labour, unlikely ever to marry, and all in need of fleeting intimacy. They had had little real choice in the matter, just as the women they turned to had not grow up dreaming of prostituting themselves to strangers. He was prompted by my silence.

"Of course, things are better now than before, but you can't always predict the outcome of every reform, can you?" No, I agreed. "Life's all 'markets, markets....' Do you read the *People's Daily*? The reforms are going to go ahead even faster, even though we Old Hundred Surnames are unhappy at how we've been left behind. We are already being squeezed so much that the morning can't guarantee the evening." Mr Hu's bespectacled face floated into my mind's eye. He too had thought of himself as Old Hundred Surnames, but he had vehemently backed Grandpa Wen and his reforms.

"I'd guess this Mr Hu has connections," opined the old man. "Today it's all power and money, and you must have *both* – if you haven't one you can't have the other. If you have neither, then you eat bitterness – education, medical fees, housing, all bitter." He counted off life's bitternesses precisely as the ship chandler had done in Yizheng, as though people along the canal, this microcosm of China, had agreed together on what the nation's problems were and how to enunciate them.

"Is it okay to criticize Party policy like this?" I asked.

"To a foreigner like you, as a friend, of course. I don't criticize on paper or shout it out on the streets. Why would I do that? I'm not a journalist, or in a position to publicize my views. This isn't North Korea, you know; people are openly offering criticism of the reforms now, and so long as they don't go too far and say that the Party has no right to be in power then it has to be put up with."

His granddaughter skipped across to us and spoke to me with the frank curiosity of childhood: "Old Foreign, what are you doing in Shaobo?" I told them of my research, and of Shaobo's reputation. The man raised a wry eyebrow.

"You speak with reason – the Grand Canal was once central to Shaobo, but the town lives by other means now. We have companies that make all kinds of things – not just barges, but vehicle chassis, hydraulic equipment, electronic components, artificial fibres, toys, clothes – and we export them all over the world. You've probably bought something made here. All along the Grand Canal it has been the same story: first there was the canal, then came the officials to manage it, then came wealth, and the literati...."

As each community had blossomed and diversified, so they had outgrown their utter reliance on it. It mattered little that his explanation was crude, for he had an elegant way of phrasing his ideas, full of idiom and the simplicity of the classical language, a pleasure to listen to. He had been a political cadre before retiring, he explained. These days he played with his granddaughter Shuangshuang and flew his kite as the barges plodded by.

There was nothing to be found of the Grand Canal's first double slipway, nor of the pound lock that had replaced it. Where they might have stood, its angles softened by lawns and shaded by cassia, the thousands of tons of concrete and steel that composed Shaobo's modern shiplock sank meekly into the earth. From high upon its gantries, the far shore of

Lake Shaobo was invisible. In its place the sky settled down to meet the water in a blanket of white so total that black specks floated like birds across my vision.

The lock-keeper stood on the balcony of his control room, leaning on its rusting rails. With near-pathological enthusiasm he grasped my hand in both of his and shook my arm from the shoulder when he realized where I had come from.

"Welcome! Welcome! The English are *such* scholars, *very* clever, natural scholars. Truly, welcome!" I thanked him and told him that England's illiteracy rate compared unfavourably with China's cities, even though we had only 26 letters to teach our schoolchildren and the Chinese many thousands of complex characters. He waved aside such cynicism with a cry approaching hurt. "*No!* If only the uneducated ones had a chance, they would be scholars, natural scholars! We Chinese are too poor, too backward to be the equals of the West." It was a pointless exercise to compare the two like that, I countered. The differences between them, and the variation within them, were such that one could say little of any meaning. To start out by idolizing the West (whatever that was) meant being blind both to its weaknesses and to China's strengths. It was a mistake to measure China by a foreign yardstick rather than on its own terms; nobody measured the West by Chinese standards, though it would have been no less valid an exercise.

"You've travelled all across China?" he asked. "You've come here many times? Please may I ask, what do you like about China?" More used to being asked about the outside world, as the plastic-bottle collector in Suzhou had done, the question took me by surprise. What *was* it that I liked about China? I knew our relationship was a selfish one: I enjoyed the way being in China made me feel. There was a sense of independence there, a lightheartedness, a liberation from anything other than immediate needs, and an escape from the worries that preoccupied me at home. Free to roam and with money to spare, in China my mind and body felt like a great sponge, soaking up new words, new facts, new foods. It made me feel like a child again, crouched upon the floor to copy Chinese characters like magical symbols onto the bare walls. Each day was a lesson in humility, as I constantly reassessed what I thought I understood. Two decades had barely scratched the surface, and a lifetime would not be enough. Yes, all this was why I loved China. But there on that balcony language failed me. All these reasons boiled down to the self-centredness of a rich foreign traveller. So I nodded sagely, gave a thoughtful "hmmm", and summed them up as honestly as I could.

"When I'm in China, my heart feels free."

He gave a start and widened his eyes. "Free? It's good to hear that you feel free, in such a poor country as this." If my tendency was to idealize this country that made me feel liberated, the lock-keeper was my opposite. He stooped down. When he stood up again he was holding a shoe.

"Look how poor I am – it's split all along the side, heel to toe. Chinese shoes are badly made."

I removed a boot and showed it to him. "Made in China, exported to England, and good quality." We both leaned on the railing, comical stocking-footed comrades, examining the footwear in our hands. The gate at the far end of the lock chamber began to inch open with a mechanical rumble. We slipped them back on.

"You have money to travel, you're very fortunate," he observed. "I've not much money, but I'm rich in learning, and I can pass that learning on to many people. When I'm alone here at the lock I study characters and their hidden meanings. Each character tells us something." With an index finger he drew upon his palm. "The character for 'government official' has a roof on top, and underneath it there are a mouth and a big belly. They spend all day in restaurants eating, you see? Now the character for 'Beijing' – it has a mouth in it, and from that mouth are falling these lines, the orders that we all have to listen to!" His stories were far from the true etymologies, but they were more entertaining.

Barges passed through the distant lock gate and began to feel their way along the chamber wall. Soon they came to rest below us, thirteen in all, large vessels whose holds were swathed in tarpaulins. Slowly the gate closed behind them.

"Coal from Shandong, headed for power stations in the Yangtze delta. The same barges will come back in a few days full of fly ash. It's used to make concrete for roads. In China, you see, nothing is wasted." Leaving this idea hanging in the air he ducked into the control room, where a bank of knobs and dials regulated the sluices. The water outside the gate began to writhe as submerged currents tore at its surface and the chamber emptied. The pied wagtails which had hovered to pick titbits from the flotsam started at the movement and flew up to the railings where they tapped their tails impatiently. This was the closest I had ever stood to a working lock, and I found the boiling up of the water a chilling sight. Since swimming lessons in primary school, when it had felt suffocating to submerge myself, I had always had a fear of any deep, moving water that threatened to drag you into its abyss and trap you there. Weirs, storm drains, even pictures of whirlpools made me uneasy. In a quiet suburb of York this had always been a purely theoretical phobia. Now the power of the submersed sluices made me shiver. The lock-keeper saw that my knuckles had turned white.

"Do you know how much water there is in the chamber?" he asked. I shook my head without taking my eyes off the churning water below. "Guess, approximately!" The far gate must have been 200 metres away. Shuddering at the thought of how deep down the bottom lay, I spat out the first answer that came to mind.

"About 20,000 cubic metres?"

He corrected me with a laugh: "You'd need to add a *big*

'approximately' to that! The correct answer is 37,000 cubic metres. Seven thousand tons of shipping passes through this lock every hour, and there are two locks here. Amazing, isn't it?" It made most English locks look like the work of an infant digging on a beach: with the exception of the Manchester Ship Canal most were just 24 yards long and seven feet in the beam. There had been a pound lock here at Shaobo for over 700 years before England's first was built. He nodded in thoughtful agreement, as if the germ of the idea that China was in some respects ahead of an England he so admired had been placed in fertile soil.

"Not long ago, the city government restored the canal. They pulled down the squatters' shacks on the banks and tore up their wharves, widened the bed, planted trees and grass. Now this stretch is handling 120,000,000 tons of freight each year. Without it our economy would collapse, do you know?" I nodded in sage agreement, though I had no way of knowing how accurate the figures were. Every statistic on the Grand Canal's importance seemed to resemble a telephone number with the word "tons" or "miles" appended. The figures were rising fast, often too fast to follow, and sometimes contradicted the claims of the next city down the line, as though these were more official guesses than official secrets. It didn't really seem to matter so long as they were vast.

It took quarter of an hour for the water in the lock to reach its equilibrium, and then the keeper pressed another button. As the lock gate retracted into the ground beneath our feet he stood to attention holding a red warning flag at arm's length. Loudspeakers crackled with a comforting female voice: "Please do not throw litter into the chamber. Do not bump other barges when leaving. Remember to put safety first. We will welcome you back to Shaobo shiplock next time you pass through."

It took six minutes for the gate to retract. It would have been quicker, the keeper said, but it had been damaged by a barge strike that had gone unrepaired. The barges restarted their

engines, then one by one they glided out into that peaceful
little corner of Lake Shaobo and away to their destinations.

御河

That evening passed pleasantly thanks to Ch'oe Pu's diary
and a bottle of Yunnanese wine. Its Chinese name had been
charmingly translated as Shangri-la Enduring Pulchritude.
Ch'oe Pu, I read, had one day been introduced to a parrot from
Gansu province which was gifted with the ability to understand
men's thoughts. Separated from his home, anxious and haggard
of appearance, he had felt an affinity with the poor bird. His
escort had scoffed at his melancholy: Ch'oe Pu would soon be
back home offering sacrifices to his father, and he was not at all
like a parrot that would die in a cage in a strange land. Even the
parrot had piped up, as if he too understood the difference.

An excess of pulchritude woke me during the night. A dark
form stood silhouetted against the open window. I told Lou
Yue in a mumbled whisper that we were in Shaobo, that I
had seen where the puntsman in his diary had been crushed
to death, but he only shifted from side to side as the breeze
caught the curtain.

"Who are you?" I whispered. The curtains rustled. I knew
nothing of what Lord Macartney's valet Aeneas Anderson
would actually have worn, but the shadow took on the
frock-coat and knee-length breeches of a liveried footman. I
questioned him: "Did you know that you misunderstood what
you were seeing? You thought the Yellow River in Chuzhou
was a bay of the sea. You mistook the Yangtze at Zhenjiang
for a lake, the lake at Gaoyou for an inlet of the ocean. I can't
follow the places you mention, you transcribe their names so
poorly. Where on earth was Tohiamsyn? There are no such
syllables in Mandarin."

"Thankless! I had no maps to guide me like you have, sir,
and I relied on intuition and hearsay. In those unfamiliar

surroundings, rivers assumed the form of canals, and canals expanded into an appearance of rivers. Without your atlases, do you think that *you* would be able to tell a man-made channel from a river, or a river as wide as a mile from an inlet of the sea? I did not speak Chinese, nor even Latin to converse with the Chinese priests who accompanied us. Everything I observed was of my own eye, noted in haste as sights passed us by, or dimly remembered long after we had returned home. The English were delighted by *any* description of Tartary they might be given. I was humble enough to admit that I was an unreliable witness." Anderson's tone did not broach argument. I heard myself conciliating him.

"You did well to observe as much as you did, Aeneas. Do you remember anything of the Grand Canal?"

"I recall that each stage of our voyage had its own character, constantly changing. I did not think of them as a single endeavour. Wasn't this 'Grand Canal' something else? Didn't it run from Lin-sin-choo to Hoang-tchew? North of Lin-sin-choo was a river called the Eo-ho, I believe."

"Your pronunciation of Chinese place names is hilarious, very much of its time!" I heard myself laugh aloud. Anderson was silent for a while.

"The only men who could hope to render a better account of their names were Lord Macartney and Sir George, who had maps and reliable informants amongst the Manchus."

"Sir George was a man of his time too. He believed that the Grand Canal had been built in the spirit of the European Enlightenment, to promote commerce and agriculture for the good of the Chinese people. It was no such thing. The peasants broke their backs labouring the fill the emperor's granaries." There came a banging on the wall of the room and a muffled, sleepy voice. I stayed sitting bolt upright on the bed until I recovered my senses and, vaguely embarrassed as always, lay back down to sleep.

御河

The buildings of Shaobo broke suddenly out into open countryside, and it was an easy matter the next morning to find a bargeman willing to sail a short distance north. The Grand Canal was wide here, in places 500 yards and more from dike to parallel dike, truly more like an inlet of the sea than a man-made waterway. We steered a course in a channel marked by navigation buoys: sailing outside their confines risked grounding.

The water wandered back and forth within the dikes' protective embrace, now hard against their sloping revetments, now driven back by waving acres of reedbeds. The early sun drew a light mist, shrinking the world to two lines of pale green trees. A wind whipped on the white horses under our bows, and our hull slapped across the rough surface. At a small town called Cheluo, quite 50 kilometres from the Yangtze, I stepped onto a sand wharf. That wealthy strip of land which bordered a distant river lay behind me now, that riparian China the ship chandler had considered a country within a country. The teeming wildfowl that once blackened the sky in Gaoyou were gone too. Instead the air was thick with flies that fed on the lobster shells and prawn husks left rotting in the streets. The windows of each restaurant bore the town's boast: "Fresh seafood is the pride of Gaoyou's people"; but its detritus was their shame. For a developing country, China has surprisingly few noisome insects: malaria has all but vanished and houseflies are not common; the legacy of Mao's "Destroy the four pests!" campaign has been good. Gaoyou was an exception: the drone of its bluebottles will be an abiding memory. To the gastronomic tourists they were a minor inconvenience.

"Like this, just swat them away!" The woman who shared my bench had come to try the region's specialities, to buy shrink-wrapped portions in presentation boxes for her parents. She ordered *pipa* duck prepared from a mallard that had dabbled along the lakeshore. Spatchcocked and dried, with its neck stretched out it had looked just like the Chinese lute that gave it its name. It arrived at the table unrecognizable, thin crimson slices of meat fanned out upon a circle of dark soy sauce. Next she would try the water chestnuts, the double-yolked eggs and the lotus root that together were famous as the "three treasures of the canal". Our restaurant faced onto a narrow street of Ming buildings restored with public money, a little corner of the city crafted into another phrase in the Grand Canal story. The modest homes of South Gate Avenue would never be the equal of the water village of Tongli, but then Tongli, Lanlan had rightly observed, had felt like a museum, an imitation of life. South Gate Avenue was authentic in its ordinariness, and it rarely rang with loudhailers. Few tourists came to see the postal relay station which stood at the end of the street.

Of the hundreds which were strung out across China by the late Qing, only Gaoyou's was still intact (of Suzhou's there had remained just that single, disappointing pavilion). In this remote neighbourhood, hidden away from the wrecking balls of the town planners, it had already weathered flood, fire and war. Calamity, as the Chinese say, is what blessing leans upon. There had once been squeezed onto that plot of land greater halls and lesser halls, a public lodging house, a private residence for the master, guest rooms readied with quilts and linens, cells to house prisoners in transit, stables, even a shrine to the three-eyed Mawangye, protective deity of the station's horses. A keeper of accounts had recorded the coming and going of letters, and there had been a vet, and runners, servants, cooks and sailors. On the canal, boats of all shapes and sizes were kept ready, from grain and salt junks to luxurious barges.

A great deal of imagination was needed to repopulate that station now. Courtyards once shaded by crab-apples and filled with flowers and carp pools had been stripped back to bare earth. Rooms where foreign envoys had slept had become galleries whose displays were slowly humifying in the heat. In one cabinet was a blow-up of China's first postage stamp, the *Dalong* or Great Dragon. On it an affable dragon danced with a fiery pearl above a raging sea. Its artwork, more potato print than photogravure, was naïve compared to the British postage stamp of the day, the penny red. By the time it was issued in 1878, some 200 territories had already followed Britain's lead and issued their own stamps. With the coming of the Great Dragon, an insular dynasty had opened up to the world in another small way.

A voice asked: "Are you a collector, too? A tall man was standing beside me, staring intently at the *Dalong*. Other men moved from case to case. "We're from a work unit in Nanjing, come to visit the postal museum. Have you ever seen a real *Dalong*?" I had not even known of their existence until 30 seconds before he had spoken. He sighed. "I haven't seen one either. They're very valuable. A yellow 5-*fen Dalong* can be worth up to 80,000 *yuan* in today's market. Collectors in Hong Kong see them as an investment." So Gaoyou's average worker would need to save his entire salary for a decade to buy one – not that this ill-starred city, erased from the map each time its dikes had failed, was likely to see one for sale in any case. Like a Great Dragon held up beside a penny red, its streets felt like a coarse imitation of the energy of Jiangnan. The shop façades were every bit as colourful as in the big cities down south, but here they could not hide the shabbiness of the buildings that lurked behind them. Poorly made kerbstones had crumbled to gravel under the wheels of taxis that always seemed to be waiting for fares but never going anywhere. A spume of wind-blown litter chased its tail in unswept corners. In a lean-to kitchen I ate food cooked by a woman of the Salar people, her hair bound in pretty Qinghai silks.

Gaoyou grew more threadbare as I felt my way westward. Shops stood empty, their windows daubed with offers to sublet. That single, dreaded character *chai* that would have earmarked them for demolition was conspicuous in its absence; at least it would have heralded a different future. Finally the Grand

Canal dike loomed like a solid wall above the alleyways. Yet further, and Gaoyou's poorest lived in floating shacks cobbled together from material salvaged from waste heaps. Garbage tumbled like a multi-coloured scree down the banks of the dike and into the water, where it wallowed around those pitiable moorings. Hoping for a ride north, I hung around a filling station on the bank. Brushed off time and again, I began to stroll. A little further on, a car slowed. The driver stretched out an arm and beckoned me to stop.

"Wei, we want to ask you some questions." The car smelled of fresh cigarette smoke. An officer with the silver-anchor insignia of the Water Police on his shoulders sat in the passenger seat, while a plainclothes man shared the back seat with me. We exchanged names.

He asked: "Mr Lin, please tell us frankly, did you ask bargemen to carry you as a passenger to Baoying back then?" Only a second's hesitation, then an admission of guilt. It was pointless lying, and besides, I had after all failed. The man in plain clothes asked for a passport and lit another cigarette while he studied my visa.

"Yingguo, Lundun...." He passed it to the other passenger, who hopped out and pushed open a gate. A sign read Maritime Safety Administration, a stupid place to have hitched beside. "You have no travel permit? There are bad people aboard these barges, and we're responsible for your wellbeing. Be sure to travel by road from now on." Contrition seemed the wisest route: I apologized, nodded, and thanked him. There remained the question of my camera. Thankfully the words "no images" flashed up. In my bag was another memory card, only changed that very morning, but full of photographs of locks and bridges, a complication bordering on espionage to have to explain away if discovered. The officer returned with the passport.

"We'll manage things like this for today, Mr Lin," explained the plainclothes man, and I thanked him again and apologized for my ignorance of Chinese law. As I walked away I noticed that my hands were trembling: I knew I had come close to being arrested.

御河

A part of me was relieved to have had the burden of travelling by barge lifted for the time being by some indisputable agency: the weather was steeling itself for a hot summer, and wandering along the shadeless dikes begging for rides was becoming unpleasant. At the outset it had been worthwhile: the Grand Canal was best experienced through the people who lived from it, but the novelty of the barges had faded, I felt I had learned as much as I could hope to, and now each voyage was more or less like the last.

Riding by bus along the toll road to Baoying was refreshing. It ran squarely along the top of the eastern dike, and the panorama it opened up was vivid compared with the blinkered scene I had grown used to. To our right the dike fell away into a flat plain, richly planted. Ditches and fishponds twinkled in the sunlight. Once this had been a landscape overflowing with water and speckled with junks, but then the Yellow River had departed north and her marshy lowlands had been drained. The junks had struck sail, and the wattle and daub houses had eroded away. Still the villages, though brick-built now and robust, lay well below the level of the lakes. Another breach would flood everything to a distant horizon and displace millions. When Yu the Great stilled the flood, the people had flocked to him and Heaven had made him ruler of China. Heaven had always been unkind to dynasties who neglected that most basic duty to maintain the dikes. The Qing had fallen less than a lifetime after the Yellow River floods of 1855. Today the Communist Party bore that same grave responsibility, and so far they had borne it remarkably well.

The margins of the canal become choked by reedbeds which grow and coalesce until finally they turn to dry land where saplings have taken root. The shipping channel grows narrow this far north, the traffic sparser. Regiments of trees stand in full leaf, just as Emperor Yang commanded. Tough grasses carpet their shaded floor. Reed thatch has been harvested and stands drying in ricks mottled by the sunlight that streams through the canopy. The man who sits beside me sailed here as a child, with relatives who were in the boat business. There were still junks with mat sails in those days, he says, not like the welded steel hulls of today. They have no romance anymore.

In Baoying the local street map, the publication that can normally be relied upon to boast of a place's most trivial of diversions, can manage only that there grows mile upon mile of lotus in its drowned fields. Lotus root is Baoying's mainstay – this is a county that even holds an annual lotus-root festival. Lotus-root juice is on sale at every street stall. It tastes of thin sugar syrup, not unpleasant, but with a palate-dulling vegetal quality like sweetened cabbage water. And there is a similarly bland uniformity to be perceived in these towns that I find myself passing through. With ever greater distance from the Yangtze each seems a degree shabbier, a bit more down at heel than the last. Beneath a superficial vitality the streets have become a monotony of shops selling clothing, cellphones, and beauty products. Without that holy trinity, I am unsure whether there would be a Chinese consumer boom to marvel at. Ever since the days of Marco Polo and his *Description of the World*, Europeans have imagined China as a vast marketplace for their goods. Baoying is a reminder to be realistic. It is the weakness of her domestic markets that have made China so ill-placed to weather a global downturn. Even here, in a rich coastal province, few of the goods on the shelves are imported. And Baoying might be underprivileged when set next to the cities of the Yangtze delta, but its living standards are still just an aspiration for most of China's population.

In the backstreets, away from the broad avenues, flyers are pasted to the walls. Unemployment is rising, and where legion banks will not lend, usurers might. Pawnbrokers – all too common before Mao put them out of business along with the brothels and the rickshawmen – have found their feet again along with the rest. Their preferences are distinctively Chinese: jades, scrolls, landscape paintings and bicycles. "For mortgages, loans, pledges and exchange," they promise, "your secrecy is guaranteed, our honesty assured." Across their adverts are scrawled telephone numbers. Almost every vertical surface in China seems to be blighted with them these days. The two characters that always accompany them are so predictable that they have atrophied to whip-like flourishes of spray paint. *Ban zheng*, they whisper, documents arranged. What kind of documents?

"Identity cards, passports, graduation certificates," a woman passing the wall explains. "The kind of thing you need to get on in life. Some people need to buy fake ones on the black market. People are always wanting to check your papers, but nobody cares if they're real or not." Why don't the police call the numbers, arrange a sting, and arrest the perpetrators? It is an innocent question. She gives a sarcastic grin: "The only people who can arrange most of those documents *are* the police."

御河

After one night in Baoying I rode further northward towards the city of Chuzhou, halfway up the long, coastal province of Jiangsu. The spectre of the Yellow River blanketed the dike-top road in a dust as fine as talcum powder. On the plain below, charcoal smudges stretched out where in recent days the crop stubble had been burned off. Water gushed from sluices into the fields, relaxed its frenetic pace, and wandered off slowly into the market gardens to deposit its life-giving nutrients. The canal itself roamed in long, lazy curves, now hemmed between swaying reedbeds to either side, now edging its way hard along one or other dike as woodland reclaimed the mid-channel. In chiming boatyards, barges were drawn up on the sand like the beached landing craft of a failed economic invasion.

This landscape had been so often effaced, lacerated by river channels, submerged by floodwaters that the canal's path across it was as much the fruit of nature's caprices as of man's labour. Tracing its historical course through northern Jiangsu was like trying to record the track of a raindrop running down a windowpane amid a storm. Waterways had coalesced, diverged and vanished for so long that the whole country appeared as one broad scar that shrouded its past in a winding sheet of pale silt. Cities had drifted across this land, loosening their grip on one place and grasping at another as their rivers ebbed and surged. Their names had melted away like snow and resurfaced elsewhere like a wellspring. Qingjiang, Huai'an, Huaiyin, Shanyang, names that for endless generations had evoked the canal had by turns hauled their way upstream and down, had put out new roots, had flourished or faded away. Reading those travellers' diaries, I was now forever catching glimpses of familiar faces in unfamiliar settings. Names which in their writings punctuated their routes were dispersed now across a hinterland they had not visited. Their cities had been washed clean, left high and dry, rechristened by grieving parents with the name of a drowned sibling.

Of the Chuzhou those travellers had known, there remained only the twin gullies of the old canal. They ran now at a wary distance one from the other, as if adversity had left them distrustful even of themselves. Beside them, the foundations of the sprawling palace once occupied by the director-general of grain transport lay exposed like a sparse Roman forum. In 1945, its 200 rooms had been torn down by the Communist New Fourth Army to become ammunition crates and rifle stocks. Forgotten amidst civil war and flood, its site had only been unearthed during the modernization of the town.

The sun scorched the rootless grass that clung to its ruins, glanced off discarded hunks of marble and off the pad stones that once supported a forest of columns. With closed eyes, the ceremonial procession of the director-general who had overseen the Grand Canal from these halls grew clearer. There came ahead of him the shouts of his runners, the beating of gongs, clouds of incense, and then the *Zongdu* himself arrived on a palanquin, dressed in silks and felt boots, a golden pheasant woven on his chest and a button of red coral on his cap.

For 452 years a director-general had sent out superintendents from this place to ensure his canal was kept clear, secretaries to oversee its most difficult stretches, commissioners to see its traffic ran smoothly. From this parched acre the barges had been quantified and standardized, and complex rules laid down to govern the cargoes that filled their bellies. Strict timetables had been issued to keep the grain moving and to make sure it was safely stored away in Beijing's granaries before the winter ice came. It had once taken 47,000 men to service that canal, to watch for fires, to take thieves who stole from it, and to perform all the other numberless tasks. Shoalsmen had dredged it, lock-keepers had rallied its barges, and slipwaymen had hauled them across its locks; banksmen had nurtured the trees that held its soil firm; springsmen had toiled to keep its sources free from obstructions; beacon men had marked out its channels; pondsmen had kept its reservoirs clean and deep. It was a golden age that had ended only with the turmoil of modernity. By the 1870s, disrupted by floods, its role usurped by more efficient railways and by the sea route around Shandong, the Grand Canal was carrying barely 7,000 tons of imperial grain each year. By 1902 it had seen its last grain transport and the palace in Chuzhou stood empty.

The gongs that had heralded the director-general's arrival died away into a thudding bass, and the mental image blurred behind a storm of pop music. A knot of teenagers poured cola onto the stonework and collected the ants that gathered to drink. Their great-grandfathers would have remembered this building, and their ancestors in turn might have lined the streets to watch the last director-general depart.

御河

Featureless and flat, the plain that divided Chuzhou from its sister city Huai'an had offered no resistance to the pair's slow percolation one into the other. An expanse now of industrial estates, it seemed an unlikely spot, yet somewhere in that landscape lay the site of the world's first pound lock. A schoolteacher sat beside me on the Huai'an bus. Had he heard of the lock, or of its inventor Qiao Weiyue? He shook his head apologetically.

"I grew up in Huai'an, I'm afraid," he said, as though reluctant to break the news, "and I'm interested in its history. If I haven't heard of this lock, I fear you won't be successful searching for it."

I extracted Qiao Weiyue's biography in the *History of the Song Dynasty*, hoping it might hold a clue. Like Lou Yue's diary its language was still lucid, the place names apparently clear despite the passage of time. Qiao Weiyue, it explained, a local administrator, had become frustrated at the number of grain barges whose backs were breaking while crossing the West River lock near Huai'an. When he learned that soldiers had been conniving with bandits to wreck barges and steal their spilled grain, he installed a pair of flash-lock gates just 250 feet apart. It was something that seemed not to have occurred to anyone before, but by placing two gates so close to one another Qiao had stumbled upon the pound lock in all but name. The design was safer that hauling barges across the cusp of a double slipway, less wasteful of water than a single flash lock. That had been in AD 984, eight centuries ahead of the Industrial Revolution. The teacher digested the classical Chinese and shook his head again.

"There's no 'West River' today that I know of. I don't know how you'd begin to find out where this place was."

"I'll try the New China Bookshop, or the city library." My tone was casual, as if it were unimportant, though nailing down the exact site of Qiao's lock had been a hope of mine since Hangzhou.

He gave a sheepish smile: "The New China Bookshop has been demolished, and I don't know that there *is* a public library in Huai'an. You see, the cultural conditions here are very backward." What was Huai'an's population? Left or right of 5,000,000, he guessed.

From the hotel that afternoon I called some numbers in the *Huai'an Yellow Pages*. The line to the New China Bookshop was dead; a gruff voice heavy with disturbed sleep growled that the Chuzhou Museum was closed to the public; the telephone at the Huai'an Museum rang and rang but nobody answered; the receiver at what I took to be the city library was lifted, but an angry woman hissed into it, as though it had never struck her that somebody might innocently dial a wrong number without intending to inconvenience her.

"Library? There's no library *here*! What do you think you're doing, calling *me*?" So I walked across town to the address in the directory. For a library serving a city of five million, it was less well-stocked than many an English village's. Dark and gloomy, small and hot, it smelt of fuggy paper, but the staff helped in whatever way they could. The West River, they discovered, was another name for the Sand River that had once headed westward out of Chuzhou. Where its exact route had taken it they could only guess at. They huddled to read Qiao's biography, and like the teacher on the bus they apologized for not knowing where the lock had been. They disappeared to return with armfuls of old maps, but they were too crude to show any great detail. A young woman was called in from the newspaper archive to help:

"I can only suggest you try the city museum," she said, "or else the university, or the provincial museum in Nanjing."

"You'd be wasting your time going to the city museum," said another. "It's closed for refurbishment. This lock of yours was built in, let me see... the first year of the Yongxi reign

159

period of Emperor Taizong of the Northern Song. Even if you could determine the course of the Sand River at the time, the remains of this lock will have been washed away or buried under silt." A vision of the Thames at Runnymede flashed into my mind. The exact location of the signing of Magna Carta was uncertain, though Runnymede was a placid water meadow a stone's throw from London. The maps of Huai'an laid out before us were lacerated by thin channels, pale mnemonics for the great rivers which one by one had scoured the city. The Song dynasty land surface must have lain yards beneath today's streets. There was no hope that anything tangible of Qiao's tiny wooden lock had survived.

Though the sun had made Huai'an's streets too hot to walk in comfort that day, the TV news that evening showed footage from Fujian province, 400 miles to the south, where it had been raining incessantly for weeks. The People's Liberation Army waded chest-deep into swollen rivers to mend the levees. Half closing my eyes to obscure their uniforms, I could pretend to myself to be watching the same frantic fight in the Han dynasty, the Sui, the Qing.... Then I stood at the bottom of the Shaobo shiplock, its gates towering above me but not quite meeting. Between those dark slabs of steel the water was pouring in, and in a panic I reached out to the chink of starlight still visible above them. A violent rainstorm hammered on the metal, a deafening roar to break the muggy darkness. The drops formed rivulets on the sky, merging and parting in torrents, their patterns melting away whenever I reached out to grasp them. The water in the lock rose. I lurched out at the stars as finally it smothered me, and my hand parted the slit in the curtains to touch cold glass. An endless patter of firecrackers from the street rattled the window, and the neon blinked on the karaoke bars. Huai'an hooted and throbbed in the sultry air.

Predictions of Change

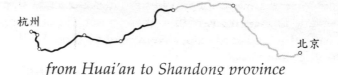

杭州　　　　　　　　　　　　　　　　　　　　　　北京

from Huai'an to Shandong province

ome Huai'an I had been travelling for a month and
had covered some 355 miles. The shipwreck survivor
Ch'oe Pu, reaching that same point in April of 1488,
saw a river three miles wide and with currents so violent
that his Chinese minders thought it bottomless. When Yu
the Great calmed the primordial waters, they told him, he
had come across the river god Wuzhiqi living in a whirlpool
there in the Huai. Wuzhiqi was a monkey with eyes of gold
and snow-white teeth. It could leap 108,000 *li*, and its mouth
spewed forth floods that deluged towns and villages. Though
it had the strength of nine elephants, Yu the Great shackled its
neck, pierced its nose with a bell, and chained it to the foot of
Turtle Mountain. Boatmen who took with them paintings of
Wuzhiqi, the Chinese said, were spared wind and wave. The
conservative Ch'oe Pu, not finding the story in the Confucian
classics, refused to believe it. The men of the Macartney
embassy were just as sceptical. They watched as their crew
sacrificed a chicken to Wuzhiqi before crossing the Huai,
wringing off its head and throwing it into the stream, then
sprinkling its blood and feathers over the vessel. Bowls of its
flesh were placed on the deck, and offerings tossed overboard
to the sound of fireworks and the burning of ghost money.
The river god placated, their barge made the far shore safely
and the captain gave three deep bows of thanks.

Today the Huai has vanished from Huai'an. The Yellow

too, that despoiler of her fellow river, long ago settled back into her northern bed to disgorge into a different sea. By night the tourist launches cruise back and forth through the silent stonework of a last flash lock. *Hongtashan* cigarettes and Rémy Martin are forced onto old comrades and a new foreign friend, to impress them, to bind them closer. The atmosphere is charmless and loud, and it drowns out a thought that has been forming. Back on the stumbling quayside, that thought quietly re-emerges from the stillness. On the outskirts of this city, barges are even now leaving these waters. Their engines are propelling them across an invisible divide into the Central Grand Canal, whose convulsions have been shaped by a more hostile environment. The waterway that has been so well-defined since Hangzhou is set to grow more mercurial.

御河

Slung back in their frames, the windows drew greedy breaths deep into the bus as it headed toward Siyang. The day was too humid for chatter, and a dozen souls sat in silence broken only by the blaring of the horn. The morning mist had reduced the scenery to a half mile of flooded paddy, like ashen mirrors set into the khaki soil. It was the season for stubble burning, and veils of smoke hung motionless like wraiths amongst the poplars. The Chinese sometimes called their Yellow River *Zhongguo de Bei'ai* – China's Sorrow – and these were its sorrowful lands, swabbed clean with wretched regularity to leave only a pale wash of greys and greens.

A slogan was painted onto the window of the Grand Canal Hotel: "Our customer is forever an emperor!" Siyang might have clanged and clattered with small-town energy, but that hotel clung like grim death to the 1970s.

Yes, it was still state-owned, the attendant mumbled as she located the room key on a fob as large as an ankle fetter, hadn't changed, she said, hadn't been renovated in 30 years.

There was no head on the shower, just a pipe sticking out from the wall. The water in the toilet's U-bend seemed to be fermenting, a threadbare carpet had given up trying to reach the walls, and Peking opera seeped through from the next room. There was a strong smell of white camphor, cigarettes and damp linen, a rare medley that tapped deep into emotions from years before. So despite the curtains which drooped in torn swags, and despite the flypaper curling from a 15-watt bulb, I felt a pang of nostalgia for the China of the early 1990s and for everything seen and done there. Lou Yue, I imagined, might soon arrive to berate me for my maudlin enjoyment of such dreariness.

The receptionist said that rain had been forecast but had failed to arrive. We both sighed: a good spell of rain was just what was needed to break the sultriness. She switched on a fan and we stood a while close together in its draught. Outside, the pounded earth of the alleys was moistened by a heavy mist. It was an exotic mud that stuck to my soles, yellow loess carried down from Gansu and Shanxi. The noonday humidity was close to suffocating, bringing my shoulder blades out in heatspots that prickled painfully. Since Huai'an the canal banks had lost their granite facings and grown ragged. A lone caravan of barges plodded upstream, its tail hidden in the hot fog that filled the sky to its zenith. The cast-off course of the Yellow River, scarcely a stream now, meandered within kissing distance of its old partner. These two aged sparring rivals now leant on each other like drunken comrades, both of them too tired to carry on their destructive carousal.

At a halal street stall I ate an evening meal of *laghman*, hand-pulled noodles piled high with tomato, green beans and strips of mutton. Old Wooden Planks counted out the change in crisp ¥1 notes. Across the plain watermark of one, beside the image of Hangzhou's West Lake, ten printed characters read "Heaven will destroy the Communist Party. Resign from the Party and ensure peace." Somewhere out there, anywhere from the Pamirs to Hong Kong to the Amur, somebody was defacing banknotes with a homemade rubber stamp. China's criminal code set a minimum of five years' imprisonment for serious cases of what it called "inciting the subversion of state authority", yet in just a few weeks two examples had passed unbidden into my hands. Their existence, and their chosen medium, implied not just disaffection but also a fear of attempting anything more conspicuous. There might have been many more that had gone noticed.

So I hurried back to the dim light of the room and threw all the banknotes I could find upon the bed. On one was a name, as though Zhou Yimin were travelling to places beyond his physical reach, a strange kind of anonymous freedom and fleeting celebrity. On another was written "Jesus loves you". Like the others they were both ¥1 notes, a sufficiently small face value to change hands often and to spread their messages widely on their evangelistic missions. Making a mental note always to check my change in future, I unscrewed a bottle of whiskey and switched on the TV. A programme was celebrating the upcoming anniversary of the Communist Party's founding.

"Without the Party there would be no modern China," the presenter declared. We could agree up to a point: without the Communists' victory in 1949 and the one-party structure that had grown out of it, China would have been very *different*, a fact undeniable by anybody who had seen how Hong Kong and Taiwan had developed over the same period. "The Party liberated us from the Japanese and ended a century of humiliation by foreign powers," she continued.

"Then it screwed up your economy with the Great Leap Forward, purged your best thinkers in the Anti-Rightist Movement, and smashed up your heritage in the Great Proletarian Cultural Revolution!" I interrupted, disappointed that she could not hear. "Why don't you tell us *that*?"

"In the fields of economics, science and culture, the leadership of the Party has allowed the Chinese people to reach new heights," she retorted. "China is producing goods for the world's marketplaces, our economy is stable, our transport and energy infrastructures are strong!" Against a background of the Yellow River cascading over the awesome waterfalls at Hukou, a military band struck up *The March of the Volunteers*. The opposing interpretations of the Party's legacy seemed irreconcilable; it had led China to such terrible depths and dizzying heights. Originally founded in Shanghai in 1921, come October 2009 it would have been in power in China for a full turn of the sexagenary cycle, through all 60 combinations of heavenly stems and earthly branches, a heavily symbolic consummation. The Communist Party of the Soviet Union had been ousted from within after 74 years, though its satellites in Eastern Europe had managed far less; the Tang dynasty had lasted for almost 300 years, the Sui had fallen after fewer than 40. The Party could not stay in power forever: no dynasty ever did. It was criminally subversive to say so, but some day it would inevitably be replaced. So who was right – the anonymous rubber stamper who predicted a violent coup? Mr Hu, who thought that almost everybody loved the Party? The Falun Gong supporter who had written on a banknote that theirs was the True Law? Perhaps there was room for all of them to be right, perhaps none. What I could say for certain was that each visit to China left a growing impression that profound change was on the way, and of tangible resentment at the dishonesty that now attached itself to every aspect of the Party's rule. So many people had complained to me over the years of the flagrant abuses that people in unelected positions indulged in – their bribery, nepotism and cronyism, their grand embezzlement of billions of dollars, their cultivation of back-door connections, their mistresses, mansions and Mercedes, their land seizures, their extortion of illegal fees for services that were part of their job, the arrests, unfair trials, beatings and even murders of local people, especially poor farmers, who so much as questioned their right to lord it over them....

"In my village we say that things are at last getting better," a farmer's son from Canton province had once joked, with a black humour typical of such anecdotes. "The People's Armed Police always used to arrive in broad daylight to smash up houses, demand money and confiscate land; now they only dare to come after dark." Even the government's own figures admitted that 1,000 officials were being found guilty of corruption each month, and though some were being gaoled and a handful executed it was still a drop in the ocean: corruption was the norm, not the exception. There was an even more pressing problem for the government. Since the Tian'anmen Square protests of 1989 there had been an unspoken contract between the Party and the people: so long as the Party provided jobs and wealth, the people would stay away from politics. Only the astronomical growth rates of the 1990s had contracted to more modest levels now as a global slump had filtered back down the chain of production. In making China the world's primary manufacturer, the Communist Party had left the economy painfully exposed to a drop in foreign spending. Now the whole artifice had begun to show signs of strain that threatened to plunge many more millions of workers into unemployment. The Party, by way of response, had thrown billions of dollars into what amounted to a New Deal for China, a colossal investment in infrastructure. By pouring money into roads, railways and canals, into power grids, airports, hospitals, schools, afforestation, drinking water, sewage treatment and a host of other mega-projects, it hoped to create enough jobs to keep growth hovering comfortably above the 8% mark, below which economists had observed that social unrest often became unstoppable.

As it was, the People's Armed Police were reacting swiftly to the most egregious of what were euphemistically called "mass incidents", be they farmers demonstrating against land seizures, factory workers demanding unpaid wages, migrants incensed at illegal detentions and police brutality.... But each year brought another 80,000 mass incidents, and the number was rising. Some were well organized and effective. Middle-class Shanghainese protesting over an extension to a railway line had used BlackBerries, cellphones and websites to spread their message. Weblogs and graffiti lionized men who had fought back against violence. One such, Yang Jia, had murdered six policemen in Shanghai in revenge for a beating that their colleagues had given him (his one-hour trial, a failed appeal, and execution by lethal injection had taken less than five months). Disparate groups wanted their dissenting voices to be heard but most dared not talk out loud. They, and hundreds of millions like them, knew that in neighbouring states – South Korea, Thailand, the Philippines, and most importantly Taiwan – autocracies had transformed into democracies, and they would not forever accept limits to their own freedoms. So some wrote their protests on banknotes. Those scraps of graffitied paper were symptoms of the tension between the Party's absolute power and the growing chorus of discontent. It was a tension that might only be relieved if reformists were willing and able to give the people a greater say in how they were governed. There were so many conflicting opinions running around my head on what might become of China in the next few years and decades, but as I lay on the bed all I could hear was Lou Yue's scolding voice once more:

"You think you know China? These people have lived their whole lives here, and yet even *they* disagree." I could not predict what was going to happen, and would have been no less surprised to awake to news of peaceful democratic revolution or of violent overthrow than to confirmation from the future that a generation hence there would still be one-party rule.

御河

Dawn's rays splayed onto the ceiling as if to remind me of the cobwebs draped there. There had been no overnight revolution. At the bus station the unlicensed cab drivers held cards scrawled with destinations. Squeezed onto a back seat with me was a pair of newly-weds, full of suggestions. One could not travel the Grand Canal without seeing the Qianlong Emperor's travelling palace at Zaohe, they said, and Little Shanghai to its north. After a few minutes of animated chatter we all sank into the torpor of the day. Before long I had fallen asleep on the bride's shoulder. She was either too polite or herself too drowsy to wake me. All the while, the Grand Canal and the old course of the Yellow River flowed a cautious distance apart. By and by they veered as one in an impulsive right angle, and between those two the city of Suqian made itself comfortable. Lake Luoma tempered the air that wafted in beneath an azure sky. After the dusty heat of Siyang it seemed like a paradise.

On Happiness Street the electric bicycles were parked three deep. From the window of Kentucky Fried Chicken the weekday traffic passed by as I sipped coffee. Taxis and trishaws wove through the pedestrians. Buses were covered top to bottom in advertisements for diamond watches from Shanghai, for flat-screen TVs from Korea. The woman perched on the next seat pondered, took a choice spoonful of ice cream, and fed it to her child.

"But our Suqian is poor as well," she insisted, "and backward." Two teenage girls walked past the window as if to defy her. They wore the tiniest of silk tops and denim hotpants and wiggled along on high heels. Our eyes followed them to the far side of the street, then lost them amongst the crowds outside the fashion boutiques, the beauty parlours, the opticians and jewellers. There was even a clothing store for the elderly called The Setting Sun is Red, its name a pun on *The East is Red*, China's national anthem during the Cultural Revolution.

"You say Suqian's backward, but what was it like ten or twenty years ago? Were any of these shops here?" She took a compact from her handbag (it pretended to be Gucci but was not a good fake) and dabbed at her nose. She was younger than me, and doubtless married if she had both a child and money – births outside marriage are rare in China, and single mothers are never wealthy. Her eyes were bright, of the perfect almond shape that Chinese women strive after. She noticed how intently I was looking at her as she applied her make-up, and the corners of her lips played flirtatiously. My shirt was dirty, my skin grimy; if she thought that just by being a Westerner I was in any position to make her better off than she already was, she was wrong.

"The shops here were all state-run, of course. There wasn't the choice there is today. Where People's Shopping Mall is, there was a branch of the state-run department store *Baihuo Dalou*. But my hometown is the provincial capital, Nanjing, and compared to there this place is still backward, I say." Until that moment I had been dismissing the small towns which lay beyond the Yangtze's rich beltway as exceptions to China's growing prosperity. But it had been wrong of me to set a benchmark with the high tide of the Yangtze delta: there were many more Suqians and Siyangs than there were Nanjings, and it was not how far they still had to go that mattered but how far they had already come. Rebuilding provinces, cities, towns and villages which after Mao's death in 1976 were close to economic collapse had been a stupefying prospect. Hurrying had not been an option: in the 1950s Mao had tried to overtake the industrialized West in one great leap, but the country had stumbled and fallen and left tens of millions dead in a criminally avoidable famine. After three decades of percolating change this young woman could still say her adopted home was backward, but it was incomparably better than it had once been. If the Party could keep delivering on that unspoken social contract, then life might continue to improve.

Yet she understood Suqian, and showing through its

sophistication were patches of what she had called backwardness. Pallid dust billowed at my heels as I walked beside the canal. Its banks had been landscaped, but neglect and drought had left them just cinder tracks punctuated by dead saplings. Most had been sawn down and carried off for fuel, leaving just a line of stumps. The water was low, its foreshore covered over with planks that led like duckboards to waiting barges. Dozens were sitting at anchor, their flanks towering above the waterline, waiting to pass through Suqian's shiplock.

I was squatting on my haunches to watch the sun set when a bargeman returning home passed by. He voiced a terse invitation to follow him, as though foreigners were commonly left high and dry and taken aboard like so much exotic flotsam. He put down his armful of vegetables, cast a beachcomber's eye over me, and correctly guessed my nationality.

"Because your clothes aren't as good as the Americans or the French," he explained. My trousers were doughy with sweat and dust, my shirt stained yellow at the collar. A skullcap perched on the back of my crown, did I not pass for a Uighur? Not close up, he chortled, not with that big nose. We drank tea and he smoked cigarette after cigarette. In the dying light we watched a man punting a lone raft on a lagoon.

"*That,*" (he pointed with his cigarette), "is what the mayor of Suqian calls 'the number one water venue on the 1,000-*li* canal'. The city government spent 120 million *yuan* on this project, but look – a failure! What can you do there? Ride a raft, or go fishing...." A landing stage on the lagoon's bank had buckled, and a banner flapped despondently. He pretended to stick a wad of cash into his back pocket, his meaning obvious: Party cadres had embezzled the money and delivered a parody of an amusement park. A hooter bellowed the end of a factory shift. As a tourist sight, it was certainly uninviting. The puntsman's wiry shoulders drove his pole into the water and his craft skittered another few yards across the ripples. The bargeman cleared his throat dramatically. "'Those who live by the mountains live off the mountains; those who live by the water live off the water.' Soon our canal will carry water from the Yangtze, and then our Suqian will have more than enough to live off."

Weeks before, a bargeman in Wuxi had touched on the Party's grand plan to transfer water from the Yangtze to the north. In the wet landscape of Jiangnan it had been hard to empathize with faraway parched fields; here, looking down at the exposed bed, it made more sense. Northern China, by nature drier than the south, had been cursed by low rainfall since the late 1990s. Two-thirds of China lay north of the Huai River basin, but only one-fifth of its water was to be found there. Once-mighty northern rivers had been reduced to blackened streams by industrial effluent and agricultural run-off. The Yellow River regularly dried up before it reached the sea. Meanwhile, of the Yangtze one trillion cubic yards were calculated to be flowing away unexploited each year into the Pacific. The bargeman flicked his stub overboard, and its glow traced an arc that phutted into mud.

"Chairman Mao had a saying: 'the south has plenty of water, the north little. If possible, it would be good to borrow some'." The Great Helmsman had made that famous meditation in 1952, against the background of his insistence that "Human plans can outweigh Heaven's". But then his Great Leap Forward had led to ruin, ten years of turmoil had followed, and nothing had come of the idea. The question of water had only become urgent under the combined pressures of industrialization and climate change. Now Beijing's aquifers were calculated to be dropping by a matter of yards with each passing year, and already it was sometimes necessary to drill down over half a mile before hitting groundwater; much of it, even then, contained dangerous levels of flourine. Beijing's population was soon expected to outstrip its water supply. Before long, the capital might be uninhabitable. Armed with earthmovers, a nation that had been capable of digging the Grand Canal with shovels could not shrink from the challenge.

The South-to-North Water Transfer Project, a solution to the drying up of China's northern cities, had been officially heralded in the *People's Daily* in October of 2000. Three routes had been planned. The western, the most physically demanding and politically sensitive, might eventually tap the headwaters of the Yangtze's tributaries on the Qinghai-Tibet plateau and funnel them into the headwaters of the Yellow River. If the project were given the go-ahead (and the diplomatic and environmental implications of diverting one of the world's largest rivers at its source might yet militate against the plan), 600 miles of tunnels would need to be blasted through the pristine wilderness of the Bayankela mountains, 11,500 feet above sea level. As for the central route, work quickly started to upgrade the Danjiangkou reservoir in Hubei province. A new canal had been dug from there to carry water to Beijing in time for the 2008 Olympics, though northern farmers had protested that their crops had been sacrificed so that the taps did not run dry during the Games.

But the principal route of the Water Transfer Project will eventually wind like a snake across eastern China, its mouth taking gulps from the Yangtze, the Grand Canal itself its sinuous body. Seventy-five pumping stations will force water lock by lock northwards – uphill – to its summit in Shandong, from where it will flow down under gravity toward Beijing. Where it meets the muddy Yellow River, an inverted siphon-tunnel 600 yards long will suck water through the bedrock under the river's belly and disgorge it clean onto her north bank. Seven million cubic yards of concrete, one billion of earth and stone, will become the project's bones. Its stomach, the Jiangsu lakes, will store ten billion cubic yards of water. In 2008 the first fruits of the eastern route project were tasted, with water from northern Jiangsu being pumped into drier Shandong. If environmental engineers can satisfy themselves that they have solved the problem of Jiangsu's industrial pollution, by the middle of the next decade more than 100 million northerners should be drinking from the Yangtze. To call the scheme an inversion of nature is no exaggeration.

The bargeman lit another cigarette and continued his train of thought. "There will be more water, and then perhaps I'll be able to make money carrying coal from Shandong. Right now, I can't take my barge north of Xuzhou for half the year – too shallow." The port running lights on a barge train passed us by in the twilight like a string of meagre rubies. We sucked at the last of our tea. The sight of thousands of tons of coal strung out along a dozen vessels had become to me almost as unexciting an event as it was to him. I turned back to the shore before the darkness fell too thickly to find my way.

御河

But for the ranks of poplars which fringed the road to Zaohe, the dry channel that had once borne the Yellow River would have been visible from the road. In their unwelcome shade, between the very trees, farmers tended their wheat. The reforestation of this flood plain had bound the soil and calmed the dust storms, but it had robbed their crops of light. A milky sunshine seeped into those groves to meld with the mist and curl about the mute trunks. Set back from the road, a village church bore a wooden cross.

"We have churches like these in England, too." I struggled to make myself heard over the truck's engine. The driver answered in a shout.

"English, are you? Why did you want to go to Zaohe?"

"Have you heard of Qianlong's travelling palace?" His eyes darted back and forth blankly between me and the road ahead. I repeated the name more clearly.

"Ah, the Temple of the Dragon King? It's very old," he observed equivocally. After an absent-minded pause during which he came close to driving over a stray dog, he smiled with recollection. "My grandmother used to call it the Temple of the Dragon King built by Imperial Command for the Calming of the Waves."

It stood apart from the unremarkable town of Zaohe, a rectangle of walls from behind which rose roofs of imperial yellow. At around the same time that Edmond Halley was describing the influence of solar heating on the movement of the monsoons, here a temple was being built so that the Son of Heaven might pray to the Dragon King for rain. China's counterpart to Queen Victoria in his longevity and accomplishments, the Qianlong Emperor visited the temple five times, such was the importance attached to the rituals he performed there. He had slept in a bed chamber dedicated to Yu the Great, stiller of the flood. Below him, the goddess Guanyin of the Southern Ocean had sat upon a lotus blossom. In the hall of the Dragon King, his reptilian majesty himself sat in gold-leafed silence flanked by eight naiads, a dignified expression playing on his wooden lips.

In the celestial symmetry demanded by tradition, two side-halls lay to the Dragon King's south, facing one another and separated by a broad courtyard. In one stood statues of the gods of the four seas and of the god of wells, in the other more statues held ceremonial writing tablets in mute attendance on the Dragon King's word. At a desk in the shadows sat a man with a wispy beard and moustache. His narrow eyes slanted neatly upward like a woodcut depiction of a Chinese sage. On his head he wore a pleated black cap with a flat brow. This was quite enough to signify his religion.

"You're a Daoist?"

He chuckled and nodded softly. The desk was spread with a yellow cloth, and on it were traced the eight trigrams and the swirling black and white raindrops of the *taiji* diagram. A bamboo tube was full of spillikins, tapered and red lacquered, each bearing a number. "I studied on Dragon Tiger Mountain. Have you heard of it? Celestial Master Zhang Ling, the originator of the teachings we call the Way of the Five Bushels of Rice, cultivated himself there in the Eastern Han dynasty." From a drawer he produced a certificate of ordination given to him on the day he had become a priest. Along with the registers of the celestial bureaucrats with whom he was entitled to negotiate, its possession confirmed that he had earned a channel to the arcane world of the spirits. He passed across a well-thumbed booklet. "Becoming a Daoist priest is a tradition in my family. Every day I have to read this aloud." The booklet was in dense, esoteric prose, each character recognizable as it stood alone but taken as a whole their meaning quite beyond my capability. Daoist liturgies were written with exactly that confusion in mind: the uninitiated would be unable to use them. His ability to perceive meaning from them was a privilege.

"I expect you understand Zhuangzi and Laozi," I ventured: like many foreign students of Chinese culture, my understanding of Daoism had been formed around those earliest Daoist texts. The philosopher Zhuangzi's writings were full of wit and anarchic spontaneity; Laozi's *Classic of the Way and the Virtue* was transcendent, hinting at ineffable truths in the most frugal of language. Both playfully subverted everything I thought of as real or important. I was surprised when he slowly shook his head: Zhuangzi and the *Classic of the Way and the Virtue* were not on the syllabus at Dragon Tiger Mountain. Today's generation of priests valued the practical application of their powers more than they did philosophical discussion. In the Temple of the Water God in Wuxi had been discarded the talismans and astronomical charts used to summon the spirits and to voyage to the stars. It was just such practices that this priest had trained for.

"There are some who understand Zhuangzi and Laozi," he apologized, "but I studied so that I could lead this life." Could he at least explain those aspects of the Water God's Temple that I had not understood? Who was the Southern Extreme

Great Emperor of Longevity, or Grand General Ni Mi? And what about these figures who dominated the hall where he spent his every waking day? "The Southern Extreme is a star, the 'old man star', one of the brightest in the sky, home to one of the emperors of the four directions. He can give you good health and long life if you travel to the star to meet him. Grand General Ni Mi? He is one of the 60 generals who control the destinies of people born in each of the 60 years of our astrological cycle. If you pray to him he will give you good fortune. And these statues?" He took in the enormous wooden carvings that lined the hall. "These are the five lake gods." I had never heard of them. He chuckled softly again, as though thoroughly contented. "Friend, even the Chinese tourists who come here have never heard of them. Every river and lake in China has a god who controls it. There are too many for anybody to know. Have you noticed that every part of this temple is associated with water? Lake Luoma is only three *li* away...."

"The Grand Canal is even closer," I interrupted, feeling an urge to stick up for it even though it was an inanimate waterway.

"Indeed, indeed, and the bargemen would stop here to pray to Guanyin for safe passage." In silent thought I toyed with the bamboo tube and its wooden tapers. There were 64 of them, one for each of the hexagrams of the *I Ching*. A book lying open next to them explained the significance of drawing at random any particular one. Generations of bargemen had come to this temple with faith that their prayers, accompanied by sufficient and visible offerings, would be answered. They had believed that as individuals the Way of Nature within them resonated with the cosmos, and that the fall of bamboo tapers could chime with that resonance and give insights into their destiny. Like anybody else who has spent long in China I had occasionally drawn lots at a temple or had my physiognomy read on a street corner. A part of me had always wanted to believe it was true.

"Could you read my fortune if I drew lots?" I asked. Unexpectedly, he chuckled and waved the suggestion away. He might have named his price, but he seemed to have too much respect for his practices to want them trivialized by somebody who by his questions had made it clear he was no believer.

"This is for *Chinese* people, you understand. You foreigners have your religious beliefs, and we have ours." Just how much money was he refusing? "Different sums. People might pay 50, 80, 100 *yuan*. I read faces and palms as well as interpreting the lots. If people get a good reading they might pay well, to ensure that their reading comes true." He thought for a moment. "One businessman had a very good reading and left 1,000 *yuan*. It's better than working in an office." To that businessman, ¥1,000 would have been an investment in good fortune, a reciprocal bond that obliged its cosmic recipient just as the banquets he held for clients would bind them together in mutual obligation. The sponsors of the dragon screen and the laughing Buddha in the Fuyan Temple had bound their fortunes just the same.

"Isn't it all officially superstition? Aren't you Chinese meant to have a 'scientific developmental outlook' these days?" The phrase was one of the Party's latest buzzphrases, an indicator that reformist factions were in the ascendant in Beijing.

"It's what the authorities call superstition, yes, but we call it *tujiao*, a religion of the native soil." What then did he think of the fact that Chinese Christians were praying to a foreign god in a village just a few miles away? For the first time the amused twinkle left his eyes. "They should stick to the religion of their native soil," he said gravely. "Cultures should not mix."

"Cultures should not mix?" repeated Jiangbing, in whose car I found myself riding later that day. "I disagree. I've been overseas as a construction worker, and I learned a lot. In the

Middle East I learned to speak a little Arabic, a little Russian. Do you speak Arabic?"

"I can say *salaam aleikum*, and *inshallah*."

"What about Russian?" Of an O-level from twenty years before there still survived a smattering of words. "Let's speak Russian, then," he suggested. *"Kak tebya zavut?"*

"Menya zavut Liam."

"Menya zavut Jiangbing." Together we called out the numbers from one to ten, then I asked him the time. "Liam, I tell you, I can't tell the time in Russian." No matter. After years in which my only foreign language had been Mandarin, I had forgotten how complex Indo-European grammars could be. In spoken Chinese, 5.30 became simply "five dots half". Over the Amur River we would have needed to use a masculine genitive singular ordinal adjectival declension to express that same idea. It seemed pointlessly elaborate now. "I tell you," Jiangbing went on. "The Russians will never have a good economy like the Chinese. You know why? They're happy to work each day until they have enough money to buy vodka, then they go and drink their wages away. The next day the same. The Arabs, well, I know less about them, but they don't work as hard as we Chinese. We work hard, save our money, and invest it."

It was intriguing, how one of the most-widely travelled Chinese men I had ever met should have been loitering by the roadside with his friends, earning money by occasionally hiring out his car. He had offered to drive me to a town called Yaowan, once a flourishing little port, and that was how we had come to be riding together. How had he been able to get the passport and documentation to leave China to work? Surely he must have had connections?

"It's no secret. China has contracts for construction projects with governments in the Middle East. Through the Party I knew people who needed workers. I did my military service, and when I'd finished I could have gone looking for work in

China, but the wages are too low. There are people who work in clothing factories in Fujian province for twelve hours a day, seven days a week. Do you know how much they earn? Eight hundred *kuai*."

"Each week?"

"Each month." At less than 20p an hour, it was unsurprising that the British clothing industry had moved its production wholesale to China. "Yes, but the cost of clothes in Britain is lower now than before, *dui ma?* If you want to keep your domestic industries you have to be willing to pay higher prices. You can't compete with unskilled peasant workers on wages." He switched on the car radio. A soccer match was being broadcast. He tutted: the Chinese national squad was hopeless; they'd even been knocked out in the group stages of their own Olympics, their best result a draw against tiny New Zealand.

"We Chinese are no good at soccer. Do you know why? The Chinese FA isn't independent: it answers to the Party. How can a government expect to run a league? And there's no club loyalty in China. In England you have Manchester United, Liverpool and the rest, and local people support their local club; here each club is named after the company that owns it, and they change their name each time they change owners. You support Jianlibao Soft Drinks, then find that next season they've changed their name to Kingway Beer! And there's nowhere to play – no grass, no open ground, not even in the villages. It's all been concreted over. Just look at the pollution on this road...." The exhausts on a convoy of trucks belched unfiltered into our path. "When I was a child I used to fish in these streams by the roadside. There are no fish anymore. All dead. We Old Hundred Surnames really regret the environmental damage." He pointed out into the countryside. "There used to be an ancient gingko tree over there, hundreds of years old. It was cut down because a company wanted to build on the land. In Caoqiao a temple of 100 *mu* was destroyed back in the Cultural Revolution, but you see we're *still* destroying the heritage we ought to be protecting."

"The pollution's not too bad here," I consoled him. "It's far worse south of the Yangtze." I had read a newspaper report about a Hangzhou bargeman who had been badly burned when methane bubbling up from the putrid canal had ignited and caused an explosion. Jiangbing gave a snort of amused recognition.

"Still, in Yaowan there's been too much destruction in recent years. Things have changed. We'll be there soon and you'll see. When I was a child they made a kind of local wine, Green Bean Spirit. The Qianlong Emperor himself gave it the name. You could buy a bottle for two *kuai*, and it was distilled from 108 kinds of medicinal herbs. Now it's made by a big company. They don't use nearly as many herbs, and it costs 100 *kuai* a bottle. They've spoilt it for the sake of profit. There's a saying: 'if you know what's sufficient, you'll always be happy'. We Chinese used to be satisfied with a little, but now it's always 'walk towards money!' and we'll never again be satisfied with what we've got."

The road to Yaowan took us through a land of wide irrigation channels that made cars inconvenient, more than tripling the distance as the crow flew. The newly-weds on the Suqian bus had made me promise to see this Grand Canal town they called Little Shanghai. Jiangbing agreed it would be worth it.

"They spoke the truth. Yaowan used to be so prosperous, so free-and-easy." Yaowan's remoteness – it lay squarely at the junction of three legal jurisdictions and was reachable only by water – had given it somewhat of a reputation. Bargemen would stop to relax there, and its ambiguous name could mean Bay of Kilns or Bay of Brothels as they wished. Merchants from across China had built provincial guildhalls and agency offices in the styles of their homelands, and by the end there had been Britons, Americans, Frenchmen and

Japanese walking its streets. Muslim traders had worshipped in mosques, Christians had opened churches. Then Liberation had seen the businesses closed down and the foreigners expelled. Jiangbing stopped his car on the waterfront.

"When the water's low you can see how the canal was dug in terraced steps. Very interesting, but the water's too high right now." Yaowan sound, a mile wide, bristled with derricks. Each was mounted on a barge and rose tens of yards into the blue sky. A filigree of guy lines supported their trunks. The entire horizon of the lake, once my eyes had learned to pick them from the haze, was thick with their filaments. "Sand dredgers. They suck sand from the bottom of the lake and sell it to construction companies. I tell you, it's illegal to suck sand from the lake here, but these dredgers are safe so long as the right people get paid."

We walked Yaowan's streets looking for traces of the past. Back in Tongli, canny developers had smelt out the money to be earned in keeping that water village just the way it was; impoverished Yaowan had demolished its old houses just to turn a quick profit building new ones. By the time people had begun to see the value in preserving them, most had gone. Film crews had once come here to use them as backdrops for costume dramas, but now a single street was all that was left. Jiangbing declared himself to be very disappointed. The little that survived was not charming like Tongli, but it was original, and original wooden buildings from imperial China are remarkably rare, given how there was nothing else just a century ago. Each opened onto that one narrow street through moveable panels which by day were lifted out and tidied away, and by night were set home and locked together. Their eaves overhung the road. Under those beetling brows hung nameboards carved in fat characters. But where in Tongli the wood had been restored and recarved, here it was bowed and worm-bored. The lime mortar which bound the iron-blue bricks was flaking, and it tumbled from between the courses.

Very soon, Yaowan would have to decide whether it wanted to make those houses part of the Grand Canal story or finally knock them down and move on.

Jiangbing offered to drive on to Pizhou. In the half-hour it took to reach the town, we passed three churches. Each was no more than a one-storey house dressed in the standard greys of the region, but each bore a painted cross. There were so many for such a remote rural corner. Jiangbing saw them too.

"I'm not an exclusivist, Liam, but it gives me an uncomfortable feeling to think that Chinese people are looking for foreign religions when they have such strong traditions. As for me, I'm a Communist Party member, so I don't have a religion."

"Isn't communism like a religion?" I teased. "Aren't Marx and Lenin like gods? Isn't the *Communist Manifesto* like a holy scripture?"

He took my teasing in good spirit: "You could say that. I became a Party member after doing military service. I was so happy when I was finally admitted. It was what I'd been heading for all my life." Even if his political beliefs did not amount to a faith, he had chosen to couch his joyfulness at Party membership in almost religious terms. Had he been a Christian, though, his conversion would not have secured him the contacts to work abroad that the Party had. We were both quiet for a time, as though Jiangbing's revelation had been a touch too personal. Eventually it was he who spoke again.

"This landscape is very historic. The farmers are forever digging up treasures, but they don't realize how much they're worth. I have a friend who buys them up for a few *kuai* and then sells them on with official customs seals for a fortune. General Cao Cao of the Three Kingdoms fought battles here, and the Huaihai Campaign that defeated the Kuomintang was fought nearby. The Americans were very unhappy when the Kuomintang armies were wiped out: they'd supported Chiang Kai-shek through the civil war, but he'd been beaten by Mao. What were the Americans doing, supporting the Kuomintang? It makes me so angry, Liam, to know that America is always causing wars in other countries – Korea, Vietnam, and now Afghanistan and Iraq. They would not dare start a war with China, I tell you. We have an indomitable spirit, and if the Americans started a war with us over the question of Taiwanese independence, they would lose. They have the better technology, but we have the better morale."

To my mind it was unimaginable that the US would go to war with China over Taiwan, no matter what assurances passed from Washington to Taibei: the US had too much to lose in attacking a country which held hundreds of billions of dollars of its national debt and still manufactured most of its imports. The election in Taiwan of Ma Ying-jeou and his disavowal of independence meant that the US was far less likely to be called upon to stand by its promises anyhow. Besides, it was common knowledge that the Chinese now had anti-satellite missiles and submarines. The People's Liberation Army would not be the poorly armed pushover it had been in the 1950s, and the US knew it.

"Isn't some kind of civil chaos more likely than war with America?" I suggested. "There'll soon be 40 million Chinese men without a woman to marry, and there are tens of millions unemployed. Even the government admits that there are hundreds of mass incidents every day. Look at your history – China has periods of unity and periods of division. The periods of unity always end with violent protests just like these. Perhaps there's division ahead?" It wasn't that I thought civil war the likely outcome: the military was not fractured into regional power bases as it had been after the 1911 Revolution, and transport and communications had shrunk China like they had every other country. But there seemed to be so many potential faultlines in this country that might yet open up. There were strong secessionist tendencies in Tibet and Xinjiang, both of which autonomous regions had seen serious unrest in the media-saturated run-up to the Beijing Olympics. Ethnic identities in the southwest aligned themselves with neighbours such as the Thais, while powerhouses like Shanghai, Hong Kong and Canton could easily go it alone as independent city states. The thought of China's internal breakdown haunted the Party, and my question had been deliberately provocative, but Jiangbing was no more easily provoked than he was teased. He proved himself to be a firm believer in what the Party taught about the repercussions of loosening its hold on China.

"You speak with reason – China has always had periods of chaos. But society is thoroughly saturated with the organs of the Party now, so where would such chaos begin? The Party is in firm control." It was an important observation. Travelling in China during the SARS outbreak of 2003, the speed with which the Party had mobilized its foot soldiers had impressed me. Once Beijing had belatedly admitted that SARS posed a serious threat, within hours every communal stairwell and public space had borne a poster warning of the symptoms; electronic thermometers were distributed overnight to transport hubs, hotels and schools, and suspected cases were whisked into quarantine. "Here's a concrete example," Jiangbing added. "This highway to Pizhou runs all the way to western Xinjiang, and there's another that runs from Fujian all the way to Beijing. In the past there were not these structures in place to keep China so closely bound. No, the Party's control is too tight for China to break apart like it did after 1911. Liam, if you consider the alternative, the chaos, it is a *good* thing for China that the Party's supremacy is not challenged."

御河

The meanings behind the names of China's biggest cities are familiar – Beijing is the northern Capital, Nanjing its southern twin; Hong Kong is a Fragrant Harbour, and Chungking marks the Double Celebration of an emperor's accession. Every place I had passed through had held some story in its characters – Tangqi had provided a Resting Place on the Dike, Zhenjiang was well placed to Guard the Yangtze, Huai'an had prayed for a Huai River at Peace.... But come the farthest reaches of northern Jiangsu and the fringes of Confucius' ancient state of Lu, the cities began to betray their high antiquity in the semantic uniqueness of their names. In even the largest of dictionaries, the characters that had identified them for millennia had no wider definitions; they had arisen seemingly out of nowhere and had absorbed no other shades of meaning. Pizhou – the region of Pi – was such a place. It was the same for Tan, and for Yun, and Zhou and Juan and dozens more scattered across the pages of an atlas. Living in constant England I had grown up with the idea that cities were static entities on the landscape. China's geography had shaped hers quite differently. The powdery ploughland around Pizhou was flecked with archaeological sites where that city had rested for a while before moving on. Name and substance had drifted across the countryside for 3,000 years and had only finally settled down a little way above Lake Luoma.

The spring harvest had been gathered in, the stubble burned off and the fields flooded once more. Machines had clawed their way through the sodden earth, churning water and ash to an oily black. The evening was warm, the sky clear and the air pleasantly free of the mugginess of farther south. Pizhou was friendly. On the windows of every street-corner hammam were pictures of Western women squeezed into bikinis, as though the city were awash with unseen blondes. Of its avenues, one or two shaded with plane trees were left, but mostly modernity had brought with it its wide streets and cloned shops. Almost instinctively by now I headed down to the canal: travelling by road had left me all the more eager to see it at every opportunity.

Its water was low, and this far north only an occasional

vessel plodded past. A gangplank led to the deck of a converted barge, and a sign promised tea. It was sparsely furnished inside, spotlessly clean, and cool. An air-conditioner hummed in a corner. A dozen tables were laid out with ashtrays ready for the evening's customers, and the bulbs on a primitive fruit machine flickered. On a radio a comedy programme had started, all quick-fire wordplay that I could make little sense of. At one table sat a couple, too engrossed in their game of cards to pay it any mind. They went on husking sunflower seeds with their tongues and spitting the shells onto the floor. A middle-aged man stood up.

"Come in, come in! A drink of tea for you. My name is Jiang Liu, a very fitting name." He drew it; it meant "the river flows". He fetched a flask of boiling water, and a glass into which he dropped a large pinch of green leaves. "This is dragon well tea, from Lion Peak in Longjing. It's not superfine grade, but it is *first* grade. With the water we must use in Pizhou, only the best of connoisseurs could tell the difference." The village of Longjing, home to some of China's finest teas, was also the source of the streams which kept the West Lake full in Hangzhou. Its tea smelled of fresh honey, with a musky sweetness that lingered on the edge of the tongue. I had crossed Jiang Liu's gangplank hoping to learn something more of the canal north of Pizhou. Its route and its history became confused up here in northernmost Jiangsu, with courses of different ages forever subdividing and dying back. Jiang Liu regretted he would be of little help.

"I'm no boatman. My younger brother and I were both told we were required to 'go off duty' when our state-run factory was sold to a private investor. We bought this old barge as a home and a business, somewhere that boatmen and townspeople could come to drink tea and talk." A pock-marked man entered, chivvied by an elderly woman. Jiang Liu addressed him. "Ah, Didi. Our friend has come from England to travel our canal." Didi, his younger brother, spoke, but his accent was strong. Jiang Liu interpreted.

"He says that we live on this barge with our little sister and our mother. Didi's son lives here too. Below deck there are living rooms and bedrooms, private space for us. Didi used to drive a big car when he had a job at the factory." Didi pretended to hold an oversized steering wheel. I asked him where the canal ran after it left Pizhou. "It forks about 30 *li* further on. One branch goes to Tai'erzhuang, the other to Xuzhou." And after that? Did the two stay separate? Did they both go to Jining? The two conferred.

"We can't say for sure. Perhaps by the Weishan Lakes the water gets too low for barges to pass." When he heard this, the seed-eating card player turned to us.

"If you want to sail to Jining, then you must go to Tai'erzhuang. If you go to Xuzhou you'll find the water too low to go any further when you reach the Weishan Lakes." He turned back and went on with his game. I pulled some dog-eared photocopies from a pocket and set them on the table beside him. A blue line left Pizhou, clearly described a broad arc to the northwest, then turned to follow the edge of the Weishan Lakes all the way to Jining. Tai'erzhuang didn't come into it. He fingered the paper. "That's not right. You should follow *this* channel." He traced a line through Tai'erzhuang, then straight across the centre of the lakes to Jining.

"Across the middle of the lakes? Is that possible?" His face remained impassive, as if the question were meaningless. My maps, almost new, were wrong. At the largest scale, the Grand Canal was a fifteen-inch blue line, simple and unchanging. Up close, though, it was less clear-cut. I let out a deep sigh. Didi broke the silence that followed:

"Elder brother, you know how to sing *Lake Weishan*, don't you? Sing for our friend!"

"My friend," Jiang Liu began, "after the Japanese bandits invaded our country, the first real defeat they suffered was at Tai'erzhuang, very close to here." He closed his eyes and sang

187

in a quavering baritone.

> *The sun will soon be setting in the west,*
> *It is quiet and still on Lake Weishan.*
> *Play! oh beloved lute of my home,*
> *Sing that ballad that moves me!*
> *Climb aboard the speeding train,*
> *Just like mounting a galloping steed.*
> *The station, the railway tracks,*
> *Are fine places to slaughter our foe.*
> *Onto the train there – unleash the machinegun!*
> *Rush to the train there – blow up the bridge!*
> *When the devils hear, they are stricken,*
> *Like cold steel thrust into their breast.*
> *The sun will soon be setting in the west,*
> *The devils' last day is upon them.*
> *Play! oh beloved lute of my home,*
> *Sing that ballad that moves me!*

Through the window that sun was setting as Jiang Liu sang. Its red orb made the sheet metal of the oil barge moored beside us burn with a dazzling beauty. As though it had been cued in, the radio beeped the hour, and from Beijing there came the first notes of *The March of the Volunteers*.

> *Arise, you who would not be slaves!*
> *Let our flesh and blood become a new Great Wall!*
> *We people of China have reached our most perilous time,*
> *Each one forced to cry out this final roar –*
> *Arise! Arise! Arise!*
> *Our myriad hearts are one.*
> *Braving the enemy's cannon, march on!*
> *Braving the enemy's cannon, march on!*
> *March on! March on! On!*

The national anthem of the People's Republic had been written in 1934, when that enemy was Japan. By the time *Enola Gay* and *Bockscar* brought the Pacific war to a close, the Japanese Imperial Army had murdered up to 35 million people during its fourteen-year occupation of China, treating men, women and children with equal brutality. By comparison, around 100,000 US servicemen died fighting the Japanese, a number comparable to British Empire losses. Though it had ended before most Chinese now living were even born, and though Japan was now China's largest aid donor, what they called the War of Resistance against Japanese Aggression still scarred the Chinese psyche. They had a nickname for Japan's red-sun flag: the sanitary towel. Every schoolchild was expected to sing *The March of the Volunteers* each Monday morning at the raising of the flag. In school they learned about the Nanjing Massacre, and in newspapers they read of how right-wing Japanese statesmen still refused to admit any responsibility for the war. Pointing an accusing finger out across the Yellow Sea in the hope that people would rally around the Chinese flag, the Party would not lightly let people forget the struggle that was the foundation-stone of its legitimacy.

That night a knock on the door woke me. After a few more furtive raps with no response there was quiet, then somebody tried the handle and, failing to turn it, barged the door with their shoulder. I groped for my sheath knife and shouted, and they went away. As I fell asleep the telephone rang.

"Do you want a girl?" a woman asked. No, I told her. Hours later, there was a furious banging on the door.

I shouted: "What do you *want*?"

"Do you want any drinks?"

"It's 3am! Go to your grandmother! You'll die without shame!" Those expletives stilled whoever it was, and I slept late the next morning. Only after I had dressed and gone downstairs to check out did I realize I had taken a room in the International Beautiful Women Club. The staff must have wondered why on earth I hadn't wanted my prostitute.

I called Jiangbing. His military service had exposed him to people from all over China and, like Lanlan and Meigui, his Mandarin was crisp and lucid. It was better to wait for him than be saddled with a driver who spoke only with the heavy local accent. He suggested what we might do with the day:

"Liam, I've looked on a map and I think you might like to see Nian Village." And so we met, and as we drove out into the khaki countryside he talked about his time in uniform.

"I was eighteen when I volunteered for the People's Liberation Army," he explained. "I went for my physical as soon as I was old enough. I tell you, it says in our national constitution that it's the sacred duty of every citizen to protect our homeland and resist invasion, and I'd always wanted to do my duty. I was based in Fujian province for twelve years."

"And after that you worked in the Middle East in construction?"

Jiangbing nodded. "I joined the Party after I'd left the army, then I got a job abroad. That's how I earned the money to buy this Volkswagen." He rolled up the windows and turned the air-conditioning on. We both let out contented sighs and wafted the cold air up at our faces. In seconds we had forgotten the heat of the road. It had not struck me the day before that his submission to the Party structure, his faith that it was too pervasive now for China to fall apart, might have been learned during his military service. It seemed obvious now: the Party was rooted deeply into every regiment and platoon, each soldier given a thorough education in Party ideology. To judge from his age – we had both been born in 1970 – his training must have begun a year before the Tian'anmen Square protests. Neither of the army groups which had entered Beijing that summer had been based in Fujian, but still he must have felt the full force of the war that was waged within the PLA in its aftermath, the push to guarantee that there would be no questioning of one-party rule and that tomorrow's soldiers too would open fire. The matter of what the PLA had done that year was too big to broach: once, an unthinking comment to a friend in Beijing, a student in the late 1980s, that there were still bullet craters visible on the Gate of Heavenly Peace had brought to his eyes a silent glaze of tears. We reached Nian Village, and Jiangbing pointed out an obelisk soaring above monumental foliage.

"This is a memorial to the Battle of Nian Village. I tell you, when I was a soldier I enjoyed learning about the fighting our field armies did in this countryside. I grew up here, you understand, so it was like learning the history of my own home." He had seemed so worldly and open-minded the previous day; now a little of his warmth seemed to leave him when he talked about the Chinese Civil War. He spoke like a commissar lecturing a roomful of recruits. "The Huaihai Campaign of 1948, in which the People's Liberation Army defeated the Kuomintang, was fought all across this region. The Kuomintang suffered 178,000 casualties."

It was a sickeningly large number, more than the entire Allied death count on the Somme. Perhaps statistics like this explained China's seeming blindness to the suffering of the individual; perhaps they were a symptom of it. Nian Village had been the campaign's pivotal killing field, yet who outside China had heard of Nian Village? With tens of thousands of Kuomintang troops trapped in a salient hemmed in by branches of the Grand Canal, two Kuomintang commanders, Communist infiltrators, had switched sides at a vital moment. The PLA had encircled and annihilated the Kuomintang as though they were shooting fish in a barrel. Jiangbing was thoroughly satisfied with the outcome.

"Our forces routed the Kuomintang here. By the time we took Xuzhou, their losses in the Huaihai Campaign were over 500,000. They lost every last piece of territory north of the Yangtze, and never recovered. This place is where the Civil

War was won."

"They were all Chinese, all of them your brothers."

"They were fighting against the revolution of the proletariat."

We drove further. The fourteen-mile section of canal which formed the southern edge of the battlefield had survived from some ancient course. Jiangbing knew nothing about its provenance.

"It's marked on this map as 'Ancient Grand Canal', that's all I know," he admitted as we stood looking over its abandoned length. Emperor Yang, Kublai Khan and the rest had all dug here. Then a great flood had severed what remained of their handiwork, leaving amputated limbs like this still littering the landscape. We drove on to the canal's present-day trunk and stood at the point where it divided, where the seed-eating bargeman had said it would. To the westward lay the big city of Xuzhou, to the north the much smaller Tai'erzhuang. Either would lead in short order to the expanses of the Weishan Lakes. I pulled a ¥1 coin from a pocket.

"Front says Tai'erzhuang, back says Xuxhou...." The coin landed with its chrysanthemum uppermost: Xuzhou. The decision lightly made, we pored over the map for places to stop on the way. The shiplock at Liushan was at no great distance, but when we reached it there were just the familiar concrete chambers lifting barges a few feet further up the slope toward Shandong, and a police launch in the blue and white livery of the Maritime Safety Administration. The same people who had stopped me from hitching in Gaoyou also had the authority to waive travel permits, to indulge their hospitality. One of the officers took the letter of introduction that had failed to secure entry to the Yangtze shiplocks. Out here in the countryside it merited scarcely a glance.

"Come, come aboard, we'll take you," he said. "You can be our foreign friend."

Soon we are racing west, passing lines of coal barges. There are no more construction materials here, no bricks that will soon be towering above Yangzhou or concrete for factories in Huai'an, just these half-submerged Jugannaths toiling under hundreds of tons of pulverized coal. This featureless land gives up twenty million tons each year. China is bringing two new power stations online each week, and this is how they are fed.

"See, the canal's main responsibility here is to carry coal to generate electricity," observes the officer. "Xuzhou City has so much that we call it 'the 100-*li* coalfield'. The canal runs straight through it. The seams are metres thick and very close to the surface." The strata here hold tens of billions of tons. He mimics the grasping action of a dragline with his hand. "Does your country have canals?" he asks. I have with me a postcard of Hatton Locks on the Grand Union Canal. It is a wonderful sight, 21 chambers rising like a staircase out of the valley of the River Avon. As an engineering achievement it excels the summit section in Shandong, clambering up 146 feet in just two miles compared to the Grand Canal's steady, 400-mile ascent to just 138 feet. But it is Victorian rather than thirteenth century, and I wait with a feeling of nervous expectation, keen to impress a Chinese waterman with what England has to show him. He screws up his face to concentrate on a thin strip of water barely visible between the lock gates and the painted narrowboats. He looks bewildered. "So small. Like a child's toy...."

"You should look at the question this way," I urge him. "Each of those barges could carry 30 tons of coal, and still Britain became the first nation to have an industrial revolution. Your barges carry 1,000 tons or more." He nods in agreement.

"The future will be better."

御河

It is said that before the legendary ruler Shun died he chose as his successor Yu the Great, the man who had risen from a humble background to still the mythic flood. With bronze that had been offered to him from the nine provinces of the Chinese world, Yu cast nine cauldrons, each decorated with the flora and fauna of its home. Passed down from king to king, from the Xia dynasty to the Shang to the Zhou, for two millennia those cauldrons symbolized the legitimacy of each ruling house. Then in 255 BC, as the Zhou dynasty drew to a close, the armies of the state of Qin advanced eastward and looted them. As they crossed the Si River in the city of Pengcheng, a storm threw one of the bronzes into the depths.

Thirty-six years passed before the victorious First Emperor visited Pengcheng. Anxious to possess the missing cauldron and the legitimacy it would bring, he commanded a thousand men to fetch it. As they were hauling it out of the river, a dragon appeared from the water and bit through their ropes. The cauldron vanished again below the waves, and the Qin dynasty lasted just a few more years. Today nobody knows for sure the course the Si River once took through Pengcheng, but if the legend is true, then somewhere in the yards of silt beneath the centre of today's Xuzhou there lies buried a mighty cauldron of tarnished bronze.

From my fifteenth-floor window, ripples on the Xuzhou skyline marked the first hills I had seen since crossing the Yangtze. A cloud of dust and fumes cloaked the office blocks, while below it the city seethed in its rat runs. Xuzhou's natives say that the history of their city is the history of the Grand Canal, and when its grain flowed past the tombs of Han princelings that was true. But then the Yellow River retreated north, the barges left for higher ground, and now the nearest branch flows far from the city centre. Just a cast-off course still traces a path through the farthest suburbs. Causeways thrown up across its unmoving water have divided it into fishponds, turning it into a broken line that seems to imply a lost continuity, like dots at the end of an unfinished thought: "I once flowed here...." That night in Xuzhou was spent far from the canal that had been so close to me for over a month. There seemed little reason to stay any longer.

Next morning, the highway north crossed the railway tracks at a village called Lianghong. This place had given me my first sight of the Grand Canal, in the late summer of 1991, when the click clack of the rails had evaporated into the darkness as we crossed a railway bridge of latticed iron. A country still subdued by the events in Tian'anmen Square just two years before had otherwise rattled past unseen that night. Now a train in the olive-drab livery of China Railways was pulling out of Xuzhou. Tentatively the carriages crossed the bridge, five miles now from the station platforms but still only slowly gaining momentum. The passengers' faces were clean and expectant, and in twelve hours they would be in Beijing. Out in the open the day was already hot. The black of coal dust was ground into the roadway, a devil's black fingerprint smeared across the countryside. Along the banks extended coal heaps from which every scintilla of colour had been drawn. Pitch-black cairns as tall as houses jostled for space at the waterfront, were pushed here and there by tarry bulldozers and tweaked into shape by the tarry men with tarry shovels who swarmed over them. The depots had stained black the roads that dared to approach them, the fringes of poplars that bounded them in the distance, the barges that suckled the bank like pot-bellied piglets. Even the blue of the morning sky was dark above them, as though the coal were sucking the very light from the air around it.

On the road northward, the fields stretched away to end at a fringe of trees. They bore no crops, their flatness broken only by clustered pimples of grave mounds from which bristled the gnarled remains of funeral wreaths. One after another, each swollen with the heavy rains that had been falling further inland, the road crossed the rivers that fed a great waterway. I mistook it for my own Grand Canal.

"*Bu, bu!*" the driver corrected. "This one carries coal from the Peixian coalfield. It goes no further." It is easy to let our preconceptions colour what our eyes see. My maps, printed with domestic tourists in mind and lyrical of the most meagre diversion, gave an impression of Peixian as a historic county, rich with folklore and pitted with archaeology dating back to the Han dynasty. This was not how most of China saw it. Nowadays Peixian was Jiangsu's Rotherham, its Welsh valleys, pitted with mines and moulded around coal. The pitheads began to reveal themselves now, pairs of wheels peeping out above the treeline, spinning in noiseless counterpoint to lower men down to the face.

A pit's headgear, and the slagheaps it had spat out, loomed over the town centre. Its twin wheels whirled silently round. Hot mists had again risen, and the afternoon was wretched. Passers-by stared: Peixian was too small, too poor despite its coal reserves, to attract many outsiders. On Hantai Road, on the ground there, beneath a tree, lay a beggar on his back. He wore only a pair of ragged trousers and his eyes were half closed, his mouth hanging open. His muscle tone had sagged, his belly retracted. The passers-by paid no attention to him. How does one unobtrusively check whether or not a man is dead? Already on Hantai Road an old man with a sack spread out before him had barked at me for mistaking him for a plastic-bottle collector. He had practically exploded, accusing me of implying he needed that minuscule charity. Would a sleeping beggar react badly to a tentative prod of the foot? And if he really was dead, then there was nothing I could have done anyway except perhaps find a policeman to cart away his corpse. So instead I turned away, found a low wall beside an ice-cream cart from where I could see him if he stirred, and opened my notebook. Thoughts had been collecting, and the beggar had jolted some of them free. I scribbled a heading – *Dickensian China*.

Being in China was like witnessing the making of my own country. Images that might have been stolen from Henry

Mayhew's famous exposés of Victorian London had been all around me since Hangzhou: child beggars had stood imploringly outside the window of Dio Coffee, and then there were the teenage prostitutes, the shoeshiners, and the infants who traipsed behind their parents gleaning from litter bins. Soon China would have more billionaires than anywhere other than the US, but they shared their cities with the rural detritus of a deferred Agrarian Revolution, toiling in factories that could have been modelled on *Hard Times*. It was just those conditions, Marx had reasoned at his desk in the British Library, that would lead to revolution. Like the enclosures that had robbed Britons of their common grazing, often these workers' lands had been seized by local officials and sold to developers over their heads. The transport infrastructure that had carried them to the cities was growing at an incredible pace, as though the government were working hard to compress Britain's canal boom of the 1700s, the railway mania of the 1840s and Margaret Thatcher's road-building programme into a single frenzy of construction.

China was like Victorian Britain in other ways, too. As the chandler in Yizheng had said, with little by way of a social safety net the fate of the poor, the disabled and the sick fell to overwhelmed charities, to family and friends, and ultimately to nobody. Each day the morning papers advertised patent nostrums to desperate people too poor for health insurance, treatments like the oil of the *yadanzi* tree, "Guaranteed to cure cancer!" Sharing shelf space with those quack medicines were the handiworks of counterfeiters and adulterators. People were watching fake DVDs, drinking fake Coca Cola, popping fake vitamin pills, driving fake cars, dying because their medicines had been cut with icing sugar or blinded by beer laced with methanol. They paid with fake banknotes (though the banks bore banners reminding people of their patriotic duty to stamp out forgeries). Like Mr Kellogg with his personal signature, legitimate industry was anxious to reassure customers that its brands were safe, that they were, so to speak, the original and best. The battle was summed up by humble toilet paper: expensive brands had begun to be sealed with a holographic sticker to guarantee their authenticity, and so now even those holographic stickers were being faked in an arms race of counterfeit one-upmanship that nobody seemed able to stop.

The Victorians had finally succeeded in eradicating adulteration and fakery through their strong and independent judiciary. China though was a society trapped in the corruptible hiatus between autocracy and the rule of law, evolving only woefully slowly from one to the other, if at all. Power still lay firmly in the gift of the individual.

"A Party cadre was playing golf at one of those expensive country clubs," a student from southern China had once told me, "when his golf buggy overturned on the fairway, crushing him to death. At his funeral, so the joke went, the eulogy recorded that he had been 'bravely martyred in the course of his official duties'. There's another story, too, about the cadre who's challenged about his enormous belly. 'That,' he answers, 'is a work-related injury'." His point was simple: you could achieve little of any importance in China – organized crime included – without treating your local Party boss to a game of golf and a slap-up meal. Anybody who has sat in hotel rooms watching endless Chinese TV has seen the Public Security Bureau crushing pirated DVDs beneath road rollers or destroying illegal fireworks in colossal explosions. Despite those headline crackdowns, the outside world has long been banging its head against a wall of official indifference to copyright infringement, forever outmanoeuvred by the master-forgers who are as thick as thieves with grass-roots decision-makers.

China's endemic corruption had even had effects beyond its borders, as sick people worldwide died from batches of fake medicines and the healthy were poisoned by foods given spurious hygiene certificates. Panamanians had been killed by the antifreeze in their cough syrup; American children had ingested lead from their toys; European customs officers had seized fake HIV drugs; fake Tamiflu had failed to treat avian influenza. But worst of all was the effect on China itself, where 300,000 infants had been made seriously ill, and six had died, after one of China's biggest baby formula manufacturers had knowingly used melamine to make its milk appear healthier. Sanlu executives and their suppliers had been handed down heavy sentences, some of them capital. Similar scandals were being exposed all the time. Only once a problem had reached this kind of nadir were the higher authorities willing to smash down doors and make arrests. Even the head of China's food and drug administration had eventually been sentenced to death on live TV for accepting millions of *renminbi* in bribes to license substandard medicines. Yes, Zheng Xiaoyu had been guilty, but it was no secret that he was just one of the myriad who took bribes to turn a blind eye. "*Shan gao, di yuan,*" people had often explained: "The mountains are high, the emperor distant." Beijing was too busy worrying about macropolitics to spend time on such minutiae until the clamour grew too loud to ignore.

I turned to the ice-cream vendor: "Do you ever see fake ice cream being sold?"

She thought for a moment, then smiled: "You do hear of people selling cheap Chinese ice cream in Häagen-Dazs or Wall's packaging, but *my* ice cream's genuine."

"Do you get many tourists coming here?"

She weighed her answer: "We say that Peixian is 'the land of a thousand ancient flying dragons, home to emperors, kings, generals and ministers', but not too many tourists come here to try to understand this history. People called Liu come to burn incense at Liu Bang's temple...." Liu Bang, a local boy made good, had become the first emperor of the Han dynasty in 206 BC. His votive temple rose behind the rooftops, founded by his son and heir so that offerings might be made to his father's soul for all time. It had been destroyed in the ten-year turmoil and rebuilt only recently, and it had become a Mecca for men with the surname Liu who wanted to honour their distant ancestor. "... But most come here to eat dog meat," she added.

"Do you locals really eat that much dog meat?" Peixian had a reputation for eating dogs, but I had assumed it was cultivated as a tourist gimmick. Attitudes to animals were slowly changing in China as people grew richer and more exposed to Western norms. In the big cities, people kept lapdogs as pets. Canine beauty parlours had begun to spring up. The ice-cream vendor gave a derisive grin when I mentioned poodles with dyed hair and jewelled collars.

"What do Beijingers know? We don't take our dogs to beauty parlours, we eat them, but now in the summer less so. Why? Because dog is a warming meat, it stimulates you. 'With a bowl of dog in your belly, suddenly your whole body feels warm and cosy', we say."

When you enter the village, the Chinese also say, you follow the customs. The checkout girls at the Farmers', Workers' & Merchants' Supermarket were eager to recommend *Liu Bang's Turtle Sauce Dog Meat*.

"This is the best, the traditional recipe, it *must* contain turtle." Turtles that were farmed in the Weishan Lakes, they said, and they laughed away my fears that they were endangered.

"There are no wild animals in Peixian anymore," said one, making my argument for me.

"Do they sell dog-meat burgers in McDonald's in Peixian?" I joked.

"McDonald's?" hooted one of the girls. "Peixian doesn't even have a branch of Yonghe Soymilk King!"

That evening I sat on the bed pondering whether to open the meat. Its story was printed on its back, like some royal warrant to justify eating it.

The young Liu Bang was a farmer, the story went, and very

fond of dog meat. The dog butcher Fan Guai did a good trade, but Liu Bang was poor and would always disappear without paying. Fan Guai began to hide from Liu Bang whenever he saw him coming. One day, unable to find Fan Guai in town, Liu Bang went down to the river and there he spied him on the far bank. With no way of crossing, he was downcast. But Heaven took pity on him and sent a giant turtle. Riding on its back, Liu Bang crossed the river and stole some of Fan Guai's meat. When the butcher realized what had happened he was furious. Trapping the turtle, he cut it up and cooked it in the same pot he used to cook his dogs. Never again would it come to Liu Bang's aid! Only when the turtle had cooked through did he find to his delight that it made his dog meat taste even better. Years later Liu Bang would lead the revolt which overturned the First Emperor's brutal Qin dynasty, and the recipe he had inspired would become famed throughout China.

The mist that had risen to fill the air that day at last congealed into storm clouds, and as I toyed with the packaging the skies parted and there began a truly biblical downpour. The first raps on the door could have been mistaken for cracks of thunder. Outside stood two policemen.

"Mr Lin Jie?" asked one. "We need to arrange an Aliens' Temporary Residence Permit for you." They seemed unsurprised when told of how I was researching the Grand Canal, as if they already knew my itinerary. The second officer plastered his fringe across a wet forehead as he spoke.

"The Chinese government places a good deal of importance on the history of the Grand Canal. We say it is a great engineering project created by our nation's labouring people in ancient times, a precious article of material and spiritual wealth handed down to us by our ancestors, a living, flowing and vital piece of mankind's heritage. It is important that the cultural traditions of the places it passes through are not forgotten."

I recognized those words: they had been the opening lines

of the *Hangzhou Declaration*, displayed in the Grand Canal Museum at the start of my journey. So they were well-versed in the canal, these officers, but could they say truthfully how much farther it was navigable?

"To Tianjin?" suggested one uncertainly.

"Tianjin," agreed the second, "if the water is plentiful enough." This scenario seemed exceptionally unlikely: experienced bargemen had answered Xuzhou, the Weishan Lakes, perhaps even Jining. Tianjin lay hundreds of miles further north across the dry North China Plain, the least likely stretch to have enough water to float a paper boat, let alone a steel barge. The true situation was bound to make itself known before too long. I answered their questions and they gave me permission to stay overnight.

"Mr Lin, we are happy to welcome you to Peixian," said the first as they stood to leave. "Your study will allow foreigners to understand more about our country. 'Let Peixian move towards the world, and let the world understand Peixian', isn't that right?" It was a common formula, adopted and adapted all across China as a guiding principle of opening up to foreign markets.

"I hope I shall be able to help the world to understand Peixian," I replied. As he was leaving, the second officer spied the silvery foil packet.

"You like to eat this? Of course, this mass-production technology is not as good as eating the meat fresh." So I was left holding the dog, unsure what to do with it. Of course I had eaten it before, but that had been during a freezing winter, the meat fresh and at its best in a garlicky hotpot. This time it felt sorry and clinical, far removed from the joy of communal eating. The rain went on falling in stair rods. It was dark, and the lights from the apartments opposite made of each raindrop on the window a tiny, sparkling diamond. Alone in a room with only man's best friend for company, I tore open the packet and took a pair of chopsticks from my bag.

Perhaps the dog meat had warmed my constitution too much or had overstimulated my brain, but that night's dream was the most vivid since Hangzhou. The talent show *No Ding, No Stop!* was being filmed on Tian'anmen Square. I was in the audience, sitting on one of the podiums reserved for Party dignitaries to watch parades process down the Avenue of Eternal Peace. The others sat cross-legged, meditating, their hands together in prayer and their eyes closed. Two boys danced around holding up placards of the Grand Canal and the Great Wall, and a third laughed maniacally while he set fire to a pile of Japanese flags.

"*Ni dong ma?*" Lou Yue was seated beside me.

"Do I understand what?"

"The emperor is telling these stories to his people."

"*Tian'a*, make sense, for heaven's sake!"

"Yu the Great allowed the rivers to flow away to the sea. *That* is how he calmed the floods. He would never have taken water from the Yangtze to irrigate northern fields. It is unnatural. The emperor does these things to make his people feel proud."

"What things?"

"His Grand Canal is coming back to life, and his people are proud of it. If they are proud of it, they will also be proud of him. He is a shrewd storyteller. In my time, too, he rallied us against the Japanese dwarves. Now he fears the Mandate of Heaven is coming to an end, that he will soon be overthrown, and he will not let his people forget what he has done for them. *Bu wang bainian guochi!* he says – Do not forget the century of national humiliation! He is desperate. He tells stories both to rouse them and to bind them together...."

I sat up, conscious of my surroundings now, flicked the light on, and reached for the pen and paper on the bedside table. The Communist Party's telling of the Grand Canal story had started back in Hangzhou, with the museum that had risen from the rubble of the old wharves. Then in Jiaxing there had been the

Museum of Boat Culture, and the restoration of the Pavilion for Lowering Sails. Wujiang's Long Bridge had been rebuilt, the water village of Tongli preserved. The *Blue Wave* plied a route between Suzhou and Hangzhou each day, and in Gaoyou the canal's last relay station had been renovated. Everywhere, the Grand Canal had been beautified with promenades and statues. Only the previous evening a policeman had said such poetic things about how it was a precious article for China, a symbol of what its people could achieve.

Just a century ago that story had been so different. The Chinese had almost stopped believing in themselves. By 1902 when, inefficient and in disrepair, it had been closed to imperial grain barges, the Grand Canal had become a symbol of China's foundering political system; a decade later the Qing dynasty had fallen. By 1933 the *Handbook for China*, that vade-mecum which had once been what the *Rough Guide* and *Lonely Planet* are today, could note that after 1,300 years the canal had been usurped by steamships and railways – both foreign inventions – and that its usefulness was less than ever.

Now though, history was turning full circle. With China's rulers eager to unite a discontented population behind them, easily understood symbols were needed – symbols of unity and strength that the Party might make its own, just as it had made the defeat of the Japanese its own, and the ending of 100 years of national humiliation. The forbidding Great Wall was the most powerful of those symbols, a ubiquitous sight on banknotes and official insignia, but the Grand Canal was another. Complementary like *yin* and *yang*, straddling the land like the character for "human", together they encouraged China to remember that it was capable both of defending itself and of relying on its native culture alone.

But these were dubious symbols. Did a physical and mental barrier like the wall really symbolize the outward-looking seafarers of Fujian and Canton, or the Manchurians, the Mongolians and the Tungusic hunters who lived in that one-fifth of China that lay beyond its watchtowers? And why should the Yunnanese hill tribes that had danced on TV weeks before, or the mountain-dwelling Tibetans, or Xinjiang's Turkic Muslims, feel any pride in a waterway that lay thousands of miles from their homes and in whose digging their ancestors had played no part? China had such a stunning diversity of cultures and histories, yet the Party was offering up such a narrow vision of what it meant to be Chinese, a vision dominated by its Han majority. I myself was guilty of talking unthinkingly about "China", as though those five letters were capable of containing its infinite variety, but the Chinese Communist Party itself was not above such easy reductionism. More ominously, into that simplistic vision were being mixed the seeds of a rousing chauvinism. Good people like Mr Hu the fur trader, like Jiang Liu and Didi with their anti-Japanese songs, and like Jiangbing the ex-soldier with his resentment of American warmongering, all were being encouraged to vent their feelings on targets outside China in the hope that they would not vent them on ones closer to home.

Why did any of this bother me like it did? Would it make any difference, sitting up in bed during a rainstorm to think it through? The Chinese after all were inured to the Party's ways, perfectly able to sift through the chaff of its propaganda. But I knew it bothered me because I feared fearing China, this place where my heart felt free. There was a fine line between patriotism and xenophobia, and it sometimes felt that that line might be crossed within my own lifetime. It had happened before, most murderously during the Boxer Rebellion of 1900 but again after 1949, when foreigners were ejected and Mao turned a nation in on itself. A repeat of that kind of thinking was not inconceivable; it is a mentality that only ever worsens as an economy contracts and easy scapegoats are sought. I had come to know China during a period of stability and security. Now though unemployment was rising, and the government was beginning to peddle the idea that it was foreign consumers, with their reckless spending and credit crunches, who were responsible. In recent years there had been stories of mobs rampaging around cities looking for Japanese businessmen to beat up after rumours that the licentious behaviour of some had insulted China. Young chatroom users – the so-called Angry Youth – had reportedly reacted to the World Trade Center attacks with cries of "cool!", so easily did their understanding of international politics spill over into a general conviction that the US was no friend. Beijing youths had attacked the US embassy after a Stealth Bomber had mistakenly targeted the Chinese embassy in Belgrade, yet the authorities had turned a blind eye to the violence. Chillingly, a young American had only narrowly escaped death at the hands of a mob, incensed at him for shopping in the supermarket Carrefour after French protesters had given the Olympic torch a hard time on its progress through Europe. Even non-Han minorities within China had not escaped: violence between Tibetans and Han paramilitaries had conspicuously come to the boil in the run-up to the 2008 Olympic Games; more seriously, long-simmering resentments in the northwest would soon lead to riots by the indigenous Muslim Uighurs and counter-protests by Han immigrants in which hundreds would be killed and injured. Many thousands of Han, historically recent arrivals in Xinjiang, had paraded through the streets of the capital Urumchi brandishing improvised weapons and chanting anti-Uighur slogans, knowing full well that a Han-dominated government in Beijing would support them over and above the restive natives.

But casually violent xenophobia born of boredom and alienation, the kind sadly common in Europe, was for now almost unheard of. In China, no matter where or when I had made an appearance, I had only ever been the victim of excessively well-meaning curiosity. Except for a few petty thieves, this country had always treated me with nothing but kindness. From the bottom of my heart I did not want that to fade, yet it was beyond my power to stop it. "Han nationalism" was fast becoming a familiar phrase, something to take into account when thinking about China. Wide awake by now, at three in the morning and weeks into my trip, the Grand Canal's place within a changing China made sense, and I knew too why it mattered to me personally. Bloated from my supper of dog meat, unable to sleep for the pounding of the rain, there was nothing to do but watch TV – a war film about the Japanese invasion of Manchuria.

御河

"I used to eat dog," admitted the taxi driver I flagged down the next morning, "but then one day I ate some and three dogs followed me all the way home. Even now there's an alley where I don't dare walk, in case the dogs see me. They start barking – *wang wang wang!* – and I swear they stare at me." The rain hammered against the windscreen. After being in Jiangsu ever since leaving Wangjiangjing and its eye-watering pollution, Shandong province was now just a few minutes away. The driver grinned. "You Westerners say that dogs are mankind's best friend, don't you, and that you wouldn't beat your best friend to death and then eat him?"

I was not the average Westerner, I told him, and had eaten dog only the night before, only it had not lived up to my memories. *Liu Bang's Turtle Sauce Dog Meat* had been a slimy stew of meat and gravy, with a whiff of dog food about it and one or two stiff hairs that had put me off. I had finished it rather than throw it away – there would have been something heartless in just tossing it into a bin – but I had not enjoyed it.

"Hundreds of farmers in this county farm dogs. Since the reforms and opening up began it's become very important for our economy. You know of Fan Guai the butcher? A direct descendant of his is still living in Peixian, still raising dogs."

"Do you know his name?"

He knotted his brow: "I don't recall. None of the dog gets wasted, you know. The fur goes to make clothes, the teeth are taken out and sold, the bones are powdered to make medicine, the penis is good for flaccidness of the *yang*. Brains, tail, liver, everything is used. Yes, and then there are the 'treasures of the dog'."

"Testicles?"

He laughed aloud at my artlessness: "*Bu, bu, bu*, they're found here," and he pointed higher up. "They're like little stones." Mr Hu the fur trader sprang to mind. He had been a Shandongnese, and it must have been entrepreneurs like him who bought the skins – and the gallstones – from dog farmers in these rural counties. We turned off the main road and onto a smaller one which led to the Weishan Lakes. Beneath the white exhalations from a power station we passed into Shandong.

A causeway dam stretched out before us, but where I had expected to see a great body of water there was only fields. The lakebed was unmistakeable enough, a shallow bowl stretching out to a ridge of higher ground in the distance, but it was dry. The sluice gates of the dam stood marooned amongst vegetable plots.

"The Grand Canal?" echoed the man who collected the tolls. He pointed far out into the fields, and we drove on.

"This Weishan Dam was a failure." The driver gave a derisive snort as we drove along its crest. "It was finished in the seventies, when there was water in the lakes, but now it's useless. It used to produce hydroelectric power, but not any more. The climate's changing, and the drought gets worse each year."

On paper at least, the Weishan Dam divided Lake Weishan, largest and southernmost of the four eponymous lakes, from Lake Zhaoyang to its north. In doing so it divided the Central Grand Canal from the Shandong Grand Canal which ran – again on paper – up to the border of Hebei. In reality the dam's piles strode across solid land. Only once, halfway along its length, did the fields become for a moment waterlogged.

A strip of silver flashed under the roadway. We got out and peered down in curiosity. A small lock was raising a barge into what remained of Lake Zhaoyang. After the vast chambers of Jianbi and Shaobo, such a Lilliputian structure seemed undignified. We called to a bargeman. Yes, he said, as though just as disappointed, no mistake, this was the Grand Canal.

Lake Zhaoyang had shrunk to just a basin of water, its shore fringed with soil stained black to its depths. Expanses of oily, pulverized coal were spread out like molehills across wharves which had solidified from the drying lakebed. In creeks of grey slurry, coal barges sank at awkward angles into the mud. In a stall made from pallets and tarpaulin, a knot of men gathered around a table to eat. They stared as they might have stared at an alien, my skin jade-white compared to their coal-grimy complexions. One of their number, a wiry man with a large cyst protruding from inside one ear, invited us to sit. With the taxi driver translating for these rural boatmen they told us what had happened.

As the lakes had withered only the deepest channels in their midst had remained navigable. The canal this far north was dying, and only the water transfer project would save it. Then perhaps there would be enough water to take big barges up to Jining all year round. Right now it could take at most a 100-ton barge, tiny by the standards of Jiangsu. Their coal, they said, that lay in those lustrous heaps all around us, came from close by, brought here by lorry from the mines of the coalfield that surrounded us. It was a sweet coal, they said, that burned hot, and it was in much demand. They disagreed about how much further the canal ran. To Tianjin, said the noodle maker; rubbish, said the diners: they were as proud as he was, but it was dust-dry beyond Jining. They seemed to know what they were saying. I would be in Jining in no time – it lay only 50 miles away – and then what?

Water, but no Boats

杭州

北京

from the Weishan Lakes to Hebei province

Straddling Jiangsu and Shandong provinces, the Weishan Lakes lie precisely halfway between Hangzhou and Beijing. On today's maps they are a distinct feature in the landscape, so large that they might be mistaken for a remnant of the great flood of Chinese mythology. Yet when the bronze-laden tombs of Liu Bang's Western Han dynasty were being dug into this yellow earth in the first and second centuries BC, the Weishan Lakes did not exist. In their place, the Si River followed a path of least resistance through a gently sloping landscape. But the Yellow River, greedily eyeing the easy course the Si had found for itself, again and again stole into its channel. They made poor bedfellows, those two, thrashing unpredictably across a narrow flood plain, depositing shoals of silt and making navigation fearful. One stretch of perennial white water, the Lüliang Flood, was especially dreaded by sailors. So fierce was its current, wrote the Daoist philosopher Zhuangzi, that not even fish could swim in it. Imperial grain barges were often wrecked there, for the Grand Canal and the Yellow River were once one and the same waterway in this border region. So engineers surveyed the landscape and dug new channels, and, as each was dug, gradually they made for the canal a life distinct from that of the inconstant river. The Yellow ploughed on in the bed of the Si, and with time their floods coalesced into what are now the four Weishan Lakes.

Now a channel had been dredged clean through Lake

Zhaoyang between marshy fields of lotus. I dared ride the canal once more, now that Jiangsu and its inquisitive policemen were behind me. A barge left the coal wharf bound for the town of Nanyang, her owner a young man. The lake was still deep, he said, but it was hard to tally his drawling dialect to the evidence of my eyes. Perhaps I had misunderstood; perhaps he meant that in its very lowest tracts, when the rains had swollen the lake to a flood, it could be deep. It was not at all deep now, otherwise how could lines of trees and acres of reedbeds be following our barge like the scenery of the Fens when we were supposed to be five miles from the shore?

The rain pattered, and he sat on his stool holding a line between marker buoys. They turned a long, smooth curve to port, while to starboard the horizon seemed to drop. There the trees were fewer and farther away, the ground less firm. A true lake seemed to be forming itself from the marshes. The foothills of the Shandong massif appeared for the first time as a dull strip against the rain clouds.

"Lake Dushan," the young man announced. "You know, in China we say that Shandong has 'one mountain, one water, one sage'. The mountain is Mount Tai, the sage is Confucius, and the water is the Weishan Lakes. Two or three years ago there was a flood, and everything here was under water as though this were all lakes again. Now sometimes the only water left is here in the shipping channel. The fishermen have no work." The lakes, a sheet of sky blue in the *Atlas of Shandong Province*, had proved more a geographic aspiration than a reflection of reality. A few years ago they had covered the area of 85 Windermeres, but now the climate was consistently too dry to sustain them. "To port it's all solid ground now, but there are no roads yet. If people want to cross it they must use a small boat to find a way through the channels."

A way through the channels, a way through their tangled history.... I squatted down with a lapful of maps. It was hard to tease a story from the many canals that had flowed here at one time or another. Ahead lay Nanyang, guarding the throat of the northernmost lake. By Emperor Yang's day it had blossomed into a rich port. Then under the Ming dynasty a fresh series of Yellow River floods had so ravaged the landscape that in 1566 the New Nanyang Canal had been opened to avoid them. From Nanyang it had struck out across country to Xuzhou. My best guess was that we were sailing along it now, the original cut made broad by dredging. The bargeman pored over the maps, but he could not relate my question marks and scrawls to the scene before him. He steered from the images in his mind's eye, he said, not from a chart.

Nanyang when we reached it was a low spur of earth, an insular township left landlocked now as the lake had dried up around it. Only a web of waterways connected it to the solid ground of the old lakeshore. At a grassless spit I scrambled up the bank and looked back. The channel I had taken vanished into a gap amongst the trees, where not long ago there had been fishing nets. A file of barges was laid to, their holds piled with coal. A shack offered their skippers a scattering of necessities – *baijiu* spirit, instant noodles, cooking oil, cigarettes. The driver of a minivan squatted and smoked. Bargemen often wanted to head into Yutai, and would gather until there were a few of them to split the fare. He had hung around all day, but nobody was interested. While we spoke, a younger man stood at his side with a look of distaste on his face. His lip was curled into a sneer at the behaviour of this stranger who appeared from nowhere and had the money to ride the minivan into town alone. He tutted as I stumbled over my words. When I had left that little shanty behind, I regretted that I had not tried to talk to him. I had resented how he had discomforted me, though I had not even smiled and said hello.

The farmland around Yutai was a jigsaw of flooded paddy, a liquid diorama, like a shrine to the memory of lakes that had once been. The villages came sporadically now, not in that seamless wall that characterized Jiangnan. Down there they had been of concrete and plaster, their roofs jet black and with windows of expensive blue glass to allay the sun. Here they were of penniless orange brick with caps of reed thatch. A woman like Mrs Du seemed out of place. She had hovered at the bus station until, with sudden resolve, she strode over as though to greet an old friend.

"My son has just sat his national college entrance exams, you see," she enlightened me apropos of nothing. "He's thinking of studying at a foreign university. How much does it cost to study in England?"

"Between five and ten thousand pounds each year, depending on the university and the course." Her eyes widened in disbelief. I added: "My wife is a university lecturer, you see." She furled her brow.

"In US dollars? *Zheme gui!* So expensive! It's best if he goes to a university in the Ukraine after all. The fees are only US$1,000 each year. What's the Ukraine like?" I shrugged. "He's a musician, my son. He plays the *sakesifeng*, you see, and he wants to study music. The *sakesifeng*? Do you know Kenny G? We both like his music."

"I like Kenny G, too," I lied. The bus driver arrived, and we all filed on board.

If her son had just sat the national *gaokao* exam then Mrs Du must have been in her mid-forties. She had a soft perm, tinted with auburn; her foundation was thick, hiding lines that suggested she had once lived a harder life; her lipstick and eyeliner were applied liberally, but neatly. So, what was she doing in Yutai? It was after all quite a remote town. She took out a business card.

"Do you know Amway?" she asked, and seemed surprised that I did not. Understandably unfamiliar with the world beyond China, she was willing to credit me with more knowledge of it than was deserved. "It's an American direct-sales company. I'm the franchisee for this region." On the back of the card were pictures of the range she sold – nutritional supplements, beauty products, dental care – all made in China under licence. "I go to Yutai regularly to see my buyers."

The bus left Yutai behind, whose functional shop units ended abruptly. The highway to Jining was new. Labourers still squatted by the roadside like wide-eyed baby birds who had fallen from a nest, unsure what to do with themselves. Their clothes were tattered, and each wore a safety helmet that looked too flimsy for words, perched high and perfunctory upon manes of unwashed hair.

"What are the economic conditions like here?" I asked.

"The economy's not that good. Yes, there are billboards and advertisements all over, and there's this new road to Jining, but the economy is substandard. You need to be in business like me to really *feel* how a place is doing."

In Yutai there had been a good number of utter destitutes on the streets, and an old man who begged for money for a boy with cerebral palsy, pulling him along in a playpen on wheels. I knew that seeing life here through a polarizing lens of simplistic antagonisms – richness and poverty, progress and backwardness, equality and disparity – only meant being blind to everything that fell between those stark extremes. Still, wasn't spending money on Coenzyme Q10 Complex wrong, when neighbours like these were still so wretched? Wasn't it exactly that widening gap that was making Chinese society so dangerously unstable? Mrs Du disabused me with cool poise.

"People simply want to buy foreign products like these because they trust them. In China our standards are very low, but higher standards cost money. Take this bus." She pulled at the handle attached to the seat in front and it came away. Its iron screws had rusted away, but galvanized screws would have cost more. "Now look outside. This road has only just been finished, but already they're repairing it. Why? *Fubai* – corruption. The city government will ask companies to bid for the contract, but the winner will be whichever of their friends can 'walk through the back door'. Then, if the contractor is given 1,000,000 *kuai* to buy the materials, he'll spend just half that cutting corners and they'll split the rest. Even these repairs will be no good, and somebody will earn yet more money repairing them."

In other respects Chinese manufacturing was world class. My camera was Japanese, but it had been made in China, and my Chinese-made boots had already impressed a lock-keeper. Mrs Du laughed.

"That's because the quality-control managers for these factories are *foreign!*" What about the Qinghai-Tibet Railway, then? I asked: China had recently built the world's highest railway across 700 miles of moonlike scree and marginal permafrost, at altitudes approaching half that of a commercial airliner. It was an astonishing piece of engineering for any country to achieve. Tibet, always a flashpoint of anti-government rioting, had been bound ever more closely to its master. Mrs Du's patriotism lay not far beneath her love of foreign quality. "Of course we're all very proud of the *Qing-Zang Tielu*. It's pressurized, they say, and there's oxygen for the passengers, like on a plane."

"And it was built by Chinese?" Mrs Du nodded her agreement. "And what about the Pudong maglev railway, the high-speed trains from Beijing to Shanghai, the *Shenzhou* spacecraft? Then there are the Bird's Nest stadium and the Water Cube swimming pool in the Olympic Park...." At that moment our engine noise dropped. The sudden stillness made us both aware of the world outside as the bus crossed a river as wide as the Thames. It was man-made, the driver said, dug with revolutionary fervour at the height of the ten-year turmoil to carry floodwater from the Yellow River into the Weishan Lakes. It was unknown outside China, unknown even to most Chinese, just another reminder of how Chinese civilization was at its most brilliant when organizing monumental projects. Modernity had only made it bolder – the line between Golmud and Lhasa had been laid in just over four years. Perhaps under dynasties to come it would be looked upon as the Grand Canal or the Great Wall of its age; or perhaps it would be remembered as the costly vanity project of a regime that had ultimately failed China. The bus rattled into the treeline. "... And the Yangtze has the biggest hydroelectric dam in the world."

Mrs Du was less sanguine about the Three Gorges Dam – there were limits to what the Party should be spending money on. "A waste," she grumbled. "A failure. Only built so that the Party would get the glory." How many of Old Hundred Surnames under the Sui dynasty had nursed the same misgivings about Emperor Yang's schemes? It was a different world then, less forgiving of dissent than today. Mrs Du was not the kind of person who wasted her time complaining, though. She had been working hard, and admitted with false modesty to earning 300,000 *renminbi* each year, enough to send her son abroad. "But these farmers," she said, pointing to the stick figures bent double in the fields, "earn about 800 *yuan* a year. That's not enough to live on." At twelve times less than an indentured factory worker earned in Fujian, no wonder they had been leaving the fields in their millions to look for work in the cities.

Mrs Du got off the bus on the edge of Jining, where the road was sliced by the tracks of factory sidings. Convoys of coal trucks passed by like columns of black ants. As for the Grand Canal, it glanced straight-sided off the city like a tangent to a circle. Its two enormous levees lay far apart, useless now that the water between them had confined itself to a single, emaciated channel. Amongst the market gardens that had overrun its bed, heaps of coal were being loaded onto barges for the voyage south. Jining was still 286 miles' sailing from Beijing. I did not yet know it, but these would be the last barges I would see.

御河

Li Bai, arguably China's most famous poet, came to live in Jining with his wife and daughter in AD 736. There he drank copiously and composed some of the finest verse in the Chinese language, an enviable lifestyle. His favourite spot had been a wine shop close by his home. Rebuilt time and again since Li Bai drowned in a river grasping drunkenly for the moon, the Taibai Pavilion stood now on a low prominence overlooking the old canal.

It had been a day of blue skies. The sun as it set steeped the pavilion's colonnaded façade in a coral light. It did not matter that the balustrades were peeling – Jining did, after all, bake in the summer and freeze in winter – or that the park to its rear was covered in rubble. What mattered was that the world seemed a few decibels quieter from its balcony, that you could hear the chirruping of sparrows. Twilight fell, and soon the curving eaves were picked out in strings of light. Had Jiugao been there, I would have told him that this place was beautiful.

It was July 1st now, and on Grand Canal Cultural Square the Chinese Communist Party's birthday celebrations were being held. Performers danced, and sang revolutionary songs. The canal flowed behind them, its lithe ribbon threading itself under bridges, running around the city like the girdles that encircled the dancers' slender waists. Jining had brought to it a distinct change of mood. Gouged deeply into thick, yellow soil, it seemed to steel itself for the challenge of crossing the approaching watershed, to coil itself as if it were readying to bound across the summit. It was silent now, its surface unruffled by boats, and its quiet restraint made it hard to believe that this had once been a world-leading feat of engineering whose very existence had determined the position of China's capital city.

For Beijing, if you think about it, is an odd place for a capital.

It sits upon a plain far from the Yellow River, that traditional seat of ancient dynasties, and even farther removed from the rice basket of the Yangtze delta. Though we accept it now without question, it was not until the thirteenth century that Beijing became the site of the capital city of a unified China, a role it has maintained almost constantly since. That it is now one of the world's most important cities, and not just a remote town set amid one of China's poorer provinces, is down to the Grand Canal.

By 1276, Kublai Khan's armies had captured the Southern Song dynasty's capital at Hangzhou and gained control of the entire Grand Canal and its grain supply. The canal, flowing still on the alignment that Emperor Yang had decreed, in those days headed first north-westward, pushing far inland to the cities of the Yellow River before doubling back north-eastward to what is now Beijing. So when Kublai Khan chose to site his new capital close to his homeland in the Mongolian steppe, he was faced with the problem that barges from the south were forced to make a long and effortful detour to reach his granaries. A mathematician named Guo Shoujing was dispatched to survey the Shandong massif to find a more direct route for them.

Guo was a skilled astronomer, the deviser of an accurate solar calendar long before the West's Gregorian system. He was also an expert in hydrology, and an accomplished surveyor who understood how to use altazimuth-mounted sights, the magnetic compass, and bamboo theodolites that floated upon a fragile meniscus of water. By the time his hydrological survey was complete he had determined the lie of the land in Shandong and decided how to cross its watershed. His plans approved by the Khan, a military engineer named Oqruqci was tasked with overseeing the construction. Oqruqci was no cruel taskmaster like Ma the Barbarous, and it took a full two years to complete the world's first summit canal. When it was finished in 1283 it led uphill from Jining, over the watershed at a village called Nanwang, and down to the Yellow River fifty miles away.

But it was impossible now for me to sail any further north. The shallow-draught barges that could reach Jining had nothing – no coal, no sand – to tempt them onwards, and fishing nets blocked their path. They loaded up and turned their bows about. The levees carried on without them, a Grand Canal still in name but in truth too shallow to be navigable.

Beyond the city, where dredging and restoration had brought it back to life as a sparkling centrepiece, Oqruqci's summit canal was bone-dry. The road to the watershed followed its convolutions through a sandy land, a semi-desert of windbreak trees and villages baking under a white sun. The thirsty rice of lower elevations would not grow here, and in its place stretched fields of maize. The landscape had given no intimation that it had been steadily mounting since the Yangtze. To reach Nanwang it had been rising by one imperceptible inch for every 400 yards it travelled. The theory of surveying was simple enough, with its triangulations and its benchmarks, but if the driver had stopped his bus and refused to go on until I had calculated our gradient we would never have got to Nanwang. For to my eye, even this, the steepest section since Hangzhou, was incurably, unarguably, flat.

In my mind's eye this moment had been quite different, as though the only way to make sense of that geography had been to compress its features into a single mental frame, a caricature in landscape. The Nanwang of my imagination had been a crown of high ground against a backdrop of foothills, from where the Wen River tumbled down. How, if it were any less evident, could any mortal man have known where to dig? But when the bus door clanged back, the hills were so low and so distant as to be invisible, and the Wen was just a parched wadi. Nanwang village itself was one strip of dusty shops amongst many, connected to the world by a line of telegraph poles which leant at drunken angles into the soft earth. There I began to search for the Dragon King Temple of the Dividing of the Waters, the one sight I was most anxious to see.

All of the travellers who had passed this way had been struck by the temple and had recorded it in their diaries. Ch'oe Pu, for one, had arrived in Nanwang and watched his Chinese escorts go ashore to burn incense. They had ordered Ch'oe Pu to do the same, but he had refused: as a Korean he sacrificed only to his ancestors, never to the lofty gods of mountains and rivers.

"This is the altar of the Dragon King who once appeared here," he was told firmly. "For that reason, everyone who passes here sacrifices most respectfully before going on. Otherwise there would surely be trouble with the wind and the waves."

"One who has looked at the sea," answered Ch'oe Pu, "is not easily impressed by other waters. I have passed through an ocean of tens of thousands of *li* and violent waves. The water of rivers like these, here in the land, is not enough to scare me."

Neither did it scare Sir George Staunton, deputy to Lord Macartney on the British embassy of 1793, who had passed through an even greater ocean. Still, Sir George was deeply impressed, describing how from that perfect high point the Wen divided to flow both north and south. The Chinese asserted, he recalled, that a bundle of sticks tossed into it would be separated and sent in opposite directions, part ending up in the Bohai Gulf and part in the Yangtze. In Staunton's day the marshy countryside beyond was carpeted with lotus flowers, but soon after Liberation the Wen River that watered them had stopped flowing.

An old man had stopped to watch me, and we stood together on the dry riverbed. Its banks still rose like yellow cliffs, their faces dappled by the shade of saplings whose roots bound the soil against the wind. Cicadas buzzed. At our feet, the rough-hewn slabs of granite which had been the bulwarks of this river junction lay scattered like giant mah-jong tiles, their chisel marks still crisp.

"Your honourable harvest count?" I asked as respectfully as I knew.

"Eighty-six harvests." He pointed to the west. "It was when the Wen ran dry that the new Shandong Grand Canal was dug. Now that's dry too." Still a sprightly young man when he had watched the workers' brigades assembling outside his village, he knew just where to find the Temple of the Dividing of the Waters. In a goose-speckled clearing its roofs peeped shyly from behind a wall.

The sailors and mandarins who once prayed there had immersed themselves in a sea of faith. There had been shrines to the men who built the canal, halls dedicated to the Dragon King, to the flood stiller Yu the Great, temples to Guan Yu the god of war and to the god of locusts, and pavilions raised to Guanyin the bodhisattva of mercy and to the flowing water itself. Now the geese lowered their heads and hissed, wary of strangers, but children surrounded me, calling out the few words of English they knew, shepherding me into their school. Their neat classrooms stood amongst the temple ruins. Weeds choked the temple doorways and smothered the walls; the tiles had collapsed, leaving purlins open to the sky. Beneath them hung mildewed portraits of Marx and Engels, of Lenin and Mao. From the sunshine outside came children's laughter. These ruins were their playground. When they grew up they would most likely leave Nanwang. Their village existed solely because it used to be at the summit of a canal that had now vanished.

"Most of the young people leave to find work in the cities – Jinan, Qingdao, even Beijing or Shanghai," explained the man who drove me out to the new Shandong Grand Canal. "There are hardly even farming jobs here anymore." Even the new canal led nowhere, he said. He summed it up in four neat words: *"You shui, mei chuan.* There's water, but no boats."

A bridge crossed it. We stared into the distance, where the levees met in a misty vanishing point. They were imposing, tall, and covered with mature trees, but of the quarter-mile gap between them barely 50 yards was taken up by a strip of sky-blue water. Through its undisturbed surface the bed was visible. Somebody had set posts and nets to raise fry. In a few years' time, the driver said, water from the Yangtze would flow here, and then perhaps there would be barges again.

"The government is planning to rebuild the Dragon King's Temple, to dig lakes, to turn our village into a tourist destination." Then he shook his head. "At the moment, though, Nanwang has only this dead river."

御河

That night I slept in Wenshang, the nearby county town. Lying prone on the bed I traced in my atlases what remained of the Grand Canal. On the outskirts of Jining there had been barges upon it, and life; by Nanwang there were neither. This moment had been approaching slowly, inevitably, with people along the way proffering their own hazy thoughts on how far it might be passable. Still it came as a shock to find myself suddenly with no barges, no chugging of engines, no petrolly spray. It had been a constant companion, though our relationship had been mute and one-sided. I had grown fond of each of its changing moods.

Other thoughts crowded the space behind tired eyes. Sooner or later the Yellow River would block my path. Pontoon bridges came and went as China's Sorrow chose to take them, but the nearest permanent crossing was dozens of miles downstream, far away from what was left of the canal. My journey looked to be entering a new phase. As for Hebei, the boatman in Xinfeng had warned of the immorality of its impoverished people, but then everybody in China was convinced that everywhere else was backward. With a rootless disquiet, a strange mixture of anticipation and deliverance, I went downstairs to find a drink. The hotelier was young, and he enjoyed staying up to talk. He was reassuring.

"*Ni fang xin*, put your heart at rest. The conditions in Hebei are not as good as in Jiangnan, but southerners always exaggerate the poverty of the north. There are good and bad everywhere. Jiangnan has plenty of rich people, and in my experience rich city people are more immoral than farmers. They have the opportunity – massage parlours, hair salons. They only exist for one reason, you know." We sat and drank ice-cold beer in the heat of the night. If rural Wenshang did have brothels masquerading as massage parlours and hair salons they were kept tactfully discreet.

"Do young people here in Wenshang too... *have relations* before marriage?" I did not want to offend what might have been his rural sensibilities. In the cities, premarital sex was becoming more common, but out here? His immediate reaction answered a different question, though no less illuminating.

"Why? Do you want a girl? If you want a girl I can get you one right now. Do you remember the girl who said hi to us earlier?" She had been tall and attractive. "She'll sleep with you if you want." He inserted a forefinger into a fist, just in case his meaning was unclear. Repeating the question only left us still at cross-purposes. "If unmarried men want to have a girl, it's very easy. Go on!" he urged. "I'll arrange it for you."

"What I mean to ask is do a boyfriend and girlfriend have sex before they marry, or do they wait until *after* they're married?" I began to wish I'd not asked.

"If you pay her then she'll be your girlfriend, but you needn't marry her afterwards." This confused the issue even further. "Do you have brothels in England?" It was not uncommon back home for women to be trafficked into the sex trade, I said. He nodded in sympathetic recognition. "A lot of the girls who work in our cities are from the countryside. They're naïve, they answer an advert looking for a waitress or a hairdresser, and soon they find themselves working as a *xiaojie*. They'll go as low as 20 *kuai*! Come, let's get you one."

Jiangbing's factory workers had earned only ¥28 for a twelve-hour day. Here in Wenshang the wages were even lower. I leaned back in my chair and gave a cold laugh at this hotelier's enthusiasm, and at the iniquities of a globalizing economy that made whores of village virgins here in remote Wenshang just as it did in China's big cities and back home. My shirt, unbuttoned in the heat, fell aside to reveal a small metal etching of Jesus around my neck. It had been bought back in Changzhou, in a church I had passed, and worn almost unthinkingly since then as an ornament and a safeguard. It caught the light.

"Who's that?" he asked.

"Yesu Jidu."

"Is Yesu Jidu a man or a woman?" he asked. A man, I said. "Is he from England too?" He had heard of Christianity, but had never equated it with a flesh-and-blood person and knew no more of its traditions than that Chinese Christians made the sign of the Cross over themselves all the time. How many Christians, though, knew that the Buddha had once been a real man who walked the earth? "*Aya*, I misunderstood," he apologised. "I thought you had come to Wenshang to see our *foya*, but if you believe in this Western religion then you won't be interested."

He was quite wrong: *foya* were believed to be teeth of the true Buddha, holy relics of Sakyamuni Gautama himself. There had been no intimation that this obscure town possessed such a thing. With only one or two others in existence, each of them was revered like the Shroud of Turin. And so the next morning I rose before the heat and walked to the Baoxiang Temple. In the Hall for Respectful Offerings a stairway led down to a saffron-painted tunnel. The air inside was cool.

"We excavated this tunnel after the tooth was found," said the young monk who led the way, "so that people can come to see it in its original setting." At the tunnel's end he cast his eyes upward. "The Pagoda of the Divine Relic is now above us." He stood aside with a seraphic smile on his lips. The tunnel had ended in a glass wall. Behind it, lit with bright colours, was a small case wrought from precious metal. In it rested a curved object of a dirty ivory hue, as large as a man's thumb. I hid my surprise with difficulty: surely a *foya* should conceivably have been a human tooth? Yet this looked more like a sheep's tooth, or perhaps a baby elephant's, bifurcated at one end, ridged, and worn at its crown like an ungulate's molar. Holy relics are often counterintuitive like that: the Dutch theologian Erasmus had once remarked wrily that the finger bone of Saint Peter revered in Walsingham must, to judge from its great size, have belonged to a giant, yet he had remained a believer. The monk's pride showed on his face as the *foya* stared back at us through the glass.

"How do you know it's a tooth from the Buddha?"

"You see the niche in the wall behind it? In 1994, when the pagoda was being restored, archaeologists unbricked that niche, and in it they found a stone casket. When they opened this they found inside it a golden casket, and inside that they found a silver casket bound with silver bands. Around them were statuettes of Buddha facing towards India, and bottles made of crystal. There were scriptures, and 324 *sheli*."

"*Sheli*?"

"When a Buddhist monk who has led a pure life is cremated after death, tiny coloured stones remain, like little jewels, precious relics. Now, when the archaeologists opened the silver casket they found the tooth. There was an inscription telling us that it was a *foya*, brought here from Kaifeng in 1073 and placed in the pagoda." For over 900 years that sacred hoard had lain undisturbed in its sealed chamber. Dynasties had come and gone, the temple's halls had time and again been levelled and replaced, and slowly the ground had risen to swallow the tooth's hiding place. When finally it was uncovered, the world's media had ignored the sheer romantic wonder of that pristine time capsule from the Northern Song dynasty. And for the believer there was the unsurpassable importance of a bodily relic of Sakyamuni Gautama, for Buddhists the equivalent of Christians finding a lock of Christ's hair.

When we came up again into the Hall for Respectful Offerings the morning had warmed, and we stood blinking in the doorway. The pagoda, thirteen tapering storeys of ancient, iron-hard bricks, stood beside us. With the discovery beneath its feet, Wenshang had overnight come to rank alongside the Temple of the Sacred Tooth in Sri Lanka or the Shwedagon pagoda in Myanmar, where eight hairs from the Buddha's head are worshipped. It seemed curious that such an exceptional relic should have found its way to a dusty little town like Wenshang, but then the Grand Canal had run at no great distance from here during the Northern Song; the tooth had most likely journeyed on it. The young monk smiled at the cement mixers which stood idle in the courtyard.

"You see we are rebuilding the temple. There will be a park telling the story of the Buddha's life, a museum for the holy relics, and a reclining statue of the Buddha made of pure crystal. Before the tooth was discovered there were no tourists here at all. Now there are more and more. They say that within a decade the tooth will bring one million each year. I hope it does."

His temple did not look much at that moment. Signs of construction work lay around and the air bore the dull taste of gypsum, but nothing was being done. The pagoda was certainly graceful – a structure worth seeing, but not worth going to see. Few tourists would have travelled to such a remote spot without there being something more. Something more had now been found. In one way, the Baoxiang Temple brought to mind Glastonbury Abbey. There in 1191, after a ruinous fire, the monks had stumbled upon what they swore were the graves of King Arthur and his Queen Guinevere. Within a few years they had gone from rags to riches, a piece of divine intervention which did not escape wry comment. The monks of Wenshang though were no confidence tricksters, their relic of potential interest to a far wider audience than just Buddhists. More tourists would mean more banknotes stuffed into the collection boxes, more incense and trinkets sold in the booths that lined the streets outside, but this young monk had abjured wealth and seemed unmoved by its prospect. He needed only his saffron robes, he said, smoothing a hand across them, and his shoes that picked up the dust of this transient life.

Ever since Hangzhou there had been development projects that had failed. Each town, each city, had had its sorry plots of shop units with "to let" daubed on their windows, ventures which had for a day or two tried to convince Party superiors that China was "opening up to the world". No doubt influential friends had tendered contracts and creamed off the profits, as Mrs Du had said they would. But the Baoxiang Temple's plans were driven by something deeper than political calculation. One and a half million pilgrims still visit the Irish village of Knock each year in the certain belief that Mary, Joseph and Saint John appeared there in 1879. Faith – witness the graffiti of a pagoda in Zhenjiang – was becoming an even more powerful anchor in the stormy sea that was China in the twenty-first century. Wenshang was small and underdeveloped, a county of no consequence to the rest of the nation. Like Knock, it felt like the kind of quiet place that seems favoured by the presence of the transcendent.

御河

The Yellow River, traces of whose past incarnations had been strewn across the landscape for weeks now, lay fully 40 miles by road from the temple and its tooth, and reaching it on the day of my departure from Wenshang had not been the plan: this was farther than I had travelled in a single bound for some time. But then the town of Liangshan had proved so uninspiring that I had left my things in a room there and walked back to the bus station to spend the day elsewhere. A bus was leaving, and it would be passing not far from the river.

In the fields outside Liangshan, the Shandong Grand Canal was suspended above the plain. The Yellow River in these parts carried almost as much silt as she did water, and the sediment that sank to the bottom had forced the dike builders to keep pace with an ever-rising bed. The result was twenty miles of stone-faced canal levees, running like an unscalable barrier more imposing than the Great Wall. The roadway skulked in their shadow for a while, then with a burst of self-confidence charged up the slope. There it ran out. We climbed off the bus and trooped down into a grassy void.

In just the few miles since Nanwang the canal had grown gaunt, far too small for those mighty embankments, like an emaciated man whose clothes hung loose from his frame. A makeshift bridge had been thrown up, though a running leap could have taken the more athletic of us across. The afternoon was hot, with storm clouds gathering, and we climbed the far bank in torpid silence to find another bus waiting to carry us onward.

For miles the road ran along the crest of that levee. Slowed by deep ruts of hardened mud, a journey of a few minutes lengthened into hours. The tyres pounded the earth to a powder which hung in the air and coated every surface, making of our sweat a grimy embrocation. No other passengers got down at a strip of shacks that catered to passing trade. The shopkeeper of a general store agreed to drive across country to the river. He took the map from me. Scrutinizing it for a long while, as though unused to seeing his world depicted in two dimensions, his reaction came gradually.

"*Budui, budui,*" he complained under his breath. "Wrong, wrong. There should be a road here...." His van was what the

Chinese call a *mianbaoche,* a loaf-of-bread wagon, from its boxy shape. It was battered, but the shopkeeper knew the back roads better than the cartographers in Beijing.

"These are mostly old river courses," he said presently, pointing out at a wasteland of ponds, bluffs and streams. Oqruqci's summit canal, just another overgrown riverbed without an expert's eye to guide, was amongst them, still freewheeling all but invisible now toward the Yellow. Reeds grew where water stood, and ducks dabbled. The land was neither determinedly solid nor liquid but in another elemental state – *shuihu,* the water margin. "Do you know the book *Shuihu Zhuan*?" he asked. The *Water Margin* was long; I was a lazy reader and had never got around to finishing it. Its setting was precisely this water margin of Liangshan, where the hero Song Jiang and his brotherhood of bandits could hide out in the impenetrable marshlands. The shopkeeper was at home in that schizophrenic environment, habituated to the threat of flooding, unmoved by the sight of the Yellow River levee which loomed above the trees. This grew in menace until, reaching its foot, it occupied half of the darkening sky. On the far side of that wall, the river that had drowned so many millions should have been towering over us. But when our van had growled its way to the crest, the river was still just a line on the horizon.

"This is just the outer levee," the shopkeeper explained. He pointed into the distance, to where inner levees kept the river fast-flowing and self-scouring in a narrow channel. A third levee set even farther out would keep the destruction to a minimum if both these were to fail.... "... But this hasn't happened for a long time. We haven't had serious flooding here since 1982. There's not enough water in the river anymore."

On the broad flood table, fields of maize waved in a sudden breeze. The air had been still and hot all day, but that first breath of wind brought with it a vague chill. Spotlit by a sun that found rends in the darkening clouds, the river bore a stormy expression. She pitched and lurched her way toward a sea she might never reach, her surface crumpled into ochre waves and white horses. We drove on, nearing a great bend where the river threw herself against the levee. Groynes jutted like calming fingers into the waters to dissipate their rage. Soon we reached our goal. To anyone who had seen the Grand Canal only as the bustling transport corridor of Jiangnan, it would have been unrecognizable. Even the sickly stream of earlier that day had died, leaving only trees where there ought to have been deep water. A dam gave the final coup de grâce, its guillotine gates severing the channel but closing only on thin air. In the fields beyond, the Yellow River had exorcized even that dim spectre. The contrast to China's Crossroads, where this canal had met the Yangtze, was complete. As we drove back into Liangshan there was a rumble of thunder. The shopkeeper ignored it.

"Liangshan is so backward," he mused. "I don't understand why you would want to come here...." I indulged him with platitudes. As we reached my hotel heavy drops of rain began to flop onto the pavement. Within minutes the heavens were being torn apart by an electric storm. And as always it was the rain that showed how much slack remained in China's infrastructure despite its veneer of progress. Shop assistants frantically mopped up water that seeped through ceilings onto cellphone displays. It cascaded into the street through broken guttering, struck the same spots it always had, and churned the cracked pavements into a string of maelstroms. The roads were soon under a foot of foul water as the drains backed up.

When the storm had passed and the sun broke through, unable still to cross the flooded roads people began to lift paving slabs and to toss them one by one out into the water until by means of those impromptu stepping stones they could get about. There was more water in Shuibo Road that evening than there was in the Grand Canal. More fell overnight. When a man on the first bus out of town made a throwaway comment about Liangshan's backwardness, there was no point in contradicting him, even for the sake of

politeness. A chandler in Yizheng had said that if a town had
neither mountains nor rivers then it would be poor. Liangshan
had both, but its mountain was small and denuded, quarried
through with gaping holes like a Swiss cheese, and its river
was a restless Hydra that thrashed about unmanageably. Our
tyres span in the mud. When hours later we made it to the
nearest bridge over the Yellow River there was not a single
boat to be seen, not a fishing smack or even a raft. She was
too fickle, her shifting shoals unchartable and her currents
unsailable. On the north shore our suspension banged with
skull-juddering percussion into the potholes. As a little treat I
opened a packet of fried horse-beans. This was not how I had
imagined I would be celebrating two months of marriage.

御河

Soon after Oqruqci completed his summit section in 1283, a
further canal was dug to carry grain barges onward to the Wei
River. It brought sudden prosperity to the land, and obscure
villages blossomed into ports where merchants flocked like
birds. The hardy, unsentimental people of Shandong, wittily
subverting the southerners' famous boast that "Above there
is paradise, below there are Suzhou and Hangzhou", sang
instead that "The south may have Suzhou, but we have
Linqing and Zhangqiu!" And they had the salt markets of
Echeng, too, and Qiji whose name boasted of its Seven Step
grain wharf. But then after an age contentedly flowing in his
southerly channel, the god of the Yellow River upon a whim
cast off his shackles and ran amuck on the North China Plain.
When at last he settled down it was into his old northern bed
once more. When tributary rivers began to flow again it was
in a different direction, away from the canal. The water level
fell, the ports withered, merchants moved on, and slowly the
canal here reverted to the farmland it had been dug from.

The city of Liaocheng alone was big enough to weather that

disaster. The old canal still clings on at its edge as a lengthy depression in the fields, a muddy *memento mori*. Only where the city sprawls out along four celestial boulevards has a section been dredged, dammed, and refilled, and its towpaths planted with soft willows. It runs beneath arches of glinting stone, past preserved wharves. A breeze teases a surface undisturbed by barges and untainted by litter. It is sorrowfully pretty, a scene embalmed like Sleeping Beauty in her glass sarcophagus. Beside it, the Lake of Eastern Prosperity compasses the square city just as a Chinese copper coin encircles the square hole at its centre. Nowhere has there been so much clear, bright water. The city seems to float upon the lake, mirage-like, shimmering above an expanse of azure, as if only its four narrow causeways tether it to this world. On that lakeshore, merchants from farther west once found security and friendship. Behind the walls of their guildhall, the strange dialects of this alien place were replaced with talk of the mulberries and catalpa trees of home.

A tour guide, a sweet-natured young woman, leads a knot of policemen through labyrinthine rooms. They have arrived fresh from a lunchtime banquet, it seems, for they smell of *Maotai* liquor and cigarettes. Surreptitiously I latch on to them. She strains to be heard over their boozy chatter:

"The guildhall is a unique collection of Qing-dynasty buildings, built by subscription for the merchants of Shanxi and Shaanxi. Here they had a place to sleep, to store their funds, to do business, and to entertain. They understood that 'at home you rely on your parents, but outside you rely on your friends'." We stop before a hall rich with carved wood and stone. Grey bricks drip with the kinds of auspicious symbolism which mercantile men liked to have about them. "You can see peonies," says the guide, "for wealth and distinction, and the clouds of happiness. Over there are the phoenixes of the five human virtues, and bats and kirins for good fortune." There are peaches for longevity besides, and dragons, fruits, flowers and people, all original, and exquisitely carved in deep relief, not the imperfect facsimiles we are more used to seeing in recent renovations. The policemen chat and smoke: it's too pleasant an afternoon to pay much attention to the commentary. It is the temple of the god of war that ignites their interest. Guan Yu was during his lifetime a general serving one of the warlords who succeeded the Han dynasty. Deified, he became the Chinese Mars, a paragon of loyalty and justice. He blessed the upright, punished the unrighteous, and was appealed to by Old Hundred Surnames when there were disputes to be settled. The merchants who founded the guildhall thought him an ideal focus for their bonds of brotherhood; in Hong Kong he has become a favourite both of policemen and triads. One of the policemen unwraps the cellophane from a packet of incense fully three feet long and lights the whole bunch in one go. Bowing smartly from the waist he places the smouldering sticks in front of Guan Yu. Guan Yu stands impassively, his red face unexpressive, his heavy black beard hanging motionless from his lips.

In the hall of Zhao Gongming the guide reads aloud a line from *An Encyclopaedic Inquiry into Spirits*: "'In buying and selling and seeking wealth, this god can allow you to make profit without risk. When in financial trouble, you can pray to him and the ten thousand things will be as you desire.' On his birthday, the fifth day of the fifth lunar month, the merchants would hold a celebration here in his honour." Zhao Gongming clutches ingots shaped like paper boats, their traditional form in China. The policemen fold banknotes into origami triangles and place them on his statue. He should give them riches in return. Beside him is the moustachioed Xie Xu, god of the Grand Canal and most revered of the many spirits of the Yellow River. In life a nobleman of the Southern Song, he had saved many lives after a terrible Hangzhou flood by giving away his possessions to the disaster-stricken populace. When he drowned himself rather than face the Mongol armies who invaded his land, the people of the city buried his body on Gold Dragon Mountain and raised a temple to his memory. His clothing is bedecked now with the dragons that writhe and play within his waters. The gods of the Grand Canal, of wealth, and of loyalty had made a fitting trio for this guild of merchants. But for all the symbolism of riches and prestige they surrounded themselves with, these were shrewd businessmen. Their guildhall, with its drum and bell towers, its theatre, pavilions and shrines, was a home-from-home for some exceedingly wealthy people. Renowned for being well-funded and legion, they were loyal to each other, and pragmatic financiers. Their home has been an insight into the insulated mindset of the men who made a living from the canal. Passing their days in this self-contained retreat, perhaps they forgot one year to give Xie Xu his due respect, or perhaps he decided to show them in a great flood that he could not be taken for granted? Such rhetorical reflections are easy, but empty. Xie Xu had never really existed, had he? This whole region, and millions of people who relied on a man-made artifice, had been condemned by a caprice of unfeeling Nature. One of the officers detaches himself from the party.

"I'd guessed that you understood what the guide said," he explains. I have only understood a fraction of her long lecture, but know enough to fill in some of the gaps. He has enjoyed his visit. The shrine to Guan Yu especially seems to have spoken to him. Guan Yu's reputation for loyalty, and the alcohol of a long lunch, have together stirred that bugbear which lurks so close to the surface. "We Chinese love justice, fairness and peace," he says. "We hate it when one nation is unfair to another. America is the biggest wrongdoer in this sense. The Americans attacked Iraq for no reason, armed with lies. The Japanese attacked Pearl Harbor, and we fought with the Americans against them, but now it's the Americans who are supporting the Japanese economy and dividing us over Taiwan. Why should the little Japanese be rewarded for their aggression while we Chinese are kept divided?"

"The Japanese have admitted there was a massacre in Nanjing..." but I am unsure as to the details and trail off. The Party, anxious to keep indignation against Japan's war crimes simmering, has probably not reported any such admission: the Xinhua News Agency is quick to report visits by Japanese politicians to the Yasukuni Shrine where the spirits of war criminals reside, slower to mention any attempt at reconciliation.

The policeman mutters his disinterest: "They're an aggressive nation, and I don't like them." Then he wrong-foots me with a rapid change of subject: *"Duile*, you're a European – did you watch the last World Cup? The Italians cheated, do you know? They got a penalty by diving in the box, and won the match even though the Australians were the better team. *Bu gongping* – it's unjust."

The 2006 World Cup has long passed into sporting history. Do his long-remembered views on it hide an important point in understanding China? It strikes me they might. Under the influence of Confucius' teachings, the Chinese have long understood that society must be bound together by the relationships between people – ruler and ruled, father and son, husband and wife.... Those relationships must be made real by appropriate ritual, and if done correctly then not only society but the entire cosmos will be harmonious. For to the Confucian, correct moral actions begot cosmic harmony, and immoral behaviour begot disorder. At the heart of the Chinese worldview is a deep-seated sense of fairness. Perhaps this is why the Party has been able to rouse so many of its people so easily to anger about crimes committed by the Japanese seven decades ago: it is easy to look at the politics of the Pacific Rim from within China's borders and see unfairness in the economic success of the Japanese and America's apparent support for them. Sometimes it is easier to accept that wider injustices – rather than simply six decades of communist rule – lie at the root of China's relative backwardness. Just as is the case with the Cultural Revolution, only once the Communist Party has ceased to be the sole interpreter of China's recent past will historians be free to reframe its ambiguous relationship with the US. Then, it can be hoped, will both sides realize that they have more uniting than dividing them.

For the moment, with the average man on the street unlikely to criticize the Party openly, holding tight to anti-foreign feeling is a rational path of least resistance, a safety valve for the emotions. Many people since Hangzhou have vented their opinions. Mr Hu the fur trader savoured the idea of standing up to the Americans; Jiangbing the ex-soldier boasted of China's superior fighting spirit. More apocalyptic than either of these is the man who now drives me back to my hotel.

"*Waiguoren hao!*" he says with a big thumbs up, apropos of nothing. "Foreigners are good!" Then he adds: "*Danshi wo bu xihuan Meiguoren*. But I don't like Americans. America always attacks small countries, like a bully. They wouldn't dare to attack *us*. We're a peaceful country, but if it comes to a fight with the Americans we'll fight and beat them. It doesn't matter how many Chinese die, there are always more. We are one billion more than them, and we're not afraid to die."

I have come to expect this now. The sentiment that China is a peaceful country is invariably followed by a baying for war. After fighting over Taiwan and Korea – a loss and a draw, to put it crudely – many people appear to want to bring the US down a peg or two now that China has the technology to challenge it. These hawkish sentiments are stoked in part by exposure to the reality of Iraq and Afghanistan and fears that China is similarly vulnerable to American hegemony. The TV news that night shows the close-up aftermath of yet another car bomb, limbless, flesh-spattered and heartrending, and all but invisible on Western bulletins whose producers will not show uncensored images. My TV can receive 52 channels, and that evening's schedule is a reminder of how the past is forever being raked over. A full dozen stations are showing dramas set during Japan's occupation of China or the civil war that followed. In one, Kuomintang fighters strafe Communist positions (just as Britain benefited from American military hardware, aircraft were sent to China as lend-lease in the hope that Chiang Kai-shek's Kuomintang would defeat Mao's Communists). Another channel is running a news story on how the Chinese are still unearthing caches of chemical weapons, given scant help by a Japanese government dragging its heels over where its army buried them. In Qiqihar, says the reporter, a man has been killed and 43 injured by mustard-gas bombs unearthed at a building site. Previous victims, he adds, have seen their compensation claims turned down in the Japanese courts. This is just an average evening's TV, a few more hours of entertainment in a slow drip-feeding that shapes the way many Chinese see the world. It helps clarify why people keep on volunteering their dislike of the Japanese and their resentment of American interference.

But nobody exists in a state of permanent bitterness, and everyday concerns drown out the indignation. I linger on one drama in particular. Communist guerrillas throw themselves against Japanese machine guns, but their heroism fights for space with a half-screen advertisement for a non-surgical body-odour cure: "No knives! No overnight stay! Sweat glands reduced at source!" This fades into an advert for real-estate investment opportunities. Along the head of the screen another begins to scroll and flash: "Vaginitis? Troublesome ovaries? Impotence? Low sperm count? Treat them all at our clinic." On that glowing rectangle is an almost comical conflation of China's preoccupations – body image, capitalism, procreation, and the injustices of history.

御河

The *Atlas of Shandong Province* had nothing to say about the sandy farmland between Liaocheng and the Wei River. When the Shandong Grand Canal was redug across those whey-faced flatlands, the engineers of the People's Republic chose not to follow the route laid out by the Mongols. Today it is necessary to hitch a ride some dozen miles to the west, where the sky is anaemic, featureless through 360 degrees and from its pinnacle to a horizon of lolling khaki, and where the air carries the perfume of garlic that stands drying in tall clamps.

The canal itself, waterless, and slung between massive levees south of the Yellow River, had been transformed, let into the living earth in a line so straight that only an enveloping mist hid its ends. Yesterday it had towered above the plain, imperious and impassable; today it was apologetic, invisible until you were squarely upon it. And like that it ran unchanging to the Wei, a bare storm drain now, a clinical culvert ready to carry the Yangtze northward but too narrow for navigation. Bridges crossed it carelessly, their supports wading deep into the flow in the sure knowledge that no vessel would ever strike them. That night I slept in the town of Linqing, in a good hotel where my feet sank into thick carpet. Here Shandong ended, across the Wei River lay Hebei province. The hotel had a business centre; Rebecca had sent an email. While I had celebrated our two-month wedding anniversary with a bag of horse-beans, she had dressed up and gone out for cocktails.

In a deep sleep that night I spoke to Lord Macartney's deputy, Sir George Staunton. He wore the red jacket of a common soldier – the best that my unconscious could attire him in – and enormous mutton-chop whiskers almost hid his face. With the chauvinistic indignation that I attributed to his times and his station, he refused to believe that this part of the Grand Canal was so ancient. I found myself politely insistent.

"It was, I assure you, Sir George, excavated in the Year of Our Lord 608, and by a man named Emperor Yang. He sailed to Beijing on a dragon boat by way of it. Most of his labourers, sir, were said to be women!" We sat on the deck of a grain barge, half-naked *qianfu* crowding about us. Fields of wheat stretched out into a dream-like haze. Sir George held out a hand and pointed at a wooden scaffold, the gantry of a lock. He spoke accusingly, holding the gazes of the Chinese.

"*That* is where the poor men drowned."

"Which men, Sir George?"

"I watched as the stern of a barge sheared off, so great was the press of Chinese come to see our passage. Their dying screams did not disturb these spectators, who went on gawping like fools at our costume, just as they are doing now. These men stole their clothes as they drowned."

"I have read what you wrote about that awful sight, yet you cannot blame *these* men, sir, for they were not born when you made your passage. Cathay has changed utterly since your time here. These men would help a drowning man."

"These men have been following me since Jehol, where their emperor refused to listen to my concerns. Where *is* this accursed place?"

"Linqing, sir, and the canal here has had many names: the Channel of Eternal Succour, the River of Grain Transport. The Mongol Kublai Khan called it the Emperor's River. Today people call it the Wei River, or the Southern Grand Canal, as it lies to the southward of Tianjin."

His face clouded over as he listened, as though it was he who were dreaming: "I recall the sun, most strange. It was astern and ahead many times each day so convoluted was this stream. We moved so very slowly, and always that shouting, those gongs. Those dying screams still haunt me when I sleep...."

I awoke in the early hours, a boatman's advice to beware the immoralities of the northerners running through my head. Only the bright dawn banished those dark thoughts.

御河

The heart of Linqing proved to be an architectural museum of China in the 1950s. Buildings which exhaled the excitement of the years after Liberation still stood across a wide swathe of the town. Red stars, hammers and sickles, cogs and gears, ears of corn, all those hope-filled details that have rarely survived into our day were moulded onto the façades. In Ch'oe Pu's time this had been a bustling port, a hub on the Grand Canal as important as any and more important than most. One of six imperial customs houses was sited there, close by the great lock where the wharves were thick with junks waiting to settle their dues and pass through. (It was still there, the customs house, the last example left in all of China, a clutch of Ming buildings being renovated on a muddy back alley, being crafted into another phrase in the Grand Canal story.) Then, just as in Yangzhou, the decline of the canal had left stranded in Linqing a community of Muslims, the descendants of Arabian traders. The men in the street wore skullcaps, and their sweeping Arabic script edged out the staccato characters of the Han. Their twin mosques dominated the old town. The minarets and crescents of traditional Islam, transformed by the materials and traditions of China, had become teardrop finials perched upon tapering spires. Domes had become tiled roofs and flying caves.

Christianity had had less time to soften its contours. A steeple jarred the roofline. Discreetly I pushed open the church door, only to be grasped by a middle-aged man who led me by the hand into a lofty nave. Its interior was uniformly white, save for wall hangings which hung like Buddhist temple scrolls. Banks of seats awaited a congregation, and an electric piano stood ready to lead the hymns. So eager was the man to relate their achievements that his words stumbled one against the other and he began to stammer. His face beamed.

"We b-built this church with the Lord's help. F-f-four years ago we bought the land. We paid 40,000 *renminbi* to buy this site – we'd been praying in a hut before that. T-ten thousand people in our congregation all gave money, and with God's love we raised one million *renminbi*." He took me by the hand again, up the stairs and out onto a flat rooftop. He disappeared into a door beneath the steeple, and a moment later a bell began to chime. He reappeared with a smile.

"That's how we call the *jiaoyou* together." He began to calm down from the excitement of seeing a new face in his church, and his voice came more lucidly. His round face was sincere and thoughtful, his hair thick and black, and he pushed it back each time it tumbled into his eyes. Together we stared out across the low rooftops. "My family have been Christians for over a century. My ancestors converted when the first European missionary arrived and went on practising even when the missionaries were expelled after 1949. Life was very tough then. We still have a tough time."

"In what respect?"

He thought for a long while before he spoke: "Society in general looks down on us. Being a Christian means that you are ostracized at work, and it's difficult to get on. As an official Christian worker – my name is on the list of church leaders which we submit to the police – I get no formal pay, no iron rice bowl. Ours is a state-sanctioned church, but it is not a government work unit and we do not live to make a profit. I might have food today, but sometimes I don't know if I'll eat tomorrow. The Communist Party exerts pressure on us, and that makes it harder still."

"Pressure?"

"They sometimes tell us we must change our leaders. Why? Does it benefit the Party? No, it's just that they are atheists, and they don't understand religious belief. They see it as a threat to the Party, alien to Marxism-Leninism. It worries them, and they want to keep it under tight control."

"How do they get around the fact that the constitution guarantees freedom of religion?" Article 36 was unambiguous, but still it felt naïve even to voice the question: in China the law is pretty much what the Party says it is.

"The constitution is set on high, and has little effect down here. The Party's talk of opening up is all about *economic* opening up. Religious freedom is just window-dressing, a way of attracting investment, of making foreigners feel comfortable about dealing with China. The truth is that you foreigners know *nothing* of the oppression that goes on. I tell you, we will probably be punished by the Public Security Bureau for just *talking* to you, you understand? Word will get to them somehow. But we'll cope. Whatever they do to us we'll trust in Jesus. There's nothing else we *can* do. We're powerless, but Jesus' love will to lp un," Standing on the roof of that church I felt ashamed. Around my neck was still tied that tiny metal icon, but what did it really mean? It had been bought almost superstitiously, a traveller's talisman. This man and his congregation were going to be reported to the police by their neighbours and made to suffer just for welcoming me, yet he was untroubled.

"The Chinese are always fighting," he went on as I stood in abashed silence. "They actually *enjoy* conflict. Mao talked about constant revolution, another way of saying constant conflict. 'Revolution must be done while the iron's hot, one revolution following another, ceaselessly advancing', he used to say. Now the turmoil is over, but the Chinese are still in conflict because they don't have eternity in their hearts. They see life as a window for making personal profit before they die. Our nation is led by a party which has no grounding in external leadership – the leadership of God – and so it is rudderless, going from one pointless attempt at profit to another. I joke that 'one Chinese can achieve anything, but a whole lot of Chinese can achieve nothing'. We are a great race, but we always have bad leaders. This is why China is so backward: our leaders have no spiritual goals to lead people's minds and hearts to something better than *this*...." He flicked his head back, and with that inverted nod the Chinese use indicated Linqing in its colourless entirety.

"Over there, in the distance, the Grand Canal is so polluted it's black, but what is the average man going to do? So long as he's making money he doesn't care. He used to be happy with what life gave him – a car today, but perhaps a mule tomorrow; Rémy Martin today, perhaps water tomorrow. Only with God's help are *we* different. There's a saying: 'If you know what's sufficient, you'll always be happy'." Jiangbing had said exactly the same as we drove toward Little Shanghai that day. "There's another saying: 'Look upward and you have too little, look down and you have too much'. In Iraq, people are losing their families every day, and we must keep a perspective. Our troubles are as nothing." He took my hand again. "You're hungry. Come downstairs and eat with us."

The church community, children, adults and old men, joined together around a low table. Each had a bowl of millet porridge, its blandness made palatable with fried yellow gourd, a little pork, and cloves of raw garlic. Modest steamed buns took the place of rice, leavened but dense, and tart like sourdough bread. We sat in the open in the courtyard. It was not hard to imagine why a world beyond the steel gates shied away from these people and viewed them with suspicion. Theirs was an introspective life, antagonized by officialdom and misunderstood by others who worshipped their ancestors, burned incense to Buddha, or read Marx and Lenin – or sometimes all three. I whispered to my friend:

"Do other religions have the same problems?"

"The Party only recognizes five religions," he whispered back. "Protestantism, Catholicism, Islam, Buddhism and Daoism. Anything else is anathema. Buddhists and Daoists are viewed with suspicion, but not so much as Christians. It's different with Islam: most of our Muslims are of Hui or Uighur ethnicity, and prejudice against them would mean prejudice against entire national minorities. Islam has a powerful voice in China, and it doesn't allow itself to be bullied. Believe it or not, it's even possible to be a member of the Communist Party *and* a practising Muslim."

Boiled water was offered round. It was brackish, and he saw the pinched look on my face as I drank it. "Salty? All the groundwater on the Yellow River plain tastes like that." I did not ask for a pinch of tea to mask the taste: from the way none had been offered, they might not have had the means. Plain hot water was no misfortune.

On a crooked course through town I passed what had once been a neighbourhood clinic. A slogan survived, cast in concrete. The choice of material must at one time have spoken of joyful modernity, but it had weathered and seemed designed now to contradict its optimism: "We must actively prevent and treat the diseases which afflict the people, and expand their medical and hygiene facilities!" The quotation had been taken from a report entitled *On Coalition Government*, written by Mao several years before he broke Chiang Kai-shek's Kuomintang armies at Nian Village. It seemed strange now, but back then it was Mao who had been calling for a democratic China, Chiang Kai-shek who had refused to allow multiparty elections.

"The Kuomintang talks about enacting democracy and handing government back to the people," Mao had scoffed, "yet still they cruelly suppress the people's movement for democracy and are unwilling to make even the slightest democratic reform." He had assured the National Congress that, amongst other things, China would have religious freedom, that everybody would be able to believe and practise without discrimination. His position had utterly changed the moment he had gained uncontested power. His words had been left undamaged by his Red Guards, and they remained now as if to taunt any hopes that things that had once been promised might yet come true.

御河

Rain arrived again overnight and was falling still the next morning as I strolled out to the canal. Instead of joining the Wei

245

River as it once had, it was brought up short by sluicegates in a gargantuan levee, raised during the Cultural Revolution by farmers from the people's communes which flanked the river. It was impossible now for even the smallest of vessels to pass from one waterway to the other. A park had been planted and a statue raised to the heroic engineers of the People's Republic. A man sat and read beneath the trees. Like the lock-keeper in Shaobo he greeted me like an old friend.

"Very few foreigners come to Linqing," he said, shaking my hand vigorously. "*Very* few. I spend a lot of time sitting here, and I think perhaps you are the first I have seen, the first to visit our canal." It felt unlikely that any outsider had troubled themselves to see that remote spot since there had been an emperor on the Dragon Throne. When he discovered why I was in Linqing, he traced three lines in the damp earth with the tip of a shoe. They formed a straggling letter "I", the Yellow River at its bottom, the Shandong Grand Canal its vertical stroke, the Wei River its upper bar. When Hebei province thirsted, a fraction of the Yellow River could be tapped off into the canal. Arriving here in Linqing, the water was siphoned under the bed of the Wei River through a mile-long tunnel. For the present it irrigated only Hebei, but once the water transfer project was complete another sluicegate would be opened and the Yangtze would flow toward distant, thirsty Tianjin. But the sluicegates were closed that day, the canal just a shallow trickle. It flowed crystal clear between hummocks of grass, so slow that pond skaters skimmed across the surface. It dribbled over a final weir as though reluctant to drop into the blackness of the Wei River beyond.

The Wei was a tragedy. It had risen amongst the sublime peaks of the Taihang Mountains, flowed past rank after rank of watercolour scenery. But then the Henan plains had tapped its water for industry and agriculture. In thankless return they had shed their chemical waste into it. By the time it reached Linqing, the river was violated and lifeless. Its levee stood ten yards tall. Half a mile away, the far bank became just a rank of trees through the mist. The river no longer occupied the entirety of that bed but had shrunk to just fifteen yards, blacker than ink, impenetrable to the weak daylight, and stinking of sewer gas. Its surface was unnaturally smooth, thicker somehow than everyday water. Jetties strutted out into the open air but fell far short of the river, their legs entangled by the tendrils of runner beans. Within living memory the Wei had regularly overtopped its banks; spillways had been dug to ease the pressure. The locals crossing back and forth between the two provinces no longer even stopped to look: this river was their normality. Like the pastor had said, what was the average man going to do?

A Canal Reborn

杭州

北京

the Emperor's River to Beijing

It had taken a fortnight to cross Shandong, and at every consultation the *Atlas of Shandong Province* had showed the land beyond the Wei River as a uniform grey. That must have been why I now approached Hebei with an empty feeling: those maps had been whispering to my subconscious that this land was empty, a grey terra incognita. The two provinces were joined together like the plates of a skull, the Wei River the meandering fissure between them. It was sky blue, its hatchings insistent that this was officially the Southern Grand Canal, as much a part of the iconic waterway as were the shipping lanes of Jiangnan. Its cartographers had been playing a never-ending game, it sometimes felt, often mistaken over names and confused about its course, only this was the worst deception of all, comparable to the Ordnance Survey, in some act of misplaced historical pride, marking the vanished Roman road of Ermine Street as a viable route from London to York. But to have done otherwise would have been to admit that here the Grand Canal had slid into an irreversible decline.

On its southernmost stretches, an immutable waterway had suffered cities to colonize her like mosses upon a rock. It had been possible to pass through great emporia that trailed one into the other – Wujiang, Suzhou, Wuxi, Changzhou, Danyang.... Up here a skittish river had forever pitched and bucked at any attempt to settle on her banks, and beyond Linqing she covered a similar distance without meeting

a single town of note. Even the roads had been unable to
mirror the Wei's unpredictable course, and it was impossible
to advance without first retracing a path to Liaocheng. And
so it took from dawn until dusk one damp Monday before I
was squatting down in Dezhou bus station with a local map
spread out upon the tiled floor. It held nothing of interest save
for the tomb of Sultan Paduka Batara. It had been a long day's
travel, but at least it hadn't killed me; poor Paduka Batara had
died here while returning home to the Philippines and had
been buried beside the canal. A single night in Dezhou would
allow enough time to visit his grave the next morning.

The completion of the direct route from Hangzhou to
Beijing under Kublai Khan had made Dezhou one of the most
important markets in his Eurasian empire. Its wharves had
teemed under the Ming. European guests of the Qing had
seen a pleasing land of market gardens set among tobacco
plantations (children, noted Aeneas Anderson, were taught
to smoke as soon as they had sufficient strength or dexterity
to hold a pipe) and had been amazed by the density of the
population, by towns and villages which came into sight one
after the other in an unbroken stream. Then, just as they had
each city from Jining northward, the floods of 1855 had put a
sudden end to that wealth.

The city was only now rebuilding itself. The municipal
government announced with pride that Dezhou had been
named Sun City for its production of solar-energy heating
systems, Air-con City for its air-conditioners, and Functional
Sugar City for its production of functional sugar – whatever
that was. Businessmen were arriving from the big cities, and
were demanding somewhere decent to stay. The map was
encircled by adverts for four-star hotels. After two months of
unwashed sheets and insect-stained walls, of leaking showers
and toilets that did not flush, I chose the glitziest on offer and
set out into the cool of the night.

The Guidu Hotel was luxurious, its lobby all marble and

soft, trickling water. Ignoring that irksome part of me that revelled in self-denial, I ran a bath and wallowed in suds, then lay wrapped in a fluffy dressing gown to order room service and flick through the satellite channels. I fell asleep without even thinking of the canal.

Dawn could not find the usual rends in the curtain and did not waken me the next morning. The restaurant had knives and forks, and I clumsily smeared butter onto a baguette like a child, giggling at the odd feeling of eating with cold steel. But outside, the city with its pretty neon extinguished had become another low-rise sprawl under a limewash sky. It was by then mid-July and the sun was already high. A hot breeze wafted the smell of hydrogen sulphide from the river as if to remind me of its presence.

What little remained of the Southern Grand Canal reeled aimlessly from one levee to the other with expansive, sweeping gestures, as though it had lost its way and like a blind man was trying to regain a sense of direction. It hunched its shoulders to squeeze through Dezhou's western fringe, and there it became for a moment a green glen edged with spinneys, softly curved like a glaciated valley. The merest rivulet of water wound along its bottom, now broadening into a rippled pond, now losing itself in a morass of grass dotted with flowers. It was so far from being a recognizable canal that no attempt had been made to beautify it with weirs and promenades. There was no need. It was beautiful like this, what it had unintentionally become, a broad nature reserve gouged deeply through a city. I hailed a cab, intending to visit the sultan's tomb, but the driver said it had been closed.

Instead, Dezhou railway station's cavernous waiting hall was packed with migrant workers. A screen showed Tom and Jerry cartoons, and amongst the snippets on Dezhou's history squeezed in between them was the story of Yi the Archer, the legendary local hero said to have shot down nine of the ten suns which once scorched the earth. We stood with our shirts unbuttoned, our trouser legs rolled up to our knees, and fanned the sweat from our bodies with newspapers.

The train we shared was bound for the job opportunities of Tianjin. Its hard-seat carriages were comfortably upholstered now, and air-conditioned, not like the old days when they were little more than cattle trucks. Tired heads lolled on lovers' shoulders as the Shandong border rolled away behind us. The young man sitting opposite opened our conversation as though we had been speaking for hours.

"Do you like to listen to music on the internet?"

"I don't really understand computers."

"Do you have an iPod?" I shook my head. Nor a cellphone, I confessed. He widened his eyes and uttered a softly drawn out gasp: "*Waaa*, do you come from the Stone Age?" Xiaojiang had been born in small-town Shaanxi, close by China's ancient capital Xi'an with its terracotta warriors. He wore a faded T-shirt bearing a picture of Lao Wu, a Chinese rock guitarist, and had a shock of wild hair that seemed to support its own weight inches above his head. What kind of music did he listen to?

"Mostly Chinese. I don't enjoy listening to lyrics I can't understand."

"Do you like that song *Don't Wanna Grow Up*?" I suppressed a grin – it was the song the little girl had danced to in Jiaxing. Xiaojiang had a placid nature and just smiled.

"In Chinese we call that 'saliva music'." He leaned his head to the side and pretended to dribble from the corner of his mouth. "It's worthless, pointless, part of the fast-food culture we suffer from these days." When he reached Tianjin he would be changing to a Beijing train, he said, returning to his job in a small hotel. "Lots of foreign backpackers stay there. I work in the shop, arrange trips out to the sights – the Great Wall, the Summer Palace, *deng deng*.... There's an internet connection so I can surf for free all day. I download songs, listen to music."

"If you're from Shaanxi, what have you done about your

hukou?" I asked. Soon after Liberation, a man's *hukou* – his official residency – had come to determine his life. Whether he was given a job, a house, an education, everything had been decided by his parents' social position before he was even born. In Mao's economic machine, the anonymous cogs were not free to move about in search of work. No matter what his talents, a peasant's status had condemned him to the poverty of the countryside. The benefits of an urban *hukou* were jealously guarded, and illicit rural migrants were regularly rounded up and expelled from the cities. Then the boom had come, and cities hungry for cheap labour had drawn workers from the interior. A blind eye had been turned. Now an urban underclass was living without legal protection, despised and indispensable in equal measure, a source of cheap muscle but a leaven for crime and social unrest as the economy shrank. Xiaojiang though was phlegmatic, a graduate of Xi'an University rather than a guileless farmer fit only for a hard hat and a shovel. He shrugged.

"I could swap my Xi'an *hukou* for a Beijing *hukou*, but that would cost money." It had long been my assumption that people would do almost anything to gain official residency in one of the big cities – Beijing, Shanghai, Canton, and now Shenzhen.

"Wouldn't there be advantages to being a Beijing resident?" I pressed him.

"If I had a Beijing *hukou* I'd be allowed to buy one of the apartments reserved for Beijingers, but I have a home in Shaanxi and a place to sleep at the hotel. China's changing, you see, and we don't all 'Serve the people's currency'." The phrase was a sarcastic subversion of the famous slogan – "Serve the people!" – that was on such visible display at the gateway to the Party's Beijing compound. With official corruption as it was, his rephrasing was the more apt.

"What about your work unit? Everybody still has a work unit, *dui ma*?"

"I walk my own path."

"Doesn't that create problems in your life?"

Xiaojiang shook his head softly. "People of my generation want to make lives for ourselves. We don't get handed a job in a work unit after university like our parents' generation, and we must solve our own dilemmas, but we're freer to do what we want."

It had been impossible to ignore how China's youth was becoming more open with each passing year, more willing to tell the truth as they saw it even if it might reflect badly on themselves or on their country. An older generation had been notoriously reticent of finding public fault with China, no matter what their private opinion. Xiaojiang balanced the pros and cons of a changing society in two open palms – the security of the "iron rice bowl" on one hand, and freedom from a life mapped out from cradle to grave on the other. Living amongst young backpackers had broadened his ideas of what made life worthwhile, as though he had never inherited the understandable instinct to make money that drives those who can remember the nadir of Chinese communism.

"What about when you get married and have a child? It won't be able to go to school in Beijing if you have no *hukou* there."

"Then I'll take this wife and child back to Shaanxi. Perhaps things will be different by then. The *hukou* is making it hard for labour to move freely; perhaps it will have been abolished. Perhaps I'll get a passport and study in the US."

"What about political matters?" I asked. "Are you interested?"

"It doesn't affect young people like me. The Party is above, and we are below." He held his palm out flat, reaching high above his head, and then again close to the table that divided us. "What the Party says doesn't make a difference to us. It's not important." His answer came as no surprise. The apparent impossibility of making a difference seemed to have left a whole generation disinterested in politics. So long as jobs continued to be created, there was nothing to be gained from rocking the boat. I showed him the two defaced banknotes I had hidden away. His face did not change when he read their inflammatory words. "A friend of mine told me a story. There was a telephone number, a regular number of a company or something, but when you dialled it you heard a message, all counter-revolutionary propaganda. If you heard it, he said, you had to hang up quickly before the Public Security Bureau traced your number and came to visit you."

"Did you ever hear what it said?"

"I'm not even sure it's true. You hear lots of stories like that." Of such stuff are all urban myths: grains of reality bound with paranoia. The grain of reality in his story was that there *was* more and more anti-government chatter, more violent opposition to local corruption, more people rubber-stamping banknotes with predictions of revolution; the paranoia lay in the fact that the PSB still had the power to come calling and lock you away without trial.

Outside the window, Hebei province bowled past. It was flat, covered to the horizon with emerald blades which hugged the ground for cover from the gritty wind. The ochre of the soil showed through in patches between the crops, or whenever a dry riverbed flashed beneath us. This region was scored through with man-made channels, dug after Liberation to carry floodwater away to the Bohai Gulf, as though a great comb had been drawn across the earth. In the 1950s there had been deep water in them every day of the year; nowadays it was exceptional if they flowed sparsely for a fortnight. Goats grazed where fish once swam. Every now and again a town lifted itself from the plain, shot past in orange brick and the silver silos of a chemical works, then passed into the distance. Xiaojiang went to find the dining car, and while he was gone the train slowed and pulled into Cangzhou.

御河

The door of the internet café opened onto a low-ceilinged room the size of a tennis court. Rows of terminals stretched away under a fug of cigarette smoke lit by the glow of computer screens, the sole source of light. The only sounds were of tapping keys and of the hissing that leaked from headphones, a metallic tinnitus. Like an opium den set up in Houston Mission Control, bodies lolled in their seats with faces fixed in somnolent stares. It brought to mind a dimly remembered woodblock, an oriental version of Hogarth's *Rake's Progress* that illustrated the descent of a young man from respectability into opium smoking and death. At a counter sat a young woman. She wore a low-cut top that revealed slight shoulders and a tattoo of a rose. On a shelf behind her, dressed in ancient robes, sat a statuette of the god of wealth. In front of him were a pack of smoked sausages and a glowing stick of incense.

"What does the god of wealth like to eat?" She turned to look at him.

"He likes to eat meat, any kind of meat." Her grin broadened into a smile, then into a laugh. She gave me a password. A screen burst into life with a warning from the local police: "You must not create, download, reproduce, consult, promulgate, propagate or otherwise use information of the following descriptions...." Below was a list of what the police deemed unacceptable – anything which ran contrary to the principles of the Chinese constitution, anything which damaged national unity, sovereignty or territorial integrity, which endangered security or besmirched national prestige, which incited discrimination against any of China's ethnic nationalities, threatened their unity or violated their traditions, which countered religious policies, spread false teachings or superstition, endangered public morality, "... or any other information otherwise outlawed". It was a none-too-subtle reminder that it was ultimately the Party that set the upper limits of debate. Four terminals away and in full view of others, a boy was watching hard-core pornography, strictly illegal in China. It was a reminder that this country, just like any other, was more complex than the laws which ostensibly controlled it. It was not long before Shengliang noticed me.

"I've never spoken to a foreigner before," he said shyly. He was tall and bespectacled, and like most of the other surfers was in his late teens, no older. The Grand Canal had had no shortage of internet cafés; the more obscure the town, it seemed, the more there were to be found. Yet, utterly absorbed in themselves, not once had anyone spoken to me within one, and whatever it was that enthralled these young people was still a mystery. Shengliang offered to explain things. We wandered together up and down the rows, glancing over shoulders into bright screens like vagrants looking longingly into the glow of living rooms. One girl was logged onto a dance website. She dabbed at the keys to make her little alter ego dance in time to the music playing through her headset. Its wide eyes and button nose reminded one of the coy schoolgirls in Japanese *manga*.

"Ah, but this is a South Korean website," corrected Shengliang. "We prefer to use Korean sites, because we don't like to use Japanese products." He stopped, thought for a moment, and chuckled. "There are games like *War of Resistance Online*, where you can play a guerrilla fighter and kill the Japanese bandits. In this girl's game you dance against four other players. You see, at the top of the screen is a shop where you can choose your hairstyle, your shoes, clothes, accessories." Killing Japanese invaders seemed to be no less real (or was it unreal?) than being a good consumer. Detached Xiaojiang from that morning's train would have dismissed it as worthless, part of China's fast-food culture. Like him, I didn't quite see the point.

"*Why* do they want to dance against people they don't know?" I asked. "Do they win money?" There would at least have been some point to that.

"It's just *fun*, that's all, a way to pass the time. A friend of mine once spent two whole days and nights here, then slept for three days."

"How can you spend that long in an internet café? It's impossible."

"They're open all night, and the local restaurants deliver for free." He nodded toward the wall, where the Royal Treasures Noodle Shop had posted a hand-written menu.

"So how old do you have to be to spend all your time here?"

"Didn't you see the sign on the door? It says 'under-eighteens are forbidden from entering'." I looked around; Shengliang too saw the children and anticipated my objection. "I started coming when I was in the first year of junior middle school, at thirteen. Children spend good money, and Old Wooden Planks 'watches as though he does not see'."

Beyond the junior middle-school pupils, tucked away undisturbed in the darkest corners, sat the serious gamers, the older boys who spent hours on end in role-playing sites. Shengliang looked over a few more shoulders. "This one is called *World of Devil Monsters,* an American game." At the next terminal sat a boy engrossed in an ancient Chinese cityscape. "This game is *Dreamworld Journey to the West*. It's based on the novel *Journey to the West*. There might be one and a half million players online in China at once. To get to the higher levels costs a lot of money. Both these games are addictive, you see, and you must play for weeks or months to achieve anything."

"But these are schoolboys – where do they get the money from?"

Shengliang gave a shrug. "From their parents? From part-time work? We've all heard of children who've stolen money, been caught, and ended up in the 'special population'. There are stories in the newspapers about children who've killed themselves, or died after being awake for days on end, and about teenagers becoming estranged from their families. They stop studying and their character changes. People call it 'eheroin'." Shengliang thought for a moment then broke into a belly laugh, his shoulders shaking: "I heard one story about a boy who spent so long playing games that he went to the internet café wearing a nappy so he didn't need to leave his seat to go to the toilet!" The players went on staring at their screens, ignoring him, the whole room a sea of unmoving heads. We sat back down and Shengliang typed the URL of *Dreamworld Journey to the West*.

"In this realm of dust," ran the introduction, "the pure lotus flower of human nature has withered, evil and desire have grown ever stronger and have swallowed the goodness in men's hearts, and hidden strengths have been drawn into the boundless darkness. The Rulai Buddha possesses the Tripitaka scriptures which can show men the path to goodness. They await transmission to the Eastern Lands. Yet Buddha fears that all creatures are benighted and will malign the True Word, and so he has decided to call on exceptional men to seek the scriptures. Here our game begins. Players must undergo a period of trials to discover the golden lotus which will make them fit to do Buddha's bidding and so accept the mission, to help open the eyes of the world, to restore human nature to its true state." The game was set in the days when the Tang-dynasty capital Chang'an, eastern terminus of the Silk Route, was the most populous city on earth and a melting-pot for all Asia. Its characters were familiar from the Japanese TV adaptation that had once been broadcast in the UK: there were Friar Sand, Pigsy, the mischievous Monkey King, and Xuanzang, a real-life monk who travelled to India during the Tang to collect Buddhist scriptures. Their digital world had everything the real Chang'an had had – homes and temples, palaces and monasteries, inns, sing-song parlours, gambling houses, pawnbrokers, shops selling traditional medicines and gold-flecked paper to burn for the ancestors.... Players who would never meet face to face could marry in cyberspace by trekking to the Shrine of the Mandarin Ducks and announcing their plans to the Old Man of the Moon who since their birth had tied an invisible twine of fate between them. With the help of the magical arts of *yin* and *yang* and the five elements, these teenagers spent their days fighting mythological demons. Less than 40 years ago, the cultural beliefs that now saturated *Dreamworld Journey to the West* were being denigrated as backward-looking and superstitious. People had been hounded and killed for espousing them. Had they been born around the time of Cangzhou's Liberation, the boys who were lost in these other worlds would have come of age wearing Red Guard armbands, singing *The East is Red*, and condemning such a life of leisure as bourgeois decadence. Now the historical accuracy of characters, clothing, scenery and architecture were a source of cultural pride, not shame. That day, just like every other, there was a virtual mass-mobilization of China's youth, every one of them clutching a computer mouse just as their grandparents had clutched their little red books. Back then it had been Mao who had shut the door on the past, who alone had pointed the cursor and clicked and guided 800 million people in building his idea of Utopia. Now the internet age has given a generation who never knew Mao the power to control their own imaginary worlds and to decide their own real futures. The ability to quote Mao has become an irrelevance. A thought came to me.

"Shengliang, do you own a copy of *Quotations from Chairman Mao*?" He knitted his brows and shook his head.

"Nobody owns a copy of *Mao Zhuxi Yulu* these days." Mao had died in 1976. Despite the incalculable effect his thoughts had on China during his lifetime, memorizing from *Quotations* has become of less importance to the individual than understanding the mythical menagerie of *Dreamworld Journey to the West*. Government statisticians have lost count of how many copies were eventually printed – it was certainly well into ten figures – yet sheer numbers never translated into relevance. *Chitty Chitty Bang Bang* and *Charlie & the Chocolate*

Factory, both released in the same year as *Quotations*, have more to offer the world four decades on. True, *Quotations* is still being bought, but its red plastic covers are piled high only on the stalls that cater for foreign tourists. Meanwhile China already has well over a quarter of a billion internet users, a technology that Mao could not have conceived of, and it is this revolution in information that will ultimately have a far greater impact than the misdirected fervour of an older generation. As the earthily Sichuanese Deng Xiaoping said of his own reforms, "If you open a window, some flies might get in." And so the men who patrol the Great Firewall of China are still regularly blocking foreign websites and blogs where Chinese subscribers discuss unsuitable topics. The cyber-windows are slammed shut arbitrarily, closing and opening seemingly at random and only ever preventing the tiniest fraction of possible flies from entering. China-based websites, which can more easily be visited by the men from the Ministry of Industry and Information Technology, tend to self-censor. But now the arrival in the shops of mobile technology has allowed laymen to share ideas, and even pictures and videos of public demonstrations. There are far too many flies for the authorities to swat them all.

Two hours of surfing in that internet café cost me just ¥2, a small sum even for a local teenager. In my change, once again, was a ¥1 note defaced with a homemade printing pad. Its text was longer than the others, a bold fifteen characters of blue ink: "Heaven will destroy the Chinese Communist Party. The *Nine Commentaries* are true. Resign from the Party, the Youth League and the Young Pioneers and ensure peace." As a foreigner I was largely immune to the implications of possessing such a piece of political propaganda; for a Chinese citizen it could mean trouble. Unreflexively, almost out of amused surprise at what I had just read, I shared it with the rose-tattooed young woman who had passed it to me.

"Have you read this?" I asked, stupidly. She glanced at it

261

and her face changed from a smile to a mask of wide-eyed shock. She waved a hand stiffly.

"*Mei kan guo. Bu shi wode.* I've not seen it before. It's not mine." I stuffed the note into my pocket and backed out of the café amongst a flurry of exculpations. The *Nine Commentaries* had been published a few years earlier by the New York-based *Epoch Times* newspaper. A vitriolic condemnation of communism and all its works, it considered the Party an illegitimate coterie of nothing more than bloodstained criminals who had brought nothing but violence, catastrophe and the destruction of traditional culture to a country who had never wished for them in the first place. The *Epoch Times* had earned a reputation for its support of the banned Falun Gong and had made itself a willing enemy of the Communist Party in the process. With this final clue in my hand, it seemed clear that all the graffitied banknotes that had come into my possession had been inspired by the *Times'* stance. Even the call to resign could be traced to its online campaign to convince Party members to hand in their membership cards. Whether or not the rubber stamps had been manufactured by activists living far away in the US or right here in Cangzhou it was impossible to tell.

Outside on Transport Avenue I blinked in the bright sunlight and set off to visit the canal, half reluctantly now, like one might visit an ailing relation in a nursing home. Today at least it seemed a little sprightlier than at my last visit, well-watered where it ran through the city centre, and somebody had brought lotus flowers to brighten up its bed. But tomorrow, I knew, out in the countryside beyond, it would have fallen back into its geriatric melancholy.

御河

These days it is the Wei River alone in whose bed the Southern Grand Canal flows, but there were times when another river, the Zhang, joined the Wei in its middle reaches. The Zhang contributed such a volume of water that together they often overtopped the banks to flood farm and city. So the Chinese dug spillways to relieve the pressure, and over those low parapets gushed the excess long before it had a chance to breach the levees. One such spillway ran from an otherwise inconsequential village called Jiedi out to the Bohai Gulf, leading floodwater harmlessly out to sea. The Grand Canal here had never recovered from the floods of 1855, and the works at Jiedi were said to be preserved like an insect trapped in amber.

The taxi driver who drove me out to Jiedi was perplexed at quite how far I had travelled to be there; for years there had not been a canal worth the name, she complained:

"I'm 50 years old. My grandfather used to tell me about when he was a boy, before they enjoyed piped water. They took water from the canal with a bucket and used that for drinking water, he used to say. Sometimes the water carried so much silt that they had to leave it to settle before drinking it." When she talked of drinking the water she used the word *chi* – to eat. It was a linguistic quirk of these northerners, and it made the silt sound so much more palatable. "You couldn't eat the water now, though – too poisonous. There were fish then, and people made a living as fishermen. When it was cold the water would freeze and ice merchants would come to chisel blocks off. They'd put them in ice houses and sell them the next summer when it was hot...." Her train of thought stopped and she went quiet for a moment. "It's strange to think that people like my grandfather never lived to see the bottom of the canal. It was always full when he was amongst the generations. Now we're more familiar with its dry bed."

"Will the water transfer project make a difference?" I asked. Her forehead wrinkled as though she were trying to remember something.

"No, not here, I don't *think* so...."

We drove slowly south alongside the railway line. Jiedi village was not far, but it was market day and the roads were choked with stalls. We turned down mud-shod alleys, the sky above our heads sliced into tiny triangles of blue by the wires that brought telephones and cable TV. Then suddenly we broke into open country and fields of maize stretched away once more. Far upstream from the weirs which made of it a florid parkland in the city centre, the canal was dry. Its grassy banks, emerald like a bowling green, sagged down into the earth as though a giant ball had been rolled across the countryside to leave a broad, shallow impression. It is said that the Qianlong Emperor, passing by here on an imperial tour of inspection, had awoken from a sleep. When he had asked the village's name, a fawning attendant had replied that it was called The Majestic Dragon Awakes. Impressed, Qianlong had landed to inspect the spillway and to leave a sample of his calligraphy upon a block of stone. A villager led us along the towpath to where it stood. Sheltered beneath a tiny roof, like a roadside shrine to the Virgin, it had been scoured illegible by the weather. A goat was tethered at its foot to munch on the corn husks tossed there. The villager kicked at them.

"There always used to be a lot of water here, twenty feet deep or more. When the flow from the Yellow River is diverted to irrigate Tianjin we have water for a month or two, but otherwise it's dry."

"Do you have enough to grow crops?"

"Oh, we have enough, enough, but it's polluted, and each year it gets less. In a decade the South-to-North Water Transfer Project will bring more from the Yangtze, then life will be a little better."

"The project won't go through Cangzhou," interrupted the driver with unnecessary brusqueness. The villager looked taken aback at this challenge to his wisdom and his livelihood.

"*Hui'a!* Yes, it will! The water will flow through Jiedi and on to Tianjin!" And there I lost the thread of their argument. Wandering off, I scratched about some rubble piled by the spillway. One brick, half buried in the grass, carried a strip of embossed characters. It had been made at the Linqing brickworks by an overseer named Wu in the tenth year of Yongzheng of the Great Qing – 1732 by our calendar. The Chinese were good at quality control back then, Mrs Du would have been happy to learn, and Wu's name was less a boast for eternity and more a way of holding him to account if his bricks failed. It was still as hard as steel. I scrambled down the bank to the riverbed. Grassy walls reared up on both sides, muffling the hubbub from the market. That channel, like a patient safety valve, would stay dry and unused like its builders had intended until the day came when the water transfer project brought so much water north that its excess once more needed to be carried away to the sea.

"That man spoke with reason," the driver admitted as we headed back to town. "I guess he was right." It seemed reasonable that a farmer should have a keener sense of such issues than a city-dwelling taxi driver. "Did you know," she went on, "that the price of water in Cangzhou has doubled? Every year less, every year more expensive."

The countryside looked so dry. It was hard to believe that a longer stretch of the Grand Canal lay in Cangzhou than in any other city on its entire length. More than one tenth of it – alone longer than Britain's longest, the Grand Union – was to be found within the city limits, yet it seemed that its water would scarcely have filled one of Beijing's Olympic swimming pools. The situation was just as grave across the whole of the north. By the Chinese government's own admission, one in three villagers no longer had access to clean drinking water. Half of those, they said, had dangerous pollutants in their water, and 2,000,000 were already living with diseases caused by drinking it. The water transfer project when it came might be a dangerous inversion of nature in the minds of many environmentalists and, like the Three Gorges Dam and the Qinghai-Tibet Railway, a propaganda coup for the Party, but for the villagers of Jiedi it could not come quickly enough.

御河

The giant bowling ball had rolled on across the North China plain, compacting a broad swathe of soil and leaving its shallow depression in the fields. Nothing more remained of the canal. Would it ever again look like it once had, like the teeming shipping lanes of Jiangnan? Of course not. Renovating its entire length north of Jining where it ran dry – the equivalent of London to Inverness, or Manhattan to Quebec – would be an absurd conceit even for a country so anxious to laud the canal as one of its greatest achievements. It had been dry for too long. The cities of these plains had withered once the floods of 1855 had cut off their economic lifeblood, and they had never truly recovered. With the end of empire in 1911 and the capital's sojourn in the Yangtze valley, there was no longer any need for a canal bringing imperial grain to Beijing. Down south the Grand Canal might have been reborn as part of a modern transport network, but this far north economic demands were meagre. Within a decade the canal might at least find new life as the water transfer project channelled the Yangtze north, but to make it navigable again shiplocks would need to be built, hundreds of bridges would need to be re-engineered to let shipping pass, and the convolutions of the Wei River would have to be straightened if today's straggling barge trains were to negotiate them. Back in Changzhou US$375,000,000 had been spent excavating a short bypass; many billions would be needed to resurrect this lifeless form up here in the north, and what would be the result of such expense? A latter-day Emperor's River which could still not compete with the tarmac and the continuous-welded rail that had overtaken it. The highway passed over its lifeless frame twice more before the white needle of the Tianjin TV tower pricked the skyline. By that time the last trace of it had vanished from the landscape.

Tianjin was the biggest city I had seen since setting out from Hangzhou. Eleven million people called it home. This was the China of foreign correspondents, all office blocks, grand hotels, and fashionable boutiques. Imported SUVs sat in gridlocked traffic, their drivers in sunglasses and sports-casual clothing as though ready for a day at the country club. After months on a Chinese road less travelled it all seemed the embodiment of every documentary and newspaper article on China's economic miracle, and it all felt quite alien. What would Jiugao the rickshawman have made of its wealth, or Mr and Mrs Yao aboard the *021 Cargo* with its greasy wheelhouse and thin mattress? The Guans on the *Jiaxing River Cargo 0312* would have been unable to understand the spoken language here, a thousand miles from fellow speakers of Wu. As they too might have done, I stood sheepish at the roadside like just another out-of-towner in search of work. Then for the first time since crossing the Yangtze I saw another foreigner, spoke in English, and felt the weeks of cultural isolation fall away. Tianjin's foreign businessmen did their shopping at Wal-Mart, he said, watched Sky Sports in ex-pat bars, lived in serviced apartments. Why would anyone want to take such a long and filthy journey, he asked, when they could get a job working for a British firm here? He admitted with a self-effacing laugh to not knowing any Mandarin beyond "salt-and-pepper spare ribs" – his knowledge of stocks and shares was what was in demand here, not his hopeless language skills – and that his only experience of China beyond Tianjin was through the screens that showed the rise and fall of its markets. It was another hot day, and sweat patches showed through his suit jacket.

Wandering Tianjin for the first time, my mind imagined the ghosts of streets that had gone, conjured up the vanished houses of foreign concessions that had once been indistinguishable from suburban Britain. The street-names – Elgin Avenue, Bromley Road, Victoria Road – might have been lifted from my own town. But they had been renamed, become memorials not to lords and monarchs but instead to Liberation and to the People. A young woman caught me in a deep reverie, eyes open but staring straight through the present and deep into the past.

"Wo keyi bangzhu ni ma?"

"Thank you, I'm fine, no need of help. Just daydreaming..." that China might stand still for a moment so that I could taste it as it was, instead of feeling that it was always just beyond my reach, vanishing as I rounded each familiar corner, changing as I turned my back. I did not take that businessman up on his offer of a night out clubbing. Rather than spend as much on a bottle of imported beer as on a cheap room, I called him to say no thanks and shut myself away. With a glass of tea I settled down to the last pages of the diaries.

The men of the Macartney embassy had arrived in Tianjin early one August morning, and despite the hour – it was barely six o'clock – so many locals had turned out on the banks of the Hai River to see them that they had declared their numbers to be incalculable. Soldiers lined the shore waving flags and pennants, and a salute of three petards was fired. In a theatre set up near the residence of Tianjin's chief mandarin they were treated to a display of martial arts on a stage adorned with ribbons and silken streamers. Later that day a magnificent dinner was sent onto the embassy's yachts, and the chief mandarin sent silks to be distributed amongst the embassy, but it was of a very indifferent quality compared to what British merchants were already exporting through Canton. The barbarians, he must have thought, would not be able to tell the difference, and there was no point in playing the harp to an ox. I fell asleep wishing I could have seen China as Macartney, Anderson and the rest had seen it, when the Celestial Empire still looked upon foreigners with an assurance of utter superiority, before the British and the French had blown open its gates, shattered the calm, and left China distrustful. Lou Yue did not show up to scold me for idealizing the past; I had already realized to myself anything he might have said. Instead, the traffic on the street woke me in the early hours in the middle of another rainstorm. By morning the downpour had mellowed into a cooling summer drizzle.

御河

In his *Classic of the Way and the Virtue*, the Daoist philosopher Laozi wrote that a journey of a thousand *li* starts beneath one's feet. Already this one had taken me three times as far. Standing on the empty waterfront, the Hai seemed small for a river that drained an area larger than the British Isles. Old Uncle in Heaven had made it tidal to Tianjin and far beyond, though the locks and dams at its mouth more often than not held it in a state of suspended animation these days. Today was such a day, and the water level was high. Anglers sat and waited for the fish to bite, no shipping to startle their prey. Before the canal here was mothballed, grain barges heading to Beijing entered the Hai at just that point, turned sharply to port, then sailed upstream for a good mile. There they would tack to starboard and enter the maws of the Northern Grand Canal for the last stretch. A swelling tide and an onshore wind would hurry them along toward their final goal. Beyond the Hai's highest tidal reach, 70 miles inland at Willow Village, the *qianfu* might have an easy time of it so long as the dragons sent down plentiful rain. Then as the year wore on into late autumn and the streams began to dwindle, its gravelly bed would begin to show and the *qianfu* knew they would soon be dragging wooden bottoms over the shallows until winter came and the way froze solid.

For hundreds of yards, demolition gangs had flattened the hub of Tianjin's old Chinese city. Just a few homes, their occupants refusing to accept the compensation offered them, stood isolated amidst a sea of yellow soil like pitiful atomic domes rising above the ruins of Hiroshima. *"Dingzi wu"*, they called them, "nail houses", for the way they stuck up and refused to be hammered down. Sooner or later though, the People's Armed Police would arrive to make sure that individuals like these did not hold up the city's plans. I walked on upstream.

"Beijing kuai dao le...." After three months of Mandarin I was dreaming it, sleeptalking it, mumbling it to myself when alone. "Almost in Beijing...."

The sole settlement of any size between Tianjin and the capital, Willow Village was not far, half an hour by road rather than the full morning it had taken Macartney and his embassy to ride on the rising tideway. There the canal was suddenly whole again, like the departed appearing in a dream, full of youth and vigour but liable just as a dream to fade. The shacks on its shore had been dismantled, their inhabitants promised compensation and evicted, and once-tumbling banks had been neatly edged with stones and willows. The water was clean and deep. A willow leaf floated upon it, unmoving: this was no longer a true canal, more a cosmetic pool of water piled up behind a small dam. A man watched me as I watched the leaf. The district government had wanted Willow Village to look good before the start of the Olympic Games, he said, and so 80 million *renminbi* of public money had been spent on this project. Back in Hangzhou I might have been scornful had I seen such legerdemain; here it did not trouble me that the health of the canal was an illusion, all smoke and mirrors for the sake of civic self-promotion: it was preferable to stagnation. But this was not my home. He sighed and shook his head at the expense.

"What was the use of looking good for the Olympic Games?

No tourists came to see our Willow Village. We know why this work was *really* done...." He slipped an imaginary bribe into his back pocket, just like the bargeman in Suqian had done. He sighed again. "China is changing. Willow Village must 'walk towards the world', *dui ma?*"

I gave a nod and a thoughtful hmmm of agreement. What had that policeman said? "Let Peixian move towards the world, and let the world understand Peixian." It was just a slogan, but the aspiration was far better than retreating into paranoid isolation again as China had under Mao.

"I think your canal looks beautiful," I told him.

He pursed his lips and nodded: "Yes, it does look beautiful."

An hour's walk farther, where Willow Village sank back into the dampening plain, the expressway traffic glided overhead. The lie of the land had conspired to fill the canal to that point and no further, in imitation of vanished tides. Then its manicured banks ended without warning, and it snaked through the fields toward Beijing a trickle once more. Out there in the open, quite alone, I sat upon the grass and thought.

For seven years before 2008, the Olympic Games had dominated the Chinese horizon, had hovered in the near future like a punctuation mark, a great intersection toward which all roads, all effort seemed to converge. Projects of all sizes had been rushed to completion, from the Three Gorges Dam and the Qinghai-Tibet Railway to the thousands of Olympic cultural parks that had been laid out up and down China to feast on the reflected glory. In each town and city it passed through, the Grand Canal had been beautified with promenades and willows so that it might look its best when on the eighth day of the eighth month of the eighth year the world's cameras had turned upon China. Its rude health would be one more proof of success. Then the Games had passed into history in a blaze of pyrotechnics in the Beijing sky, the roads had diverged on their far side, and the cresting wave of pride and expectancy had broken, crashed, and fallen back to leave a tangible tidemark across an entire country.

御河

On reaching Tongzhou the stream broadened gratifyingly into a wide river, shallow and straight sided. Its accumulated silt, a brown soil carried there from mountains brushed by the dust of the Gobi, had only recently been dredged away. It lay piled in caramel hills now, a dark contrast to the loess that clung to my trouser hems like some exotic cargo. Summer was drawing from the earth a mist thick enough to make of the far bank a monotone pencil-sketch. The damp air moistened the thin fabric of my clothes. I ran a hand over the dew that wetted my scalp, and smiled. Tongzhou lay within the sixth ring road: I had made it to Beijing.

The plain which spread like a blanket at Beijing's eastern gateway had looked poor, as though few crumbs had fallen from the capital's banqueting tables. Mute villages had come and gone. Then from miles away I had watched hungrily as white pinpricks first coalesced into a line above the treetops then reared up as a wall of tiles and glass. There was something about the way the pedestrians held themselves here. The streets were well paved, the drivers self-assured. It was clear that this was the edge of a rich metropolis.

Tongzhou was proud to be the starting point of Chang'an Avenue, the celestial axis of Eternal Peace that bisected the heart of Beijing. It was here too that the Grand Canal officially began its descent to Hangzhou. At the exact confluence of the two, a powerfully symbolic site, a swathe of parkland had become Grand Canal Cultural Square. Where had I heard that name before? Of course – there had been another beside Bowing to the Emperor Bridge in Hangzhou that torrential spring day. More than a thousand miles now separated them.

"Sir, can you guess what *that* is?" The voice at my shoulder belonged to an elderly man, a picture of urbane gentility in his charcoal suit, cardigan and trilby. He pointed to a derrick from which there appeared to billow a rhombus of stiff, white metal. There were many more of them. "They're meant to be a fleet of junks in full sail, but I'm not sure I quite see it." His Mandarin was clipped and toned, gently rising and falling like the sea. He removed his hat to reveal white hair and a forehead speckled with liver spots. He was Yang Daren: willow-tree *yang*, great *da*, and kind-heartedness *ren*, he explained (the Chinese language has so many homophones that it is normal to expound a little upon the correct writing of one's name). On a palm he traced his surname with an index finger. It was the same one that the canal-builder Emperor Yang had been born with, before the first emperor of the Tang had mockingly altered its written form to mean not "willow tree" but "scorching". Together we strolled further into the park, stopping beside a circular feature set into the greensward. It could not have been less than 150 yards in diameter.

"This disc is the sun," he said. "In the distance is another, the moon." This was impossible to discern through the mist, which made a wet washing-day of the junks' white sails. "A processional way joins them, a kilometre and more long, and there's a statue of the Spirit of the Grand Canal."

China's ritual architecture, designed to reflect the workings of heaven, was often built on such a scale that it could only truly be understood from above. Like the Temple of Heaven or the Forbidden City, this square was the ritual architecture of its age, only put to work now for the glory of socialism with Chinese characteristics rather than for an emperor. Yet the sun and the moon seemed to have nothing to do with the Grand Canal, so what did it all signify?

He chuckled: "It's all very important. *Very* important." Then he smiled broadly, giving the distinct impression that he thought it not at all important. "The sun rises every day in the east, *dui ma?* Beijing too is rising, as is the Grand Canal that starts here. Just across the highway you will find another square, Olympic Cultural Square. If Beijing and the Grand Canal together are being reborn, it is the Olympic Games that proved to be the driving force in their rebirth. The sun and moon are aligned here, and everything is in harmony." Then his face fell a little. "There was already a beautiful park here before the decision was made to hold the Olympic Games in Beijing," he mused. "We Tongzhou folk used to enjoy coming here. Our district government are all rustics, you understand, and uncultured. They've found themselves in charge of part of our expanding capital city, but in truth they're just rural boors with money to spend. They can't hide the fact that it was Old Hundred Surnames' taxes that paid for it." He paused for a while to think. "Ah, we will wait and see," he said finally. "Perhaps I will forgive them their short-sightedness!" He spoke with a smile playing on his lips, with the magnanimous sufferance of the powerless.

He listened patiently to the roll-call of places I had seen since Hangzhou, and how each had had its own plans to enliven its little stretch of waterfront. He understood why. "The Grand Canal is a symbol of Chinese achievement. It is listed by the government as a cultural relic. Now scholars are recording its heritage, its traditions, and cities are keen to make their own little stretch as beautiful as they can."

Long since retired, Mr Yang had time on his hands, but he did not enjoy playing endless games of bridge and chess like other octogenarians. He had become an avid devourer of newspapers. He had read of a symposium, he recalled. The delegates had all signed the *Hangzhou Declaration*, that brief statement summarizing the importance of the Grand Canal and urging their government to apply for World Heritage status. It had been a shrewd tactic that had claimed for the Communist Party the stewardship of the canal and all that it symbolized. That same *Hangzhou Declaration* had been given pride of place in the Grand Canal Museum at the very start of my journey. It had been skilfully crafted, intended to leave no doubt that the Grand Canal, like the Great Wall, was a crowning achievement of Chinese civilization. No imperial grain had flowed upon it for over a century now, yet still China's rulers were feeding upon the canal's symbolism just as their predecessors had fed upon its substance.

Since Jining the canal had been unnavigable, grand in name only, but even this had not stopped the towns along its banks from adding their voices to the chorus of support. If anything, the manicured banks and pretty promenades of Liaocheng, Linqing, Cangzhou, Willow Village and now Tongzhou said more about China's pride in the Grand Canal than all the splendour of Jiangnan. Down there where the canal was whole, it was an easy matter to make a tourist attraction of a Precious Belt Bridge or a water village like Tongli; it took conviction to refill the lakes at the summit and to lay out the beautifully symbolic park where we now sat. It was in these abandoned stretches of canal that the story had become more than just a statement of fact. here it was a promise that the canal had not just a past but a future too.

But could the Party really succeed in winning World Heritage status for the Grand Canal, like it had the Great Wall? So much more than just a strip of water bound by earth banks, it would first need to be quantified. Its main channel was only the consummation of the countless waterways which gave it life, no more to be separated from them than an artery might be excised from its flesh and still go on pulsing. Like a hard-worked rope that lashed the north of China to the south, the canal was forever unbraiding and reforming, leaving an impression here or a tattered strand of itself there. The dry bed of Oqruqci's summit canal and the ghastliness of the Wei River were both as worthy of recognition, if not affection, as the serene arched bridges of Zhejiang. If an application were to have any hope of success, a corridor 1,100 miles long and dozens wide would need to be sketched out. Every historic site would need to be officially recorded, and steps taken to insulate them from change. Many of its cities were ranked amongst the most dynamic on earth; they would be unlikely to accept restraints on their development for the sake of heritage, no matter how much patriotism was used to sugar-coat the pill. It was the pace of reform, the *Declaration* warned, of modernization and of urbanization, that had brought profound and unwelcome changes. Unless steps were taken, very soon much of the Grand Canal's historic fabric would be gone. And that, the delegates agreed, would be an irreplaceable loss for China and the world.

Mr Yang finished speaking: "There is so much work to be done, but it will be worth it. I might seem like an old man who complains a lot, but like all Chinese I am very proud of our Grand Canal."

御河

Henry Eades, a quiet man and an ingenious metalworker, had persuaded Lord Macartney to engage him for his coming embassy to China. Despite terrible seasickness, he refused to turn back at Madeira. He never saw Beijing. It took eleven months to reach Tongzhou, but it was there in August of 1793 that Henry died of dysentery. His body was buried with full military honours in a Chinese cemetery, the first of what would be many funerals before the British left the following year. The embassy's orchestra played a dirge, and the people of the city turned out to watch the outlandish spectacle. Leaving Henry Eades to rest forever in Tongzhou's soil, the embassy made its entrance into Beijing in unsprung horse-carts. Lord Macartney had hoped to sail proudly up the Grand Canal into the heart of the Chinese capital, but even by his day such a passage had been impossible.

On a clear day, if the forest of office blocks permits, it is possible to stand in downtown Beijing and make out a ridge of low mountains to the north-west. Up there, not far from the rock-hewn tombs of the Ming emperors, the White Spring once gushed from the earth. In 1293 the polymath Guo Shoujing, Kublai Khan's surveyor of the Shandong watershed, coaxed that springwater down to the foot of the mountains. There it met the headwaters of other streams, its volume grew, and finally it tumbled into Khanbaliq where it unfurled itself into a broad lake named Jishuitan, the Pool Where the Waters Gather. Jishuitan became the hub of the Khan's capital, where barges spilled forth luxuries from across empire and oceans. When under the Ming emperors the imperial city was extended, the pool was immured within its forbidden precincts. The place where the waters had once gathered became a pleasure garden for the nobility. Its wharves given over to courtly dissipation, that northernmost section of the Grand Canal simply stagnated.

Now the last ashlars of its locks lay scattered like discarded Lego. Beside them, the canal itself had become unrecognizable, just a storm drain for a city's sprawling suburbs. Swollen by the overnight rain, its torrent sprinted past. I had had some romantic notion about finding a horse and cart to ride in dubious triumph into the capital like the Macartney embassy had, but carts had been banned from Beijing's busy boulevards. Instead I set out on foot.

Before the start of Deng Xiaoping's reforms, the dozen miles between the village of Tongzhou and the city of Beijing had been open fields. Now creeping modernity had blanketed the soil and the temperate crops, had felled the broadleaf trees, changed the skyline, and smothered all the age-old differences that had once made Beijing as distinct from Hangzhou as northern Europe is from its south. It was impossible to say now what had grown on fields that lay beneath tarmac, whether it had been dry wheat or wet rice. The willows might have been leading me back toward the Qiantang River. Swallows dipped to catch mosquitoes just like their cousins on the towpath in Tangqi.

At Eight Li Bridge the bed widened to allow Beijing's dirty water room to pass. Motorways soared overhead on massive concrete piles. The bridge itself, one last scrap of history, looked vulnerable, its frail arches like the work of a child beside those striding monsters. But to Beijing's commuters Eight Li Bridge was just another stop on the Batong Line. The strap-hangers were riding downtown in their white shirts, and together we spilled out onto the platform at Beijing Railway Station. The storm drain joined the city moat in the long shadow cast by the city wall, and there it disappeared beneath the streets. I telephoned my wife, then went to say a final goodbye to the Grand Canal.

At Jishuitan the fishermen sat in silence on the banks, their air of lazy anticipation heightened by the chirruping of cicadas. A statue of Guo Shoujing extended a hand as if to calm the streams he had led there. Above him, the Shrine of the Swirling Waters caught the last of the daylight. The water trickled through the mouth of a stone dragon into a jade-green pond, and there the grandest of canals ended, beside a scarlet pavilion set amongst the trees.

China's communist experiment too – for better or for worse – will eventually come to an end, but the Grand Canal will always be something the Chinese can be proud of, the unique achievement of a unique nation. Once, in Wuxi, a bargeman had tapped his temple and told me that the Grand Canal was more a concept than a route. China's present-day rulers had taken that concept, this waterway dug by millions of ordinary men and women, and had woven it into the story of their country. And when the last of them has closed his book and left the podium, the Chinese will still have that remarkable story to tell themselves.

As for my own story, that solitary blue thread traced in a hotel room in Tangqi had unwound into a skein of contrasting colours. A Chinese author, the radical intellectual Lu Xun, once penned a memorable line in a short story called *My Old Home*: "Hope is like a path across the earth," he wrote. "Actually, the earth had no paths to begin with, but when many people pass the same way, a path is made." In the coming years, China will tread a great many such paths. Along the route of the Grand Canal it might prove to be one of cultural protection, or of raw economics; of policies that have already degraded the Chinese environment, or policies that might yet save it. More likely these paths and others will forever run beside one another, merging and splitting just like the canal.

My own path through China had given me something that time and progress could not change. While one by one the places that had entwined themselves into my memories were disappearing, the canal would remain the same so long as there was demand for its cargoes. For as long as I was alive to see it, it would ring with boat engines and smell of diesel fuel, a touchstone of the senses to try my memories against. When I am gone, some future lover of China will perhaps set out from the West Lake, that enchanting model for the cover of *Beginning Chinese*, and feel a sense of loss at how a China yet to come into being has in its turn changed. And the water, serenely oblivious to our fleeting human attachments, will flow peacefully on.

I climbed a winding path to the top of a hill and watched the sun sink behind the Western Mountains. When it had set, when the Pool Where the Waters Gather had grown invisible in the twilight, I could still hear the Grand Canal bubbling and chuckling above the noise of the great, darkening city.

Appendix

Author's Note & Acknowledgements

My trip was completed over three months in 2006. In the following three years I returned to China several times to fill out aspects of the story as changing events dictated, and so the journey as related contains some details which are strictly speaking out of sequence.

Navigating the Grand Canal required the help and assistance of many people, many of whom broke China's reasonable and necessary safety regulations by doing so. I've modified names and barge registrations to make them untraceable. One outspoken Christian has been given as much anonymity as possible by placing him and his community in Linqing, a few miles along the Wei River from where our meeting actually took place.

My sincere thanks to the people I met on my journey, both those I've stayed in contact with and those whose names I did not ask. My eternal love and thanks especially to Becky my wife and Rachel my mother for funding this book. Thanks also to Jamie Coleman for his invaluable input, to Jon Foster-Smith, Elizabeth Corrin and Carl Thelin, to Ryan Wang and the other volunteers at the *Jing-Hang Yunhe Lianyihui*, to Bing Ling, Shengliang Hsu, 'Billy' Hao Ma, Eddie Y and Liu Jie for various help, advice and translations, to Professor Linda Walton for material on Lou Yue, and not least to Rene Carroll for her sempstressing.

横渡大运河得到了很多人的帮助，　其中很多人甚至破了一些在中国认为是合理而必要的安全规定。我已经更改了他们的名字和船只的注册号码，使他们无法被追踪。我还隐去了一位直率敢言的基督教徒和他的教会的名字，并把他安在了离我们真实会面地点几十英里的临清。

Glossary of Terms

dan	A traditional measure of dry grain, 133lbs.
getihu	Private businessman or business.
Jiangnan	The land "South of the Yangtze", especially referring to southern Jiangsu and Anhui, and northern Zhejiang and Jiangxi.
laowai	"Old Foreign", informal name for a foreigner or foreigners in general.
li	A unit of measurement, one third of a mile.
qianfu	Man or men employed to haul barges.

Money

The currency of the PRC is officially called the *Renminbi*. Its basic unit, the *yuan* (¥), commonly called the *kuai*, is divided into 10 *mao*. At the time of writing, £1 varied from ¥11-15, and US$1 from ¥7-8.

Chronology

The following list of Chinese dynasties covers only those in the text.

Xia	21st?–16th? century BC
Shang	16th? century–1045? BC
Zhou	1045?–256 BC
Spring and Autumn period	770–476 BC
Warring States period	475–221 BC
Qin	221–206 BC
Western Han	202 BC–AD 23
Eastern Han	25–220
Southern Liang	502–557
Sui	581–618
Tang	618–907
Northern Song	960–1127
Southern Song	1127–1279
Yuan (Mongol)	1279–1368
Ming	1368–1644
Qing (Manchu)	1644–1911
Republic of China	1912–1949 (then on Taiwan)
People's Republic of China	1949–?

eyeSight

Our greatest fear is not that we are inadequate, our greatest fear is that we are powerful beyond measure. By shining your light, you subconsciously give permission to others to shine theirs.
Nelson Mandela

Travel can be a liberating experience, as it was for me in 1990, when I was just one hundred yards from Nelson Mandela as he was released from prison. I watched this monumental occasion from on top of a traffic light, amidst a sea of enthralled onlookers.

This was the 'green light' moment that inspired the creation of Eye Books. From the chaos of that day arose an appreciation of the opportunities that the world around us offers, and the desire within me to shine a light for those whose reaction to opportunity is 'can't and don't'.

Our world has been built on dreams, but the drive is often diluted by the corporate and commercial interests offering to live those dreams for us, through celebrity culture and the increasing mechanisation and automation of our lives. Inspiration comes now from those who live outside our daily routines, from those who *challenge the way we see things*.

Eye Books was born to tell the stories of *'ordinary' people doing 'extraordinary' things*. With no experience of publishing, or the constraints that the book 'industry' imposes, Eye Books created a genre of publishing to champion those who live out their dreams.

Twelve years on, and sixty stories later, Eye Books has the same ethos. We believe that ethical publishing matters. It is not about just trying to make a quick hit, it is about publishing the stories that affect our lives and the lives of others positively. We publish the books we believe will shine a light on the lives of some and enlighten the lives of many for years to come.

Join us in the Eye Books community, and share the power these stories evoke.

Dan Hiscocks
Founder and Publisher
Eye Books

www.eye-books.com

eyeCommunity

At Eye Books we are constantly challenging the way we see things and do things. But we cannot do this alone. To that end we have created an online club, a community, where members can inspire and be inspired, share knowledge and exchange ideas. Membership is free, and you can join by visiting www.eye-books.com, where you will be able to find:

What we publish

Books that truly inspire, by people who have given their all, triumphed over adversity, lived their lives to the full. Visit the dedicated microsites we have for each of our books online.

Why we publish

To champion those 'ordinary' people doing extraordinary things. The real celebrities of our world who tell stories that celebrate life to the full, not just for 15 minutes. Books where fact is more compelling than fiction.

How we publish

Eye Books is committed to ethical publishing. Many of our books feature and campaign for various good causes and charities. We try to minimise our carbon footprint in the manufacturing and distribution of our books.

Who we publish

Many, indeed most of our authors have never written a book before. Many start as readers and club members. If you feel strongly that you have a book in you, and it is a book that is experience driven, inspirational and life affirming, visit the 'How to Become an Author' page on our website. We are always open to new authors.

Eye-Books.com Club is an ever-evolving community, as it should be, and benefits from all that our members contribute, with invitations to book launches, signings and author talks, plus special offers and discounts on the books we publish.

Eye Books membership is free, and it's easy to sign up. Visit our website. Registration takes less than a minute.

eyeClassics

Riding with Ghosts, Gwen Maka
£7.99

Gwen Maka's love affair with America and low budget travel began when she stepped off a plane at JFK airport in 1982 with £100 in her pocket, on her way to study underdevelopment on a Sioux reservation. This is the inspiring story of her solo cycle from Seattle to Mexico, tracing the history of Native Americans.

Also by Gwen Maka, the sequel to **_Riding With Ghosts_, _South of the Border_**

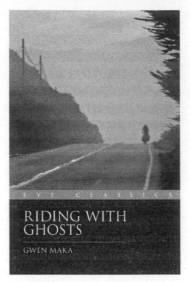

Frigid Women, Sue & Victoria Riches
£7.99

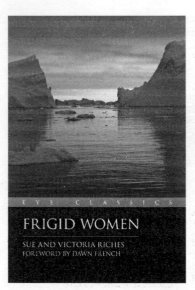

'Women wanted to walk to North Pole'. Mother and daughter, Sue & Victoria Riches never imagined how much one small advert in a newspaper would change their lives.... Within two years, they were trekking across the frozen wilderness that is the Arctic Ocean, as part of the first all-female expedition to the North Pole. At times terrifying and indescribably beautiful, it was a trip of a lifetime. Having survived cancer, it was an opportunity to discover that ANYTHING is possible if you put your mind to it, and if you WANT to succeed.

eyeClassics

Jasmine and Arnica, Nicola Naylor
£7.99

When Nicola lost her sight, her world collapsed. Institutionalised and misunderstood, she spent the next seven years coming to terms with an issue she had spent her life denying. Eventually she started to piece together her shattered life through a new found interest in massage. She decided to travel India alone, researching Indian massage techniques and holistic therapy. *Jasmine and Arnica* is the powerful and sensorial story of this seminal trip.

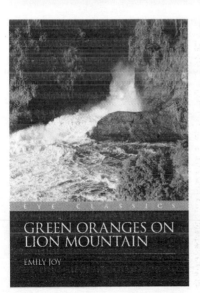

Green Oranges on Lion Mountain, Emily Joy
£7.99

When your dad can crash his aeroplane into two water buffalo, life is unlikely to go according to plan. Even so, Emily Joy puts on her rose-tinted specs, leaves behind her comfortable life as a Western doctor and heads off for two years to volunteer in a remote hospital in West Africa. This is the true account of her posting in Sierra Leone; adventure and romance were on the agenda, rebel forces and civil war were not.

Also by Emily Joy, *The Accidental Optimist's Guide to Life*

www.eye-books.com

eyeBookshelf

Good Morning Afghanistan,
Waseem Mahmood
£7.99

It is a time of chaos. Afghanistan has just witnessed the fall of the oppressive Taliban. Warlords battle each other for supremacy, while the powerless, the dispossessed, the hungry and the desperate struggle to survive. A glimmer of hope emerges in the form of a spirited breakfast radio programme. This book is a true account of how an intrepid band of media warriors help a broken nation find a voice through the radio.

Siberian Dreams,
Andy Home
£9.99

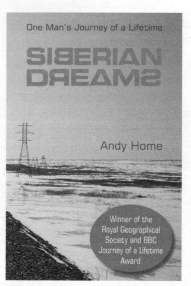

Winner of the journey of a lifetime award, Andy Home travels to Siberia, to the town of Norilsk, once both a prison camp and, later, a Soviet military base. He interviews the people in what is now not only one of the worlds most polluted cities, but also the biggest source of the metals we use everyday. What are their dreams? And in what way have their lives changed?

The Good Life,
Dorian Amos
£9.99

Dorian Amos begins the adventure of
a lifetime when he moves his family
from Cornwall to the wilderness of the
Yukon. Share in their highs and lows
on this fascinating journey as they
leave everything and everyone they're
used to, and go in search of a new
and better life.

The Good Life Gets Better,
Dorian Amos
£9.99

The sequel to the bestselling book
about leaving the UK for a new life
in the Yukon, Dorian and his growing
family get gold fever, start to stake
land and prospect for gold. Follow
them along the learning curve about
where to look for gold and how to live
in this harsh climate. It shows that with
good humour and resilience life can
only get better.

eyeAuthor

Liam D'Arcy-Brown 林杰

Liam D'Arcy-Brown was born in south-east London in 1970 and raised in Yorkshire. Sent one day into a school storeroom he discovered a discarded Mandarin primer and so his interest in China began, helped on its way by such diverse influences as oriental cookery and Roland Rat's Hong Kong summer special for TV-am.

After reading Chinese at Oxford he went on to study China's ancient history in Shanghai on a British Council scholarship. He worked as a tour escort for Voyages Jules Verne and as a sales manager at BBC Haymarket before turning to travel writing. His childhood in the historic city of York left him sensitive to the indelible past that saturates the present, a theme which recurs in his work.

His first book, *Green Dragon, Sombre Warrior*, took him from lengthy researches in the British Library and the Oriental Reading Room of the Bodleian and onward to a great 10,000-mile circuit of China's four most distant points. His more recent journey from Hangzhou to Beijing made him the first Westerner in more than two centuries to trace the length of China's Grand Canal. He lives in the beautiful town of Kenilworth, Warwickshire, with his wife Rebecca.

Also by Liam D'Arcy-Brown:

Green Dragon, Sombre Warrior

In his critically acclaimed travel-writing debut, Liam D'Arcy-Brown travels to China's four extremities, finding complex, unique, and often conflicting cultures. An essential read for anyone interested in the real China behind the formulaic headlines.

"D'Arcy Brown proves himself to be an intrepid traveller as he goes ... where few Westerners have gone before. Into his travelogue he weaves some of the history of China, and he turns out to be a very good historian ... His debut is a moving and chilling book. Let us hope there are many more to come" *The Times*

Green Dragon
Sombre Warrior
Liam D'Arcy-Brown

www.eye-books.com